Fran

InnerCities Cultural Guides

Frankfurt

Brian Melican

INNERCITIES
Signal Books

First published in 2015 by
Signal Books Limited
36 Minster Road
Oxford OX4 1LY
www.signalbooks.co.uk

A catalogue record for this book is available from the British Library

ISBN 978-1-909930-18-6 Paper

Cover Design: Imprint Digital
Production: Imprint Digital
Cover Images: © Sean Pavone/Shutterstock; A Köhler/Wikimedia Commons
Half-title page image: Eli Beckman/Wikimedia Commons
Printed in India

Contents

Introduction

Sitting in the venerable halls of the Frankfurt University building, it dawns on me that only Germany has structures which
so completely encompass the full sweep of human history,
from the most senseless brutality to the very highest peaks of intellectual achievement. The building itself is a broad sweep in shape,
too, massive in scale and gently concave, giving an impression when
inside that it may even run full circle. Its history certainly does: the
university is named after Goethe, a polymath and creator of some
of the most hauntingly beautiful arrangements of words in one of
the world's most philosophically and sentimentally rich languages.
Yet in the early 1940s some of Germany's greatest scientific minds
were at work in this building developing the gases and chambers in
which millions of human beings would meet their end.

Frankfurt has thus the dubious fame of being home both to
Germany's most beloved, most learned and most civilizing literary
influence—a towering figure of the European Enlightenment—
and to the process which became the symbol of its demise. It is
therefore fitting that the authors of *Dialectic of Enlightenment*, Max
Horkheimer and Theodor W. Adorno, who destroyed any remaining philosophical certainty that intellectual and societal progress
was irreversible, were of the so-called Frankfurt School, born of this
university.

Just as it is impossible, therefore, to understand modern
Germany without reference to its manifold cultural zeniths and
its all-encompassing historical nadir, so too is it impossible to
grasp today's country without examining Frankfurt, its historical capital and present centre. Yet Frankfurt today is viewed by
many both inside and outside Germany as a kind neutral business mecca with nothing by way of heritage and little worth
seeing beyond a parade of skyscrapers and its cavernous trade fair
halls. Readers in Britain will understand the comparison with

Frankfurt's town-twinning partner, Birmingham; in the US, the equivalent in popular culture might well be Dallas, a city known for being at the centre of the country and thus one that people pass through rather than stay in.

That is certainly the relationship I had to Frankfurt before deciding to investigate it more deeply: how many times did I change trains here, drinking a second-rate coffee and unpacking a sandwich between Hamburg and Paris or between London and Munich? A quick survey of friends both in Germany and abroad revealed that almost all of them had been to Frankfurt, but that most had seen little more of it than the airport transit areas. Those who had ventured into town between flights, or for a business meeting, remembered little more than the picture-book Römer square and the city's high-rises.

The towers: looking down westwards from the Main Tower viewing platform onto the gigantic railway station as planes come in overhead, Frankfurt can indeed seem to be little more than a pulsating transport node. Even turning towards the city centre, the gothic Eschenheimer Tor, one of the remaining gatehouse towers of the medieval city walls, seems to suggest that this place has always had a certain weakness for tall buildings. In a darker, critical frame of mind, it can be easy to reduce the city to the ant-farm of international business filled with corporate drones or, alternatively, the evil stronghold of modern turbo-capitalism on the European continent with a historical predilection for phallic expressions of financial power.

While Munich, with its beautifully preserved or reconstructed buildings, wears its historical and cultural importance on its sleeve; while the unlovingly reconstructed cities of the Rhine and Ruhr trade on their proletarian credentials and easy *bonhomie*; and while Berlin or Hamburg entice with their urban chic, open spaces and flagrant contradictions, Frankfurt is devoid of much of its original substance and can seem in many respects boringly bourgeois and overwhelmingly business-orientated.

Yet the city has so much more to offer: its history is visible to those willing to scratch below the surface, and rewards with unexpected importance. Berlin has spent, all things told, less than two centuries at the head of a united German state: Frankfurt was the *de facto* capital of the whole of Central Europe until 1800 and the birthplace of the idea of a country called Germany. Today, too, it plays such a crucial role in the life of the Federal Republic of Germany—and the European Union—that it seems almost wilfully negligent not to find out just a little more about it.

This book is an attempt to do just that, and to present what I have learned to the interested reader; and although it is therefore written from the perspective of an outsider, this seems—given the problem diagnosed above—somehow appropriate. It is my hope that you will, by the end of the book, agree with me on this point, and have developed, or in some way furthered, your own interest in this fascinating city.

Thanks

I should like to begin by thanking those who helped me research this book in their professional capacity: Thomas Worschech at the Deutsches Filmmuseum provided me not only with invaluable information and a copy of his book, but with a wealth of insights into the city. The staff of the Ernst May Haus in Römerstadt were equally willing to help beyond the remit of their specific topic areas. The city press department were efficient and friendly in setting up contacts to various museums and experts.

While it may be slightly harder to define, it would be remiss of me not to include an acknowledgement of the contribution made by personal friends living in Frankfurt to this book. I am particularly indebted to Peter Mandrella (although he is now, once again, of Düsseldorf) for his insight into publishing in the city, and to Markus Dieckmann and Christopher Krämer for sharing with me their insider's view of the Frankfurt banking world; I would like to thank all three for their various acts of generous hospitality. Claire Kudena and the staff of the Culturetranslate agency were friendly, welcoming faces and a reliable source of practical information, as was Olaf Kopmann at Frankfurter Societät.

Finally, I should like to thank James Ferguson for his confidence in me and for publishing this work (as well as for persuading me to write it in the first place), as well as my partner Nicole Runschke for putting up with my physical absence for research purposes and mental absence while writing the book; as ever, I will close by thanking my mother for her boundless interest in my work and tireless support of it.

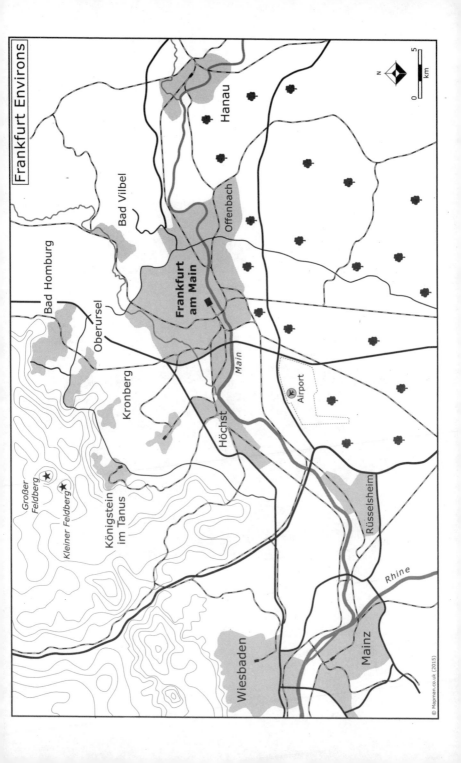

A view of Frankfurt in the 1600s by the talented founder of
the Merian dynasty (Wikimedia Commons)

1 | Contours
Geography and Topography

Until well into the nineteenth century, there was a variety of English names for Frankfurt in circulation: as well as the common Frankfort, variations such as Frankforde or Frankford were also to be found, and it is especially this latter which conveys in English the two key characteristics for which the city was named: it grew up around a ford, in the territory of the Franks.

The river in question is the Main, around 150m wide at the ancient site of the ford. The crossing is part of a slight elevation on both sides of the river, which also offered the fledgling city a view of the surrounding area and a defensive advantage. Modern Frankfurt is so built up—and so vertical in its character—that this low hillock is almost completely invisible in panoramic views of the city; but walking up from the bank of the Main to the central Römer square, its presence becomes slightly clearer. Apart from gentle slopes to long-disguised promontory points such as this, the centre is generally flat in character, comparable with those of other cities on broad river plains such as London.

Rivers

The river at Frankfurt's heart is the Main: the full German name, Frankfurt am Main, is used when the city needs to be distinguished from other Frankfurts, notably Frankfurt an der Oder on the border with Poland. The Main was and is the defining element of the city's topography. Rising some 560km (350 miles) to the east, it is one of the few central European rivers which follow a broadly east-west axis, fed by primarily north-south tributaries such as the Regnitz, which comes from Nuremberg and Bamberg to the south, and the Tauber. Its course takes it through Schweinfurt and Würzburg, Aschaffenburg and Offenbach, before—around 50km east of its confluence into the Rhine—it passes through Frankfurt.

The Main has been following its current course for around two million years, carving the valley through which it flows out of shell limestone and red sandstone. The alternation between warmer and cooler climatic periods means that the Main valley was cut in stages as various glaciers built up and melted away, leading to what geologists refer to as fluvial terraces—stepped valleys—into which the river has, at various points in the last million or so years, deposited large amounts of sediment. The relevance of this process in the short timeframe of human history are the gently sloping hillsides and fertile fluvial plains which now characterise the area, perfect for viticulture and agriculture respectively: the fecundity of the countryside around Frankfurt has always been favourable to human settlement, meaning that the area has generally had a high population—and has often awakened the interest of peoples and armies from less propitious regions.

As it enters Frankfurt from the east, the Main is roughly 100m wide and turns sharply to the south, creating an S-bend before it continues on its course westwards. The low-lying floodplains here have always made for perfect boat moorings, and the city's eastern harbour is situated just to the west of the Main bend. By the time it reaches the city centre, roughly five kilometres downstream, the Main has broadened by a half to 150 metres; in central London, by way of comparison, the Thames flows at almost double this breadth, while in New York City, the Hudson is roughly ten times as wide (by American measures, the Main is a stream). Yet as it continues west through Frankfurt, the Main makes a more or less straight bolt for one of the few European rivers of globally relevant dimensions: the Rhine, into which it flows at Mainz (named for it) approximately 30km downriver.

Although it does not flow through Frankfurt, the Rhine is also a crucial feature of its geography. Rising in Switzerland, the Rhine meets the Main at more or less the half-way point in its 1,300km journey into the North Sea. The Main empties approximately 225m^3 per second of water into the Rhine, making it its greatest right-hand tributary and fourth greatest overall; through the Rhine, the Main is directly connected to the North Sea downstream and the Swiss Alps upstream. The mighty Rhine is also responsible for the broad fluvial plain which lies to the immediate south of Frankfurt, a 30-to-50km-wide tract which stretches 240 km south into Switzerland and on which great cities such as Mannheim, Strasbourg, and

Basel have grown up. It is safe to say that, without its connection to the Rhine, the Main would never have gained the degree of importance it retains for water transport to this day, and that Frankfurt in turn would never have developed to the extent it has.

Hills and Forests

To its northwest, Frankfurt is flanked by the Taunus mountain range, of which the third tallest peak, the 798m Altkönig, lies little more than 15km away from the city centre. The Taunus range stretches for 50km north to the Lahn valley and 80km east to west, where it is divided by the Rhine from its continuation, the Hunsrück. Along with the Hunsrück, the Siebengebirge and the distant Ardennes, the Taunus forms part of the much larger Rhenish Massif, which extends for over 160km to the north of Frankfurt and remains to this day sparsely populated.

To the northeast, the undulating hills of the Wetterau stretch for around 50km, drained by the Wetter, Nidder, and Nidda rivers, which join just north of the city centre and empty into the Main as the Nidda in the western district of Frankfurt-Höchst. Beyond the Wetterau rises the dramatic Vogelsberg Massif, Germany's only extinct volcano and Europe's largest basalt formation; its highest peaks, both around 760m high, are the Taufstein and the Hoherodskopf, around 55km northeast of the city centre and visible from its skyscrapers on (rather rare) clear days with low humidity. From here on eastwards and northwards, the German central uplands stretch with little interruption all the way up to the Harz range, home of the Brocken peak made famous by Frankfurt's best-known historical progeny, Johann Wolfgang von Goethe.

Aside from witches' peaks, the classic German literary landscape is the forest, and both Frankfurt itself and its immediate surroundings are characterized by extensive woods: the Taunus mountains are covered in pine forest, while the Wetterau hills and the Rhine plain too are defined by woodlands. Within the city, trees are an important feature of the landscape: Frankfurt's southern districts are blanketed by one of Europe's most extensive urban forests, the Stadtwald, in which several suburbs and the city's airport are essentially little more than clearings, islands in seas of trees when viewed through the window of an airliner. The city centre, despite its obviously modern features, is also dotted with wooded parklands such as the Grüneburgpark to the northwest, the Riederwald in the east, and the narrow but tenacious green belt on the old city walls, known as the Wallanlagen.

It was with wood from its ample hinterland forests that Frankfurt's first permanent Main crossing was built in 1170 AD. Due to the rocky ridge across the river where today's Alte Brücke, Old Bridge, stands, the ford at Frankfurt had been the only safe passage from northern to southern Germany for several centuries by this stage, and it is this essential characteristic which made it a centre from these early post-Roman years onwards.

Bridges and Roads

At first Frankfurt was close to the centre of the Kingdom of the Franks, which covered most of the Rhineland, the Mosel area, and Belgium by 500 AD. With the navigable Main forming an east-west axis and the ford allowing north-south movement, the city was at a crossroads and gained in importance as the Franks moved east into Thuringia, south into Swabia and north into Saxony. By the time of Charlemagne, Frankfurt was a strategic pivot of the Carolingian Empire, roughly 160 kilometres from the imperial capital of Aachen to the north and the important city of Strasbourg to the south. The Carolingian heartlands, in what is today southern Belgium, Luxemburg and eastern France, were all close to hand, as were the frontiers to the east. Frankfurt was also the middle of a new north-south land axis between the empire's northern border near Hamburg and its southern territories in Lombardy.

Despite the disintegration of this territorial entity, as Christendom pushed further north and east and medieval Europe expanded, Frankfurt's position on the populated continent only became more and more central. Trade routes between what are today France and Poland, Belgium and Austria, Denmark and Switzerland all passed through Frankfurt. Regardless of how borders were drawn in the continuous flux of the Middle Ages, the city remained a crossroads.

At the height of the loosely organized Holy Roman Empire in around 1600, Frankfurt was at its precise geographical centre on both the north-south and east-west axes: it was here that the Empire's elected emperors, who came from as far afield as Spain and what is now the Czech Republic, were crowned.

After the rise of France to the west and Prussia to the north in the eighteenth and nineteenth centuries, Frankfurt shifted from being at the centre of a European patchwork to being on the frontier of nation states. With France 160km to the southwest, Prussia the same distance to the northeast and Bavaria to its south, the city found itself on the frontline in the Napoleonic Wars, its trading ties frequently severed.

Rails and Waterways

It was only with the unification of Germany under Prussian domination in the 1860s that Frankfurt was once again placed at the centre of an empire: the Second German Empire and, later, the Third Reich. Although in both of these entities, with their focus having shifted east to Berlin and the Prussian plains, Frankfurt found itself at the western extremity, its equidistant location between the new industrial metropolises of the Rhine and Ruhr to the north and the agricultural heartland of Bavaria to the south assured it once again a central position.

It was the exchange of goods and foodstuffs in the new industrialized Germany which secured Frankfurt a role it plays to this day as a transport hub. By the turn of the twentieth century, it was at the centre of Europe's longest rail network, and the advances both in shipbuilding technology and inland waterways also put it in a commanding position as a river port.

With the caesura of 1945, Frankfurt was once again part of a north-south strip in the form of the Federal German Republic, in which it played an important part as the gateway between north and south: with Berlin cut off behind the Iron Curtain, Frankfurt was a logical choice for several of the central state functions of the FRG (although its capital was 120km further north at Bonn), and as air travel boomed in the 1960s, it quickly became Germany's first airport and Europe's third in terms of passenger numbers and freight.

Air Travel and the Digital World

After the reunification of Germany and the enlargement of the European Union into the east, Frankfurt has once again regained its topographical centrality: it is now 40km west of the geographic centre of the EU, only 320km away from Brussels, 420km from Berlin and Prague, just under 500km away from Paris, and 580km away from Vienna and Milan. With the Schengen open borders agreement, it is now possible—and perfectly ordinary—to travel between these destinations without so much as showing a passport.

Yet modern Frankfurt's centrality is not just measured in proximity to European destinations, but in flight hours: Frankfurt Airport can be reached by plane from European capitals as far apart as Madrid, Stockholm, Rome and Copenhagen in around two hours. On an even broader scale, it is roughly halfway between Dubai and New York (see Chapter 9).

For worldwide traffic of another kind, too, Frankfurt is located at a convenient global crossroads: the city's internet exchange point is the world's busiest, with a maximum throughput of more than three terabits per second. While Frankfurt's internet infrastructure is the most important gateway to and from Germany for its millions internet users, no small portion of this capacity can nonetheless safely be assumed to be occupied more or less constantly by the huge volume of automated trading on the Frankfurt Stock Exchange. Indeed, in terms of the global markets, Frankfurt shares an important characteristic with its most bitter rival on the scene, London: due to its closeness to the Greenwich meridian, Frankfurt's working day acts as a convenient link between the Far East and the United States of America: when trading starts in Frankfurt, Tokyo (eight hours ahead) is just finishing up; when Frankfurt's bankers hit the off-switch on their monitors, New Yorkers (six hours behind) have just settled down at their desks.

In both geographical and virtual topography, Frankfurt has never been as central as it is now.

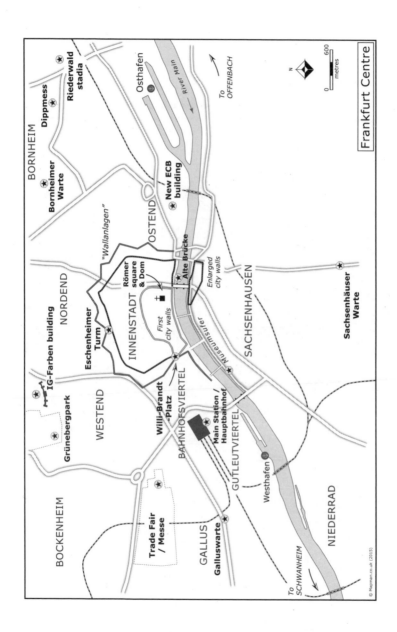

Frankfurt Centre

BORNHEIM

Dippmess

Riederwald stadia

Osthafen

River Main

To OFFENBACH

N

0 600 metres

BORNHEIM

Bornheimer Warte

New ECB building

"Wallanlagen"

OSTEND

Alte Brücke

Enlarged city walls

NORDEND

IG-Farben building

Eschenheimer Turm

Römer square & Dom

First city walls

Museumsufer

SACHSENHAUSEN

Sachsenhäuser Warte

INNENSTADT

WESTEND

Grüneberpark

Willi-Brandt -Platz

BAHNHOFSVIERTEL

Main Station / Hauptbahnhof

GUTLEUTVIERTEL

Westhafen

BOCKENHEIM

Trade Fair / Messe

GALLUS

Galluswarte

NIEDERRAD

To SCHWANHEIM

© Mapman.co.uk (2015)

Franckefort·

Chronik der Sachsen. Mainz 1492.

An early image of the city from the Chronicle of the Saxons in 1492
(Wikimedia Commons)

2 | **The Urban Map**
Growth and Development

Altstadt, Neustadt

As with so many German cities, the name Altstadt, or Old Town, can frequently lead to a brief moment of disappointment. After centuries of constant urban regeneration and the extensive destruction of the Second World War, German old towns in cities of any size are not at all comparable with those in parts of Europe passed over by both the upheaval of industrial revolution and the destruction of aerial warfare. Yet, whether their ancient origins have survived or not, German cities remain focussed on their old centres, and Frankfurt is no exception.

The core of the Altstadt is the elevation today known as Domhügel, or "cathedral hill". At the time of the first Frankish settlement in around 500 AD, however, the most important building here was not a cathedral but the royal residence: the ground would nevertheless have been consecrated early, as the Merovingian kings of the Franks were Christian and required a chapel. Indeed, the early history of the city is very much characterized by a succession of royal and ecclesiastical buildings, culminating in the Salvatorkirche of 852—on the site of which today's cathedral stands—and the Carolingian royal palace, whose existence was first recorded in 794, when Charlemagne convened the first ever *Reichstag* (literally "empire day") there. The remains of this *Pfalz* or palace were, until recently, visible in the now-buried archaeological garden in front of the cathedral.

After the decline of the Carolingians, the city experienced a brief and early period of abeyance as the royal court moved elsewhere. In the early Middle Ages, however, regal regalia returned in the form of the Hohenstaufen monarchs, who remodelled the Carolingian palace, adding a great hall, the Saalhof, and who had the first permanent river crossing built in 1170, where today's Alte Brücke, Old Bridge, is located. From 1180 onwards they had a wall erected around the city as it stood then: on today's map, the outlines of this first wall are drawn by Fahrgasse, Holzgraben, Großer Hirschgraben, and the Main quay. The 600m^2 area thus enclosed was now the city of Frankfurt. Built as it was to protect the inhabitants from marauding medieval armies, there is no small irony in the fact that the few remains of this wall today were revealed by wartime aerial bombardments: its elegant brick arches are visible at the northern end of Fahrgasse, surrounded by the kind of hastily erected post-war constructions which characterize large parts of the Altstadt today.

Nevertheless, the Old Town contains some of the finest and most historically important structures Germany has to offer, even if many, like the iconic Römerberg square and town hall, or the Paulskirche—the birthplace of German parliamentary democracy—just to the north, are actually painstaking restorations of ruined originals. Others, such as the Schirn art gallery, built largely on the site of the original royal residence, are daringly modern. Yet aside from its manifold buildings of historic or contemporary worth, much of Frankfurt's old core is covered today by relatively nondescript, four-to-five-storey housing blocks built in the frantic reconstruction of the post-war years. The streets to the immediate west of the town hall, for example, would not be out of place in any number of suburban settings across Germany: washing hangs on balconies and geraniums and pansies dangle from kitchen windows within sight of the ancient Saalhof, some of which still stands. As such, Frankfurt's Altstadt today is at once ancient and modern, spectacular and unedifying in equal measure.

Within little less than two centuries, the city was already expanding beyond this original walled area and, in 1333, was given permission to extend its fortifications accordingly. Almost quadrupling the size of the area enclosed, the new wall was to define the shape of the city for the next five centuries; so large was the expansion that areas of the Neustadt—the "New Town" behind the new wall—remained farmland well into the 1500s. This semi-rural character was made clear by the fact that the old wall was at first retained, with the city gates being shut every night around what had become by definition the Altstadt, the "Old Town". It was not until

1584 that the last piece of the Hohenstaufen wall was removed and the two towns were allowed to merge.

By this stage, the central point of the city had very clearly become the Römerberg, not far to the west of the original Domhügel, where the town hall was built on the north-south passage leading down to the ford. The most important thoroughfare of the extended city, however, quickly became the east-west Zeil, originally a country road passing just north of the Hohenstaufen wall and now part of the Neustadt enclosure. Where the north-south roads to the ford and to the old bridge crossed the Zeil, new squares sprang up, today's Hauptwache and Konstablerwache respectively. These two plazas situated at each end of the pedestrianized Zeil now have a more typically central feel than the Old Town: tourists are outnumbered by suited passers-by and shoppers laden with bags from big-name stores.

Indeed, fed by the mass transit interchanges now located beneath the two squares at its ends, the Zeil has become Frankfurt's major shopping street and is today characterized by the same placeless architecture as many a consumer strip; by and large, this generalization holds for much of the rest of the Neustadt. Despite continual reminders of its antonymic age in the form of place and street names (such as Roßmarkt, or "stud market", and Steinweg—the first street in the city to be paved) and despite the odd surviving structure from bygone eras (most notably, the Stock Exchange building of 1879), much of the Neustadt today is covered by charmless post-war buildings and inhabited by international chain shops or eateries at street level and offices in the low-rise space above.

In the Middle Ages this new, larger Frankfurt was surrounded not just by a wall, but by defensive structures of increasing complexity. Beyond the city walls and gates—of which only the classically gothic Eschenheimer Tor, the Rententurm on the river, and the Kuhhirtenturm to the south today remain—a protective mass of earthworks was erected throughout the 1400s and interspersed with fortresses, named *Warten*, of which four remain today. Stretching several miles around the city, these land defences provided both safe pasture for the townsfolk's livestock and an outer ring of fortifications in wartime. During the 1600s, an inner ring of defences was created in the form of raised bastions around the city walls, and given the expense and permanence of such constructions, it would have seemed reasonable at the time to assume that the city's outline was now quite literally set in stone.

The West, North, and East Ends

This was most definitely not the case. Their spectacular futility proven during both the Thirty Years' War of the 1600s and the Napoleonic Wars at the start of the nineteenth century, there were few who bemoaned their loss when the city's walls and bastions were torn down by the French occupiers in 1806-07. In fact, the population very quickly got into the habit of taking constitutional walks on this unused strip of greenery: writing to her son in 1808, Goethe's mother reported to him that "the old walls have been removed, the old gates torn down. The whole city is now a park. One could think oneself caught up in a fairy-tale… The very smallest peep of the sun is enough to draw countless people out." The early popularity of this "green belt" around the Neustadt anchored it in the city structure and, as a park landscape filled with trees and sculpture, what are collectively called the Wallanlagen remain a defining feature of the centre to this day.

In her letter, Goethe's mother noted that the walls would not have been torn down without the French occupiers—"the bewigged city elders would never have managed it"—but, given the gathering pace of urbanization from the 1830s onwards, the fortifications' days were already numbered. Population growth was at first slow in Germany compared to Britain and France: London passed the million mark in 1810, as did Paris in 1840, while Frankfurt did not reach 100,000 inhabitants until 1875. Yet even in the early 1800s, Frankfurt's original territory of Altstadt and Neustadt was already visibly bursting at the seams: visitors such as Henry Crabb Robinson remarked that the streets were crowded and narrow and "the houses lofty and irregularly built". At first, it was the wealthy merchant classes who moved out of the city into the surrounding greenery, turning the old grazing lands into generously-proportioned garden plots with imposing family villas along the north-west road to Bockenheim.

As trade and industry expanded in the mid-nineteenth century and urbanization sped up, the original area of the city became ever more crowded, and the authorities decided to take action: the arable areas to the west, north and east of the city centre, formerly surrounded by the outer earthworks, were divided into plots of land, given street layouts and sold to developers.

In a manner reminiscent of the growth of London, the patrician class already present in the western part of the city, known from the 1850s on as Westend, lent their area a lastingly bourgeois feel: streets were wide, houses and apartment buildings fine and land expensive. Meanwhile, the area on the north-east road to Bornheim, christened Nordend, was intended for the trade and clerical classes; building here was denser, typically in four-to-five-storey tenements, and streets were narrower. The newly baptized Ostend, meanwhile, just like London's East End, was given over to dockyards and industry—and to the workers employed there.

To a great extent, these classifications and the architecture to go with them have held true to this day: Westend is still the preferred district for wealthy bankers, featuring stately townhouses and leafy avenues, while Ostend, a colourful mixture of old industrial sites and run-down blocks documenting almost 150 years of loveless housing development trends, is currently undergoing gentrification. Nordend remains a popular mixed area for city workers, with the bonus that those of its 1850s tenement blocks which have survived are now considered highly desirable.

By the second half of the nineteenth century, with both areas of the old city now surrounded on all sides by built-up districts, the distinction between Altstadt and Neustadt had become all but meaningless. The new division was now between the original territory of the town, the interior Innenstadt, and the West, North, and East Ends, known as the Außenstadt, or exterior. Today, the term Innenstadt is still used to refer to the old city centre, while Außenstadt has fallen into disuse in favour of naming specific districts.

Sachsenhausen

In another parallel between the development of Frankfurt and London, the areas south of the city's river are almost as old as the northern city itself, have grown and changed with it, and are yet somehow quite distinct. Sachsenhausen grew up around the head of the Old Bridge on the south bank of the Main and was considered important enough to be included both in the ring of medieval land defences and in the elaborate ramparts of the 1600s. While the city to the north was expanding apace in the mid-1800s, however, Sachsenhausen remained quiet, populated by a mixture of smallholders, tradesmen and the odd wealthy family cocooned in a small mansion. Until the 1870s, Sachsenhausen housed a tenth of the city's population at most.

Then, within a decade, the area underwent a complete transformation. Its population more than doubled between 1870 and 1880 as, with the opening of the lower and upper Main bridges in 1874 and 1878 respectively, it became far better connected not just to the Innenstadt, but to the newly developing Westend and Ostend areas around it. In 1869 a footbridge had already been erected over the old ford, linking the city centre at the Römer to Sachsenhausen: known as Eiserner Steg, or the Iron Footbridge, it remains a popular point for a panorama of the city centre, as well as an everyday thoroughfare for city workers.

By the outbreak of the First World War, Sachsenhausen and the neighbouring areas south of the river were home to more than a fifth of Frankfurt's burgeoning population. After the war, a range of new and adventurous developments was built to the south as part of the "New Frankfurt" housing programme, frequently in a reformist, garden-city style which has remained popular—and exemplary—to this day, extending the city out to the natural barrier of the extensive Stadtwald forest: the long, low lines of the Heimatsiedlung blocks are the best-known of these developments. And while the overall demeanour of Sachsenhausen was and is residential, the riverfront—with its proximity to the city centre and excellent views of it—became home to some very fine *belle époque* architecture and a string of five museums. Today, these factors have combined to make Sachsenhausen one of the city's most desirable areas to live in.

Bahnhofsviertel, Gallus, Gutleutviertel

While the 1870s saw Sachsenhausen turn from a village into a suburb, they also saw the construction and rise to prominence of three completely new areas to the west of the Innenstadt which lastingly weakened the gravitational pull of the old centre and lengthened the town out along the Main. These areas did not spring up by chance, but were created by a conscious planning decision on a scale almost unimaginable in modern metropolises.

As the first railways arrived in Frankfurt in the late 1830s and 1840s, the city fortifications had only been gone for a quarter of a century: aside from the new villas of what was to become Westend, much of the land surrounding the Wallanlagen was still arable or completely unused. The region's first railway from Wiesbaden to Frankfurt came in across these fields from the west right up to where the city walls had stood; the locomotive sheds and depots were set out to the north of the line on what had previously been the gallows, and the land to the south was given over to goods lines down to the river. Other companies soon laid their tracks along the same path, and by the 1860s Frankfurt had three western rail terminals amidst a sprawl of sidings, water towers and coal bunkers.

After the Franco-Prussian War of 1871-72, Germany as a whole, and Frankfurt as an urban centre, began to expand rapidly. Vastly increased rail traffic was both a driving factor in and a symptom of Imperial Germany's breakneck economic growth, and the city was soon outgrowing its uncoordinated rail infrastructure. The town hall's answer was to shift the railhead half a mile westwards out of the city, allowing its dimensions to be vastly increased, freeing up space around the centre and offering a chance to plan an integrated river harbour with increased capacity nearby. In 1888 the gigantic Hauptbahnhof, which remains one of Europe's three largest passenger stations to this day, was opened on its current site, albeit surrounded by little more than overgrown former sidings.

In little over ten years, however, the station had been hemmed in on all sides by a dense urban landscape. As had been done in the 1850s with the Westend, Nordend and Ostend, in 1889 the city authorities gave the disused area of land between the old walls and the new station a road layout and sold off land in parcels to developers, who promptly filled them with residential property. By the outbreak of the First World War 25 years later, only the site of the old station remained undeveloped, the rest having been filled with stone-built townhouses of five to six floors in the style of the time. Although much of the turn-of-the-century architecture now considered so handsome survived the air raids of the Second World War, what soon became known as the Bahnhofsviertel is, today, down at heel. It is notorious as a red-light district, with all of the other attendant illicit activities and social ills, and has become synonymous with criminal syndicates and their turf-wars—changes which started in the late 1940s due to developments in its neighbouring area, Gutleutviertel.

Gutleutviertel—literally "Good People's Quarter"—takes its name from a sanctuary for lepers run by monks, its location outside the city walls wedged in between the gallows and the Main having been left uninhabited by Frankfurt's medieval burghers. With the arrival of the railways and the development of the harbour to the west of the city centre, the Gutleutviertel slowly lost its rural character, housing sidings and warehouses. As part of the redevelopment of the 1870s and 1880s, the city and national governments made use of its proximity to the new main station, Hauptbahnhof, and new harbour, Westhafen, for important pieces of infrastructure: the Imperial Army erected extensive barracks, the Gutleutkaserne, in 1877, while the city had the public gas and electricity works built there. Remaining spaces were given over to workers' housing, the urbane apartments of the Bahnhofsviertel being out of the financial reach of the labouring population at the time.

In an irony of history, however, the grimy Gutleutviertel would end up dragging the Bahnhofsviertel down to eye-level. After the Second World War, the US Army requisitioned the Gutleutkaserne infantry barracks and made Frankfurt its European headquarters:

American servicemen looking to spend their pay stumbled over to the pubs and bars serving the railway station, and the glory years began. When American forces moved out of Frankfurt in the 1970s, however, the area's fortunes fell as quickly as they had risen: popular clubs quickly became seedy dives, and the general post-war drain to the suburbs meant that even the area's central location was more of a hindrance than a help.

The third of Frankfurt's districts to be created with the new Hauptbahnhof was the former field of execution, Gallus. In an early piece of shameless urban regeneration-related rebranding, the name Gallus—originally the result of Frankfurt dialect eroding the word *Galgenfeld*, or gallows—was linked to St. Gall, whose Latin name is Gallus. A new, eponymous Catholic place of worship put an official seal on the arbitrary change of etymology in 1905, by which stage the gruesome history of the area had already been buried under a new goods station and other industrial developments. For much of the twentieth century, the freight terminal to the north and the main station to the south defined the limits of Gallus and determined its population: with the exception of the *Frankfurter Allgemeine Zeitung*, which set up its editorial offices next to its printing works there, Gallus was synonymous with industry and the city's working classes. With the redevelopment of the old goods station in the 2000s under the name Europaviertel, however, the area was opened up to the Messe, the world-famous trade fair area, to its north, and its proximity to the station and to the banking area has seen its character change.

The same is true of Gutleutviertel which, despite being on the proverbial wrong side of the tracks, has profited from its proximity to the city and, above all, to the banks in the western districts as urban living has once again become popular. The Westhafen docklands are now home to shiny new bankers' apartments and swanky bar-cum-restaurant locations; the Gutleutkaserne was refitted in the 1990s to house Germany's busiest tax office and other municipal entities; only the monumental heating plant on the site of the old electricity works serves as an active reminder of the area's industrial past. The Bahnhofsviertel alone has retained its louche, gritty image, although the early signs of gentrification have recently manifested themselves here, too: given its central location, literally in the shadows of the city's banking towers, the only surprise is that it has taken so long for the young and upwardly mobile to declare its shabbiness to be chic and to start paying over the odds for rentals there.

Mainhattan

The proximity of these run-down nineteenth-century apartment blocks, plastered with neon and donor kebab signage, to the city's cluster of gleaming skyscrapers is one of the contrasts that gives Frankfurt its *frisson*. Often grouped together under the punning portmanteau Mainhattan, the dozen or so core towers that form the famous skyline of the city are to be found in the southern part of Westend and the western extremity of the Innenstadt. On the map, they form a sort of inverted Y in which the two spurs begin at the Main in the south and the Messe in the west, converging at the Taunusanlage park on the former city walls and heading north past the Opera towards Nordend.

For all their apparent size, the skyscrapers which form this cluster are by American or Asian standards somewhat squat: the tallest among them, the Commerzbank Tower, stands just 259 metres (850 feet) high. Furthermore, compared to the downtowns of American metropolises, the area they cover is unremarkable: they stand on two main axes, along Mainzer Landstraße and Taunusanlage, which each measure just over a kilometre. Unlike the other European clusters in London or at Paris' La Défense, the skyscrapers are not arranged around a focal point and there is plenty of space between them by way of low-rise office blocks and greenery. Yet the effect at street level is still, at first, very much that of a bustling, high-rise financial quarter; two streets behind the strips of skyscrapers, however, the genteel banker's villas of Westend or the grimy tenements of the Bahnhofsviertel begin.

In recent years, Frankfurt's high-rise panorama has started to spread beyond its original confines in the financial district of south Westend: the 1980s and 1990s saw the extension of the northern spur onto the Messe site and into Gallus and since the millennium several towers have sprung up elsewhere in the city. The redevelopment of the Westhafen in Gutleutviertel was sealed in 2003 with a circular tower; one year previously, Sachsenhausen got its first real skyscraper in the form of the already-iconic Main Plaza Tower. Meanwhile, Ostend has seen the opening of its maiden tower, nothing lesser than the new headquarters of the European Central Bank: with its acres of brownfield land and central location, Frankfurt's Ostend will provide an interesting proposition for the next round of high-end, high-rise development. As such, the nickname "Mainhattan" may soon justly be applied to the city as a whole, rather than just the jagged skyline to the immediate west of the centre.

Niederrad, Schwanheim

Although the central axes have defined Frankfurt's skyline-based image for decades, the city has been friendly to high-rise developments elsewhere, too: most notably in the districts of Niederrad and Schwanheim, south of the river to the west of Sachsenhausen. Formerly quiet, spacious suburbs, their proximity to both the city centre and the rapidly expanding airport saw them selected for the kind of large-scale high-rise residential and commercial developments which sprung from the positivist town-planning spirit of the 1950s and 1960s. The idea was very much of its time: living quarters and working space were to be separated, and plenty of room given to large, car-friendly streets. To the east of the railway line heading south out of Frankfurt, high-rise blocks with views of the Main river and generous gardens would house those tired of the congestion, noise and stress of the city centre; to the west, a gleaming new set of offices would offer a spacious working environment right next to the autobahn, just a short taxi-ride away from the airport.

And to a certain extent, this vision has become reality: companies looking for workspace at cheap rates are glad of the Bürostadt development, while the Mainfeld high rises—although an easy target for stigmatization with their weathered brown concrete exteriors—have been spared the dystopian fate of many such a 1960s housing project worldwide. Nevertheless, the quiet, sterile, commuter-town atmosphere of the area makes it feel dated today,

THE URBAN MAP

and the rehabilitation of city-centre working and living pose questions about its future.

Bockenheim and the Messe

One suburb that is doing far better out of the resurgence of inner cities is Bockenheim, northwest of the Westend banking district and directly north of the Messe. A village settlement almost as old as Frankfurt itself, Bockenheim remained outside the earthworks erected around Frankfurt in the Middle Ages, although its citizens were given the right to flee into the city in case of danger: the Bockenheimer Warte, one of the four remaining towers marking the gates in what was the outer ring of defences, stands at the beginning of today's district, which became a part of the city of Frankfurt in 1895. By this stage, the two settlements had grown into one another: with space in Frankfurt proper limited, Bockenheim was an inviting prospect for pioneering nineteenth-century industrialists, and by the time Bockenheim was incorporated into Frankfurt, its economic importance to the city was second to none, with everything from railway carriage construction to chemical works and shoe factories located in the area. In 1912 Bockenheim also played host to Frankfurt's first airfield, and although this was soon relocated south of the Main, the landing strip remained in military usage until after the Second World War.

In the post-war years, industry rapidly deserted the city altogether, leaving space next to the Westend into which the Goethe University, founded there in 1912, soon expanded—the now defunct AfE tower was symbolic of the 1950s and 1960s architecture which accompanied the university's shift into the area. Workers gave way to students, factories were replaced by lecture halls, and lunchtime canteens made space for late-night bars: Bockenheim gained an alternative, counter-culture character in the wild 1960s, and was in many ways a ground-zero from which the philosophical and social changes which shook up German society from 1968 onwards could be said to have emanated (see "Unions and Students", page 205).

While it has retained some of this feel, Bockenheim's proximity to Westend meant that it did not go unnoticed by that district's financial services sector, also looking to expand out of the limited space there. Beginning in the late 1980s, a range of auxiliary companies set up in the area, undeterred by the area's radical reputation and attracted by the newly-expanded Messe, most of whose exhibition halls are located in the southern section of Bockenheim.

The German word *Messe* means both trade fair and mass, indicating a gathering which was originally linked to the Church calendar but rapidly became an economic event in its own right. Frankfurt's central location in both the Holy Roman Empire and Europe as a whole quickly made it a preferred location for many of medieval Europe's major annual fairs and markets, and out of this tradition developed Frankfurt's modern proliferation of trade shows and exhibitions, the most famous of which today are the Book Fair and the Motor Show.

With the vogue for large-scale exhibitions in the late nineteenth century, it became clear that the old city-centre locations used for trade fairs such as Römerberg and Roßmarkt were no longer enough to keep up with the likes of London's Crystal Palace of Paris' *Grand Palais*. Accordingly, in 1907, the city of Frankfurt founded a new company to build a hall for modern expositions in more spacious out-of-town surroundings; in 1908, the Festhalle was opened in Bockenheim, and remains at the core of the much-enlarged Messe area today. In the 1980s, with the increasing size and importance of international trade shows, a second wave of expansion saw newer and larger expo halls erected, as well as the imposing, pencil-shaped 257m (843ft) Messeturm skyscraper—Europe's tallest building from 1991 to 1997, until it was surpassed by the city-centre Commerzbank Tower.

Bornheim

The only tower of note in Bornheim (that other Frankfurt area that was once a village beginning with B and ending in -*heim*) is the Friedberger Warte, another of the four remaining towers of the medieval outer ring. The rest of this bustling district, extending northeast out of the city centre between Nordend and Ostend, is decidedly low-rise, antiquated and rural, even, in parts, making it a popular place of residence for young families and those who do not get along with overly-urban living environments. Yet the contrast between the wattle-and-daub exteriors of many of its surviving pre-modern buildings and the shiny towers rising in the distance is a popular photographic motif in its own right, too, as are the picturesque backyards and beer gardens behind these old houses.

Although this former village became the first of the surrounding settlements to be officially incorporated into Frankfurt in 1877, it retained its rural character to a far greater extent than other areas. In 1785 it had seen Germany's first experiment in manned flight when French balloon pioneer Jean-Pierre Blanchard set off on his forty-minute flight to Weilburg, yet the city's first airfield was, of course, set up in Bockenheim; and despite its tradition of artisan craft, factories, too, remained few and far between. Closer in to the city centre, newer tenement blocks replaced the old village houses along the Berger Straße—the high road that led from the old city walls out into the country, and which today forms the central axis through the district—but in the old village, today Bornheim-Mitte, little changed. Many of the popular taverns and inns there serving old-style trencherman's fayre and *Appelwoi*, Frankfurt's astringent answer to cider ("Zur Sonne" is among the best), have histories measured in centuries, while the winding roads, even filled with cars, can make both the city and the modern era generally feel very far away.

Nevertheless, Bornheim has not remained entirely untouched by the march of history. The fields on its eastern fringes at Bornheimer Hang were included in the "New Frankfurt" building plans of the 1920s: long, low-rise garden-city apartments were built, as well as a football stadium for the city's beloved Eintracht Frankfurt, with further blocks added on to counter the housing crisis following the destruction of the Second World War. In fact, it is actually through destruction rather than construction that the twentieth century made perhaps its biggest mark on Bornheim: in the years following the Second World War, the unbuilt area just past the Bornheimer Hang to the south of the football stadium was used to store the rubble of the old city following the devastating bombing raids.

Here, the city set up a not-for-profit organization to marshal the whole process of clearing, collecting, sorting and salvaging valuable materials from the detritus; from 1945 through to 1964, the *Trümmerverwertungsgesellschaft*, the first of its kind, processed an average of 1,500 cubic metres of rubble a day, producing enough recycled building materials for 100,000 new apartments and offices. Jokingly referred to by Frankfurters as *Monte Scherbelino*—an Italianate nonsense name which might translate as "Monte Shard-elino"—the concept received nationwide and international acclaim as an efficient, societally beneficial way of dealing with war damage.

After it had played its role in effacing the post-war ruins, the *Trümmerverwertungsgesellschaft* effaced itself in 1964 and the area was returned to a use perhaps more in keeping with the old medieval origins of Bornheim: staging the twice-yearly Dippemess funfair, which has been held in Frankfurt since the 1300s and which, like the city's Messe, became too big an event for the crowded city centre. Frankfurt's ice-hockey team then built its hall between this fairground and the old football stadium—which remains in use, albeit by FSV Frankfurt 1899, the city's second football team, Eintracht Frankfurt having moved to a new, far larger ground in the extensive Stadtwald forest.

Eschersheim, Heddernheim

Separated from Bornheim by the trees of the central cemetery, Frankfurt's northern quarters extend out to Eschersheim and Heddernheim, further former villages which have become an integral part of the city. At first glance, the area is an unremarkable dormitory for the centre, yet it is precisely its suburban character that makes it of interest to those looking to understand the development of the city. As the faceless parade of hastily erected 1950s houses and supermarket parking lots gives way to the shallow valley of the Nidda river, the various dreams of generation after generation of urban planners hove into view: from the early twentieth-century garden city of Römerstadt (see Chapter 12) through to the 1960s car-and-concrete-loving futurism of the workmanlike Nordwest (whose descriptive, logical name catches the spirit of the time), there is no shortage of architectural idealism here—and indeed the surrounding woods and fields make this particular slice of suburbia a not undesirable location for middle-income Frankfurters.

The Periphery: Airport, Rüsselsheim, Offenbach

Located in the middle of the extensive forests to the southwest of the city is Frankfurt Airport: Germany's largest, and third in Europe in terms of passenger numbers after London Heathrow and Paris Charles de Gaulle. Entirely surrounded by woods, with its surface area of more than 18km^2, around 80,000 workers and its own major railway station, the airport truly is an area of the city in and of itself—it even has its own municipal district within the local government structure (residential population: 200). While major airports such as Heathrow and Gatwick in London, Charles de Gaulle and Orly in Paris, or JFK and La Guardia in New York may be simple features of their gigantic urban areas, any attempt to understand Frankfurt without taking into account its outsized airport is doomed to failure: this city of little more than 700,000 inhabitants can handle 65 million air passengers a year (which compares to a figure of 75 million for Heathrow, in a city whose population is well over eight million), while the airport organization directly employs more people than any other single company in the surrounding federal state. Frankfurt's gigantic airport is therefore one of the city's key economic factors, and is as such viewed with pride by some and bitterly fought against as a symptom of the ills of capitalism and globalization by others: the German Green Party, for example, was born out of the 1980s protest against a new take-off runway (see Chapter 4, page 110).

Another employer both of considerable size and of symbolic importance for all of Germany resides just west of the airport in Rüsselsheim on the Main: Adam Opel AG. While German car-makers such as BMW, Mercedes and Audi have gone from strength to strength, mid-market Opel has seen its profit margins continuously sink since the early 1990s and was only kept afloat by a state bailout in 2009. Owned by the American giant General Motors and forced for decades to limit its exports to Europe alone, Opel's turbulent history and uncertain future show that if Frankfurt Airport is enjoying the upside of globalization, Rüsselsheim's carmaker is suffering from the same thing. Nevertheless, this compact, ancient, and resourceful town's highly-skilled workforce has attracted other international automotive concerns—as has its closeness to the airport. Although not a part of Frankfurt, the fortunes of nondescript, take-it-as-you-find-it Rüsselsheim are very much dependent on what happens a few miles upriver.

The same might be said of Offenbach, located to the southeast of Frankfurt. The two cities have more or less merged into each other, with only a few fields remaining between them on the floodplain to the south of the Main; Frankfurt's Ostend is joined directly to Offenbach by the Kaiserleibrücke across the river. As such, with its loveless post-war architecture and proliferation of concrete monstrosities, down-on-its-luck Offenbach, which suffered a sharp decline in its historic industries of leather production and electric appliances from the late 1970s onwards, is often considered Frankfurt's "problem suburb", the dirty little secret that the wealthy banking city likes to keep at arm's length. There is some truth to this "Tale of Two Cities" portrait, as many of the gleaming skyscrapers of the Frankfurt financial district are cleaned by those who live in the crumbling tower blocks of Offenbach. Yet distinct cities the two do remain, and there is no surer way to annoy both Frankfurters and Offenbachers than to claim that they are one and the same. Parts of Offenbach are recorded in writing before Frankfurt was first mentioned in 794 AD and due to the piecemeal structure of German lands until unification under Bismarck, the two cities were actually in different countries until the 1860s.

The Region: Rhine-Main and Hesse

Officialdom, however, has not failed to take note of the cities' modern dependency on one another: since 2001 Frankfurt, Offenbach and other nearby towns and cities such as Rüsselsheim, Hanau and Bad Homburg have been part of a greater urban authority called Frankfurt-Rhein-Main, which coordinates planning, transport and other matters of regional important to the altogether 2.2 million inhabitants of the area. Given the fact that Frankfurt's actual population of 700,000 rises to over one million between 8.00am and 8.00pm, it is easy to see why this kind of urban-area-wide planning is of the essence—and why outsiders could be forgiven for seeing in Frankfurt's immediate neighbours little more than suburbs.

The overarching administrative entity of which Frankfurt and its region form part, however, is the State of Hesse. Germany today is a federal republic constituted along similar lines to the United States: Berlin is the federal capital of a country composed of sixteen states, each with wide-ranging powers and their own regional assemblies. This system was imposed on Germany after the Second World War principally as an insurance policy against a renewed outbreak of totalitarianism; with powers divided across (what were, until the absorption of East Germany in 1990) ten state capitals, any resurgent dictatorship would have a tougher time staging a successful *coup d'état*. Furthermore, Germany in 1945 was divided between four main occupying powers and its territorial extent was by no means clear; several states founded by French forces were earmarked for possible integration into the Fourth Republic, for instance, with the final Saarland question only being resolved in the late 1950s. Lastly, a decentralized state harked back to the millennial tradition of the Holy Roman Empire and was welcomed by many in the German population as a return to a cosmopolitan, pluralistic and expressly non-nationalist past.

The State of Hesse was proclaimed by the United States in September 1945, and thus predates the Federal Republic of Germany, eventually constituted of the various entities established by Allied forces in their parts of Germany in 1949. Its namesake was the medieval Landgraviate of Hessia, a powerful German state situated around the ancient towns of Kassel, Marburg and Giessen to the north of Frankfurt and which, during the 1400s, established an extra-territorial dependency around Darmstadt to the south. In the sixteenth century, it waned and was partitioned into five smaller duchies and princedoms, which were eventually yoked back together under Prussian expansion in the 1860s to form the province of Hesse-Nassau: the extent of this historical entity was the rough blueprint applied by American occupying forces in creating the new state.

Nevertheless, despite its territorial position within the newly-established Hesse, Frankfurt had had little truck with historical Hessia thus far. The Hessian heartlands had always been some way to the north, and Frankfurt's immediate territorial neighbours in the Holy Roman Empire had been Hanau, by tradition more Bavarian than Hessian, and Nassau, a historically distinct entity. Although in the German Confederation of the early 1800s, these territories became part of the Duchy of Hesse and the new state of Hesse-Nassau respectively, there was little in the name; moreover, Frankfurt retained territorial independence until 1866, after which point it was annexed into the new Prussian province against its will. As such, Frankfurt—although by some margin the largest city of the region since the 1500s—was ill-suited to become the new state's capital in 1945. Not only was Frankfurt holding out for the kind of city-state status accorded to the Hanseatics Bremen and Hamburg (both federal states to this day), but it was out of the running in any case as it was simply far too damaged to host a new government apparatus. The Americans opted for the quiet spa-town of Wiesbaden, comparatively unscathed, where they had also set up their military headquarters. And so since 1945, Frankfurt has been at the economic and cultural centre of a state whose seat of government it does not host, much in the same manner as megalopolises Los Angeles and San Francisco are subordinate to tiny Sacramento as part of the State of California.

The State of Hesse today is home to six million people, meaning that more than ten per cent of its population lives within Frankfurt's city limits and that a third of its population is to be found in the surrounding urban area. In national terms, Hesse stacks up as medium-sized state both by population and territory. The giants of federal Germany are, in terms of population, North-Rhine-Westphalia, at 17.5 million (half a million higher than that of the neighbouring Netherlands), and by area, Bavaria (only slightly smaller than its sovereign neighbour, the Czech Republic). The federal dwarf, meanwhile, is Bremen, with a population

650,000 and an area of 420km², i.e. roughly the size of municipal Frankfurt.

In this way, Frankfurt is both at the heart of Hesse and yet very much independent of it, subject to its legislature but—by sheer force of population at the ballot box if nothing else—defining in its political culture. While the historical identity of being an urban *Frankfurter* is quite distinct from any notions of being provincial *Hessisch*, migration and commuting into the city mean that the two identities commingle to a great extent.

3 | Landmarks
Buildings and Styles

As a general rule, the concentration of landmarks in cities increases with proximity to their centre—and Frankfurt is no exception. The landmarks one encounters at the city's focal points, however, are not always what might be expected—or indeed quite what they seem. This dissonance is never clearer than on Römerberg, Frankfurt's central square and premier postcard motif.

Römerberg

The Römerberg square is roughly triangular, flanked on the northwest by the eponymous cardinal-hued Römer town hall, on the east by a Brothers-Grimm-style ensemble of wood-and-plaster-fronted houses, and on the south by the Nikolaikirche (St. Nicholas Church), resplendent in its bright barber-shop livery of white paint and bare red sandstone. The Römer town hall building is a kind of triptych of medieval stone façades fronting a labyrinthine set of courtyards and buildings which have been in continuous use by the city authorities since the 1400s, while the church dates back even further to the twelfth century. The view of both can be taken in from the restaurant tables in front of the charmingly irregular row of olde-world houses on the east side of the square, which bear names such as Großer und Kleiner Engel, Goldener Greif and Kleiner Dachsberg—the Big and the Small Angel, the Golden Griffin and the Little Badger Hill.

In December the square hosts Frankfurt's most popular Christmas market, while in summer the statue of Justice standing in a fountain first installed in 1611 attracts hot-and-bothered tourists for a five-minute sit-down. The visitors park their posteriors on pavement slabs set on ground which saw centuries of regal pomp as Holy Roman Emperor after Holy Roman Emperor was proclaimed in the city: whenever the assorted royalty of the Empire convened in Frankfurt to elect their new superior, the Römerberg hosted a

The central Römer Square as it was in the 1890s (Library of Congress, Washington DC)

party of truly medieval proportions, with casks of ale tapped by the minute and entire oxen being spit-roasted on the square.

So far, so historic; so far, so idyllic. Yet today's picture-postcard is, depending on how one views the matter, a poignant, lovingly-reconstructed reminder of what Frankfurt has lost—or little more than a cynical tourist trap. It is, in any case, a simulacrum, as becomes clear with a visit to the Historisches Museum in the Saalhof behind the St. Nicholas Church, where perhaps the city's most striking "landmark" can be viewed: two scale-model recon-structions of central Frankfurt (see Chapter 6). The first, roughly 2.5 × 5m (8 × 16ft), shows the city's Old Town as it was in 1927, while the second, slightly smaller diorama documents the city cen-tre as it was in 1945. While the older model—all churches, towers and narrow streets—could, in the days before computer generated imagery, easily have been used for a scene-setting bird's-eye-view shot in a medieval period drama, the second model would look more at home in a film about an apocalyptic struggle with merciless aliens: hollowed out churches stand amidst a sea of blackened walls and flattened debris. The Römerberg is in ruins, its picturesque row of wooden houses eradicated, much of the town hall in rubble and the St. Nicholas Church severely damaged.

These models are phantom landmarks, reminders of central Frankfurt's lost Old Town which, due to the picturesque nature of its buildings as well as its sheer size and extent, was once one of the archetypal old towns of central Europe—and perhaps *the* archetypal German *Altstadt*. They remind the visitor both of the achievements of the German renaissance and of the country's descent into col-lective barbarity, all the while raising the same stubborn questions regarding the proportionality, morality and effect of Allied bombing raids in the Second World War.

In another more subtle way, however, these landmarks also lay bare the debates about urban planning which have been held in Frankfurt more or less continuously since the early 1900s, and which show no signs of being resolved today. The old model was started by brothers Robert and Hermann Treuner in 1925, out of fear that the Old Town was soon to be demolished: its narrow streets and roughly 2,000 timber-framed buildings were considered by the radically progressive city authorities of the 1920s to be a hindrance to proper urban development, and they wanted much of it bulldozed to make way for brick new-builds, parks and wide roads. The Brothers Treuner, local activists and not least the Historisches Museum itself campaigned against the plans, and as a more conservative local government took over in the early 1930s, a new concept based on the upgrading and improvement of the existing structures was implemented—a concept which was swiftly co-opted by the National Socialists, obsessed as they were with all things "traditionally German".

The Nazis' conflation of architectural heritage and mythic Aryan bunkum meant that, in the years following the War, openly defending the preservation of what remained of the ruined Old Town had become a risky political business. Well into the 1970s, major cities all over Germany queued up to pour their non-Nazi credentials into concrete, with Frankfurt leading the charge. Only deeply conservative conurbations such as Munich, Münster and Dresden—or those that had just been plain lucky and escaped total destruction—seemed able to resist the temptation of *tabula rasa* solutions. In Frankfurt, the debate once again crystallized around the city authorities on the one side, dusting off modernist dreams of demolition in their 1950 planning competition, and the Historisches Museum on the other side, which put on its first post-war exhibition concurrently to plead for preservation wherever possible. This time, however, the Brothers Treuner found themselves on the other side of the debate: their second model was used in a 1946 exhibition to advocate a blank-slate solution for Frankfurt and, as such, purposefully exaggerated the degree of destruction as documented in Allied aerial photos of the time. In contrast, they kept working on their as-yet unfinished model of the Altstadt until completion in 1965: perhaps faithfully documenting what had been so damaged gave them the mental freedom to imagine something new?

As it happened, the debate between the preservationist and positivist camps was never settled, and the Römerberg is the most prominent display of this in Frankfurt. Used as a car park in the years immediately following the War, its characteristic ensemble was painstakingly reconstructed over the years while much of the rest of the Old Town was hastily cobbled together or completely redesigned. Yet all is not what it seems: the triptych façade of the town hall hides a far more modern, expansive 1950s complex, with only the Emperors' Hall—rebuilt in a far more simple fashion—remaining of the original layout. Meanwhile, the row of fairy-tale houses opposite is a complete, albeit convincing, reconstruction, as is the late-gothic Steinernes Haus across the path from them, while only the St. Nicholas Church survived well enough to be restored to its original glory with no structural changes. On the southwest corner of the square, meanwhile, stands Haus Wertheym, the only timber-framed construction to have survived the air attacks of 1943 and 1944 undamaged: its cool, damp cellars only metres away from the Main made it a crucial location for wartime firefighters who simply did not give up on it. The fact that it did not take a direct hit, however, is just good luck—and Frankfurters have been toasting it ever since in the city's oldest continuously operating pub, located in the building along with a patisserie.

In spite of such authentic credentials, for critics the Römer as a whole is a kind of Disneyland fake which negates the tortured past of both the city and the country. Yet the 1950s planning conflicts are visible on the square: on the other side of the Römer, for example, in the adjacent Salzhaus on the corner to the main thoroughfare, Braubachstraße. Variously a salt merchant's store and a debtors' jail before it was subsumed into the town hall complex in the nineteenth century, it was, in contrast to the neighbouring triptych, not faithfully rebuilt, but reconceived in a historicizing style which nods to the history of the building while including visibly modern elements: the arched base of pale carmine sandstone and the pitched slate roof are classic Frankfurt, as are the building's proportions; yet the storeys in between are square, rational, and lit by typically pre-fab post-war windows. Most strikingly, the side of the building features a mosaic of a phoenix rising from the ashes, a symbol of Frankfurt's reconstruction. Neither quite fish nor fowl, the Salzhaus was controversial when it was unveiled and has remained unloved to this day, neither looking quite original enough to please the traditionalists nor brave enough to appease the radicals. Indeed, it was to be the first and, for many years, the last tightrope-walk of its kind.

The Historisches Museum itself bears witness to the swings in planning approaches. It is located in the Saalhofkomplex on the Main, which includes parts of the Saalhofkapelle, the oldest surviving building of any kind in the city, dating from the twelfth century, and the Rententurm, a glorious gothic tower which once housed the river toll authorities; the two older structures are joined together by the patrician Bernusbau and Burnitzbau townhouses of the eighteenth and nineteenth centuries respectively. While this ensemble was faithfully restored following the war, the ruined houses between it and the St. Nicolas Church on the square were razed and the area given over to an outsized, almost entirely windowless exposed concrete museum extension. Opening in 1972, it was immediately unpopular among all but the most ardent defenders of brutalism, and especially hated by many in the museum itself. Its shadowy, looming presence over the picturesque Römer came to symbolize for many the thoughtlessness and arrogance of positivist post-war planning, and so few mourned its 2011 demise in favour of a new building. Through using sandstone and pitched roofs, the new extension is billed as a more sensitive addition to this historic square which will, as the planning speak goes, "enter into a dialogue with its surroundings" by revealing more of the historic Saalhof complex. Yet the new building will be a visibly contemporary addition and is by no means a reconstruction of any preceding structure. After decades of oscillating between slavish reconstruction and brash novelty, city planning seems once again willing to try a third way for Frankfurt's central square.

Domhügel

To the immediate east of the Römerberg, the city's other historic centrepoint, Domhügel—"cathedral hill"—has also been at the mercy of the decades-long swings of the planning pendulum. The Old Town was at its most dense in the area between the row of reconstructed houses on Römerberg and the cathedral, which were connected by two narrow thoroughfares, Bendergasse and Saalgasse, and a wealth of lanes which centred on Hühnermarkt ("Chicken Market") and the villagey cosiness of Fünffingerplätzchen ("Five Finger Place"). This entire quarter was flattened in a 1944 bombing raid and remained unbuilt wasteland until the early 1970s, when the colossal Technisches Rathaus was erected on the northern part of the site, stretching almost from the Römerberg to the cathedral. Very much like the old extension of the Historisches Museum across the square, the "Technical Town Hall" was despised by many from the moment of its inception. Composed of three squat office towers and surrounded by a seemingly impenetrable ring of tinted-window and concrete frontage, the building was nothing if not in the spirit of its time. Soon after its inauguration, Bendergasse and Saalgasse were redeveloped with new-build housing (albeit along their original routes and on a less monumental scale) but the widespread controversy surrounding the plans dogged further development of the site, especially as excavations for the new metro line running under it had revealed the foundations not only of the city's founding Carolingian palace, but of ever older Roman settlement. Only in 1986 was the last gap in the flattened quarter filled by the new Schirn Kunsthalle, a strikingly bright and lengthy strip of a building running from the Römerberg to the Domhügel and housing the city's premier public art gallery. Flanked by this new building on the south and the Technisches Rathaus on the north, the ancient remains were left untouched and open to the sky as the Archäologischer Garten, and the centre of Frankfurt was finally complete.

Yet the controversy continued. While the Schirn, its daringly horizontal form centred on a stone cylinder with something of the look of a castle keep, won grudging respect, the space-hopper-sized bulk of the Technisches Rathaus looked more and more like a misguided mistake with every passing year. Along with the old museum extension across the square, it too met its demise in 2011 as part of a new development plan, the "Dom-Römer-Projekt", the idea of which is to recreate not *the* Altstadt, but *an* Altstadt, which means a set of buildings between the Römerberg and the Domhügel somewhat truer to the original scale of the long-gone Old City. The plans called for 35 buildings, 15 of which would be reconstructions of old timber-framed buildings, yet predictably enough, the scheme has become a political football and cause for much soul-searching. The planning debate centres once again on whether it is intellectually coherent and morally right to recreate buildings which perished at the end of a shameful period of the country's history, while political issues such as the privatization of public space and scant municipal finances are slowing progress. As of 2014, however, the archaeological garden has been sealed and buried, both to avoid further damage to it (thirty years of urban pollution and rainy weather had taken their toll) and to create the space needed for the new project.

The overriding aim of the Dom-Römer-Projekt is to open up the axis from west to east between the Römerberg square and the cathedral, the Dom. There has been a place of worship on this site since the conversion of the Franks to Christianity in the sixth century; the Carolingian Salvatorkirche cemented the importance of this patch of consecrated ground, and its 1239 replacement, named Bartholomäuskirche (Church of St. Bartholomew) became by and by the place in which Holy Roman Emperors were made. The Golden Bull of 1356 named the church as the site of the election, and between 1562 and 1792, ten emperors were crowned at the altar before taking the Königsweg, Kingsway, along the narrow streets to the Römer and dining in its Kaisersaal or Emperor's Hall. Although lacking a bishop's seat and thus not technically a cathedral, the important role the Bartholomäuskirche came to play in the life of the city and the empire, as well as its growing size, made the designation "church" seem insufficient, and the building was eventually referred to as the Kaiserdom: the Emperor's Cathedral.

The structure standing today is essentially a medieval gothic church erected piecemeal between the 1200s and the 1500s, consisting of a nave and a transept forming an Orthodox cross and a wealth of smaller chapels surrounding it, culminating in the tall gothic tower at the western end. Yet little of the Dom is actually original: the Reformation back-and-forth between Catholicism and Protestantism saw much of the interior changed, while a fire in 1867 destroyed the first roof and the spire. The subsequent repair work, intended to restore the cathedral to an imagined ideal of former glory, replaced the early-gothic nave with a larger, mock high-gothic structure and led to the removal of several somewhat ramshackle buildings which had backed onto the church and which did not quite fit in with the purist Prussian concept of a great cathedral *comme il faut*. Completed in 1878, the repairs began again in 1945 after several bombs had crashed through the transept roof and gutted the interior. Even on this holy site, the battles between the city's post-war modernists and the traditionalists raged: decorative murals added during the 1870s restauration were whitewashed and the inside of the Dom received an entirely minimalist makeover, which was then peeled back in the 1990s to reveal the surviving wall paintings or painted over in brick red to mimic the medieval look of the cathedral.

Altstadt and Innenstadt

Besides the Dom, the historic core of Frankfurt is home to another church of considerable cultural importance to the life of German-speaking peoples: the Paulskirche or Church of St. Paul. Today's circular, classicizing structure was preceded by a monastery of the Order of the Discalced Friars, known in German as the *Barfüßer*, or those without shoes. These ascetic monks welcomed the Reformation and actually gifted the newly Protestant city their monastery and its chapel in 1526; by the end of the eighteenth century, however, the old church building had become so run-down that the city fathers had it demolished. The designs for its replacement were inspired by the Pantheon of Rome, and work began in 1789 (a fact which would later seem symbolic). The rotunda and dome were completed in 1802, yet before the new structure's tower and stairwells could be completed the economic crises as a result of the Napoleonic Wars put the construction work on what would turn out to be a thirty-year hold, and the new church was not consecrated until 1833.

The acoustics of the circular space made the church ideal not just for preaching, but also for parliamentary discussions, and after the German-speaking lands of Europe had elected their first democratically legitimated assembly following the revolutions of March 1848, it chose to meet there. Thus the Paulskirche was transformed into a hotbed of political radicalism as delegates hammered out a constitution for Prussia, Austria and other members of the German Confederation, united for the first time ever under the black, red and gold flag which would, a century later, become that of today's Federal Republic. As it happened, the Paulskirche constitution of 1849 was rejected by the authoritarian governments, the parliament melted away and Germany and Austria would have to wait until 1919 until the old order crumbled.

Yet stillborn as the child may have been, the church was widely remembered as the birthplace of Germany democracy, making it a site of national importance for the young Weimar Republic, and bringing conflict with the now conservative, nationalist Protestant Church, which had developed into a cornerstone of the Prussian establishment so suddenly dethroned. On his death in 1925, for example, a statue of Friedrich Ebert, the fledgling democracy's first president, was erected at the entrance to the rotunda, against which the church authorities protested vehemently. The church was, however, as with most of Frankfurt's consecrated ground, owned by the city (see Chapter 8), and the angry Paulskirche minister had to wait for the Nazis to seize power in 1933 before the statue was removed—much to his well-documented satisfaction.

Obliterated by bombing raids in 1944, the role of the Paulskirche as the cradle of German democracy made it an uncontroversial choice for reconstruction, and with the centenary of the 1848 events fast approaching, the city authorities pulled out all the stops to have the building ready by 1948. Due to the material and financial constraints of the immediate post-war period, the crowning dome was replaced by a flat roof and the interior design was starkly simplified; furthermore, the city's desire to have full use of the building as a public space led to changes in its internal structure, with a mezzanine entrance level separating an exhibition space in the lower floor and a high-ceilinged auditorium above.

Since the very first day of its post-war inauguration, the rebuilt Church of St. Paul has been consistently used to challenge, provoke and sometimes infuriate German society as it has built up its new democratic tradition. The first speech held there on the centenary of the gathering of the 1848 assembly was writer and painter Fritz von Unruh's (see page 238) *Rede an die Deutschen* (Speech to the Germans), a critical analysis of the Nazi years which proved unwelcome in a nation in which everybody seemed desperate to get back to business as usual.

Again and again, however, unsettling voices have been given use of the Paulskirche to make themselves heard: in 1955, the German Social Democrats and the Congress of Trade Unions met there to form a protest against West Germany's rearmament; the Peace Prize of the German Book Trade, awarded in the church yearly since the 1950s, has frequently gone to controversial writers facing political opprobrium in their home countries; and in 1998 the *Wehrmachtsausstellung* was hosted there on its tour through Germany. This controversial exhibition about the brutality of regular German forces during the Second World War busted the widespread myth that only the SS had been responsible for war crimes and led to one of modern Germany's most bitter historical arguments.

In June 1963, President Kennedy addressed an audience in the Paulskirche, underlining in his speech its heritage as the cradle of German democracy, and to this day it seems to fulfil this role like no other place in the country except the Bundestag itself in Berlin. The lower floor houses an exhibition about the church's history, while the entrance level features an epic allegorical mural depicting Germany's long and treacherous trudge to its current democratic state; upstairs, the minimalist auditorium symbolizes the open, rational, clear-thinking approach modern Germany seeks to hold itself to. Alongside the flags of the Federal Republic, of the City of Frankfurt and of the 16 federal states of modern Germany, the plain white walls of the upper level feature memorials to the victims of National Socialism as a collective and to Frankfurt's own Johanna Kirchner in particular (see page 223). The statue of Friedrich Ebert, destroyed by the Nazis, was recast and returned to the church in the 1950s.

A far more unassuming ecclesiastical presence is to be found due south of St. Paul's Church, in the form of the Leonhardskirche, just along from the Rententurm and Haus Wertheym on the banks of the River Main. Like these two medieval structures, the Church of St. Leonard is one of the very few buildings to have survived the air raids of 1943 and 1944 largely unscathed and is, in fact, the city's oldest completely intact pre-war building. Yet unlike either, it is somewhat inconspicuous and hemmed in on all sides by unremarkable townhouses or post-war apartments. Originally a Romanesque basilica of the 1200s, today's church was built in the gothic style in course of the fifteenth century and, aside from some renovation work in Prussian times, its structure has remained unchanged, much in contrast to its interior, which bears witness to the ravages of history. Indeed, its location on Buchgasse (Book Lane) hints at an interesting facet of its colourful past. As a Catholic place of worship, Leonhardkirche lost much of its parish with the Reformation, and although the Holy Roman Empire managed to reach an understanding in which both faiths were tolerated, occupation by the rabidly evangelical Swedes during the Thirty Years' War put a further squeeze on both its congregation and its finances. In fact, the only way the church could survive was to rent itself out as a warehouse to its neighbours in the booksellers' quarter surrounding it: for years on end, the church was unusable as a place of worship as books of all kinds, including perhaps some of those that had helped spread Protestant ideas across Europe, were stored everywhere, including on the altar. Italian merchants arriving in the 1700s brought some relief to the stricken church, only for the city to use the secularization of 1803 to strip it of many of its valuable objects, including an original Gutenberg bible today at the Frankfurt University library. It was then closed to worshippers once again during the Napoleonic Wars as the occupying French used it to lock up Prussian prisoners. Floods followed in 1845, and a small fire during the bombing raids destroyed the altar, but the interior still retains a wealth of period details from five hundred years of religious history to this day.

Central Frankfurt's fifth church of note is Katharinenkirche on Hauptwache to the northwest of the Römerberg. Like the Paulskirche, it was preceded by a cloister chapel—one belonging to a nunnery in the name of St. Catherine. With the Reformation, the nuns left the city, and their buildings were used to house women in need. In 1678 the chapel was replaced with a new church, the first to have been built in the city following the Reformation; today's structure, entirely rebuilt to the original design in the early 1950s, can appear somewhat lost on the busy Hauptwache square, but was a building of impressive proportions at the time of its construction. As the premier Protestant place of worship in the city, St. Catherine's Church attracted a string of gifted *Kapellmeister*—musical directors—including the baroque composer Georg Philipp Telemann (1681-1767). It was also the habitual place of worship of Frankfurt's most famous son, Johann Wolfgang von Goethe, whose family home was but a few streets away and is today a museum about the man often termed Germany's Shakespeare.

Much in the way that English speakers unconsciously quote Shakespeare, so many of German's most succinct, expressive and commonly-used phrases have their roots in the writings of Goethe (1749-1832), the exceptionally long-lived and continuously productive playwright and poet *par excellence*. In view of Goethe's overriding importance to German culture, the Goethe-Haus and Goethe-Museum on Großer Hirschgraben are buildings of international standing, beloved both of tourists and serious scholars. Goethe was born at the address in 1749, but the house in its present form came into being during his childhood as his father, the wealthy heir to successful inn-owners, had the family's two neighbouring timber-framed houses replaced by one single, four-storey dwelling. The young Johann-Wolfgang and his sister Cornelia received lessons in their father's custom-fitted and extensive upstairs library and played at marionettes and cut out silhouettes in their bedrooms. Apart from interludes to study at Leipzig and Strasbourg, Goethe remained in the family home until his move to Weimar in 1775. He describes his childhood home, and Frankfurt generally, in his autobiography *Dichtung und Wahrheit* (*Poetry and Truth*, see Chapter 5), recounting events at the Großer Hirschgraben house in such a lively and detailed way that, for bona fide aficionados, there is a genuine thrill to visiting the building. Sold by his mother following his father's death, the Goethe house was purchased by a charitable association in 1863 and turned into a museum for art and literature from the writer's lifetime. In 1897 the charity opened a museum to Goethe himself next door, which was itself extended and re-opened in 1932 (by none other than Nobel Prize laureate Thomas Mann, who went on to author of a fictional account of Goethe's beloved Lotte).

This expansion allowed for the Goethe house itself to be progressively returned to how it had been during the author's childhood and adolescence, albeit with very little by way of original furnishings: notable exceptions are the iron banisters engraved with the initials of Goethe's parents and a grandfather clock of truly extraordinary proportions, intricacy and functionality (it offers not only the time, but the date, a barometer, and astronomical as well as astrological readings).

The clock survived, as did much of the rest of the house's collection, in safe storage during the Second World War; the banisters were salvaged from the wreck of the house and museum. (Coincidentally, the bombing raid which destroyed them took place on 22 March 1944, the 112th anniversary of Goethe's death.) In contrast to the Paulskirche 100 metres away, however, the decision to rebuild the place of Goethe's birth was not uncontroversial. While literary figures including Hermann Hesse and Frankfurt industrialists such as Richard Merton were in favour of reconstruction, the city planning authorities were set against it, with the support of architectural associations and liberal publicists. Concerns ranged from the moral implications of reconstructing a memorial to a man so important in a culture that had gone so wrong through to simple planning considerations: reinstating buildings on such a small scale would set a precedent which would go on to hinder the city planners in their efforts to lay broader, car-friendly roadways through the centre. This clash of attitudes becomes clear at the end of Großer Hirschgraben—a street which still follows the original course of the city's first ever walls (see page 10)—where traffic from the Berliner Straße thoroughfare thunders into an underpass. Meanwhile, from the garden between the Goethe house and the museum, the aerial mast atop the 259m Commerzbank Tower is clearly visible as a reminder of how unlikely the 1951 reopening of an immaculately restored Goethe house seems in retrospect.

The city centre also houses a museum to another of Frankfurt's famed literary sons who, like Goethe, was a member of the Katharinen-kirche parish: Friedrich Stoltze (1816-1891, see Chapter 5). Although the Stoltze-Museum is also located in a reconstructed townhouse, the sixteenth-century structure is today surrounded by new-build, sand-wiched into a courtyard between Holzgraben and Töngesgasse. As such, the museums' location is a reflection of the difference between their subjects: in contrast to Goethe's worldwide prominence, Stoltze remained a largely regional figure known for his odes to Frankfurt in dialect verse and his biting satirical publications, for which he was often forced to flee his home city.

At the end of Töngesgasse, where it runs into Fahrgasse just below the unprepossessing 1950s Konstablerwache square, the sur-viving remains of Frankfurt's first city wall stand: the Staufenmauer, named after the Hohenstaufen monarchs who ruled the eastern part of the Charlemagne's Frankish kingdom and, later, the Holy Roman Empire, and who were overlords of Frankfurt during its construc-tion in the late twelfth century (see Chapter 4). Immediately behind it, outside the original city walls, was once Judengasse, the street at the centre of Frankfurt's Jewish community during the centuries of ghettoization from the mid-1400s on. It followed the walls in a curve down towards the river and was renamed Börnestraße after the Jewish population of Frankfurt had been granted the right to settle freely in 1796, moving away from the crowded and impov-erished area in their droves. Nevertheless, the centre of the Jewish community remained here until its destruction during the Nazi years.

Although the road layout was later changed completely by the post-war thoroughfare Kurt-Schumacher-Straße, today a branch of the Frankfurt Jewish Museum, the Museum Judengasse, is set into the ground floor of Börneplatz municipal offices to display the foundations of old houses once at the southern end of Juden-gasse, discovered during the construction work in the 1980s. Plans to redevelop the entire site—empty wasteland since the end of the Second World War—were defeated by Frankfurt residents, who petitioned then Mayor Wolfram Brück. Börneplatz, formerly home to both the reformist and the orthodox synagogues, now features a memorial to the vibrant Jewish community of Frankfurt extinguished by the National Socialist regime, the Gedenkstätte Neuer Börneplatz, built of bricks from old houses on Judengasse and surrounded by plane trees. The memorial is directly south of the old Jewish cemetery, whose walls are perhaps the most poignant part of the Börneplatz site, featuring 11,134 metal blocks for every Jewish victim of the Holocaust from Frankfurt – including a block for one Annelies Frank (see Chapters 8 and 10).

Museumsufer

The Jüdisches Museum Frankfurt, the central location of the Frankfurt Jewish Museum, is at the other end of the city centre on the Untermainkai (Lower Main Quay). The museum's building was originally erected as two separate townhouses for the bankers Simon Moritz von Bethmann and Joesph Isaak Speyer in the 1820s; they were then bought by the grandson of the founder of the Rothschild dynasty, becoming known as the Rothschild-Palais. In 1928 the city of Frankfurt acquired the buildings, which housed both the city and university libraries in the immediate post-war period, before becoming a branch of the Historisches Museum. On 9 November 1988, fifty years to the date after the Kristallnacht pogrom, the refurbished Rothschild buildings were reopened as the Jewish Museum.

Across the Untermainbrücke on the Sachsenhausen side of the river, the Frankfurt Museumsufer ("Museum Embankment") – begins. This unique ensemble is composed of a row of eight museums running almost consecutively along the southern bank of the Main River, beginning with the Museum Giersch in the west and comprising the Liebighaus, Städel, Museum für Kommunikation, Deutsches Architekturmuseum, Deutsches Filmmuseum and the Museum der Weltkulturen, ending with Museum für Angewandte Kunst in the east. Grouped around the impressive central Städel gallery, the remaining institutes, housed either in refitted patrician villas from the late nineteenth century or in daring new-builds, were extended and created as part of a concerted ten-year drive between 1980 and 1990 to create a cultural attraction of national and international renown. The man behind this development was Hilmar Hoffmann (born 1925), the Social Democrat city councillor for culture between 1970 and 1990, whose initiative was so popular that he was left in office by the opposing Christian Democrats after they won the 1986 local elections (he would indeed go on, as head of the Goethe-Institut, to reveal conservative tendencies of his own in use of language, signing the famous Frankfurt Appeal against the German spelling reform in 1994).

At its inception, the Museumsufer was a genuinely radical project. Not only were its sheer scale and ambition unheard of, but the Städel gallery which was to form its centre stood mighty, monumental and alone on the Main—and did not seem to either need or want neighbouring attractions to burnish its appeal. Featuring one of Germany's largest and most valuable connections, the Städel gallery dates back to the late eighteenth century, when a spice merchant's son turned banker Johann Friedrich Städel (1728-1816) started to build up an impressive collection of paintings purchased on his frequent journeys to London, Paris and Amsterdam; Goethe visited his stately townhouse on Roßmarkt more than once seeking inspiration in the collection (an iconic scene of him visiting Italy painted by Tischbein would later form part of the very same). On his death, Städel bequeathed his home, around 500 paintings principally by Dutch and German masters and a financial legacy to found a publicly accessible gallery and an art school in his name. In 1878 the much-enlarged collection was moved to its current premises, a purpose-built museum on Schaumainkai in the neo-Renaissance style, whose imposing sandstone façade with Romanesque and Florentine detail would be the blueprint for two other major Frankfurt buildings of the time: the Opera and the main station.

In his will, Städel had specifically stated that his school should be open to all aspiring artists regardless of religion, nationality or gender: the ever-growing collection, too, reflected this open approach, adding Impressionist works by the likes of Degas and Monet—and later, under the stewardship of Georg Swarzenski (1876-1957) Expressionist pieces by painters such as Edvard Munch and Max Beckmann—to the works of the masters Holbein, Vermeer and Rembrandt. The Nazi rise to power could only mean the demise of this liberal legacy. Swarzenski, director of thirty years, was forced out due to his Jewish heritage; Max Beckmann, who had been teaching at the Städel school since 1925, was also thrown out in 1933, while the works of his students were burned on the Römerberg. In 1937 the nationwide Nazi purge of "degenerate" art led to some of the Städel's finest modern works being confiscated and then sold or spirited away. While safe storage for the remaining collection saved a veritable treasure trove of pre-Modern art from the air raids, the post-war museum was faced not only with the considerable task of restoring its ruined building, but also with repurchasing the works of which it had been deprived. Some have remained elsewhere, such as Beckmann's famous *Kreuzigung*, which today hangs in New York's Museum of Modern Art, while others were bought back: to raise enough money for *Synagoge*, also by Beckmann, collections took place on the streets of the city in 1972 (see Chapter 6).

Today, after two extensions, the museum displays 600 of its 3,000 paintings and is considered one of Europe's premier collections. While the postal artefacts, telephones and computer technology shown by the neighbouring Museum for Communications may be less prestigious, the building's asymmetrical, airy spaces, designed by Günter Behnisch, the man behind the Munich 1972 Olympic Village, tempt many into exploring its collections. These include glass cases showing the progression of mobile phone models from early Motorolas through to the latest Apple models. A similar approach is found in the neighbouring Museum of German Architecture, which features a series of scale models of buildings in Frankfurt, starting with Celtic tribal huts and ending with the 1999 Main Tower skyscraper; as might be expected, the building itself is also of architectural interest in its attempt to document a brief history of styles by reshaping a late 1800s villa. The collection of the

German Film Museum, also housed in a stately pile, is a Mecca for film buffs and professionals alike, and a testament to Frankfurt's key role in explaining and democratizing cinema (see Chapter 6). Smaller museums such as the Museum of World Cultures, featuring an eclectic range of exotic objects typical of ethnographical museums of its kind, and the Museum of Applied Art, which documents how artistic movements have influenced decoration by showing nine rooms in various period styles, round off a cultural offering of exceptional breadth and density.

The Main Bridges

The last element of the Museumsufer was opened in 1990 to integrate it fully into the city centre: the Holbeinsteg, a suspension bridge for pedestrians linking the Bahnhofsviertel directly to the Städel. Much like the Millennium Bridge in London designed to encourage foot traffic to the Tate Modern, the Holbeinsteg crossing plugs an 800m gap between two road bridges, the Friedensbrücke to the west and the Untermainbrücke to the east. Unlike London, however, Frankfurt had long had a pedestrian-only crossing in its city centre, the Eiserner Steg. At the time of its inception in the 1860s, there was only one bridge across the Main in Frankfurt, and although it was becoming increasingly crowded and dangerous to pedestrians, city authorities showed little interest in expanding it or adding a second bridge. So Frankfurt businessmen decided to take matters into their own hands and raised money for a footbridge by selling bonds: pedestrians would pay a toll per crossing and, once the investors had received their dues, the bridge would be gifted to the city.

The bridge was opened in September 1869 and instantly became indispensable—both for commuters and *flâneurs*. When increasing river traffic up the Main to the east harbour led to barges getting caught below it (most famously the *Walhalla* coal transporter in 1910) the bridge was raised several metres rather than removed; Expressionist painters such as Beckmann and Kirchner glorified its elegant arcs (see Chapter 6). Dynamited along with all the other Frankfurt bridges by the retreating Wehrmacht in 1945, the Eiserner Steg was then the first to be rebuilt in 1946; in 1993, it was completely renewed and the stone steps at either end fitted with lifts. The view up and down the river from its centre is considered to be one of the classic Frankfurt panoramas, and it has been tied into the city's literary heritage with a Homeric verse in the original Greek added to the northern tower for the Goethe celebration year of 1999: "Sailing upon a wine-dark sea to people of other tongues"—a fitting inscription for a trading river in one of Europe's most international cities.

While Frankfurt may have more footbridges than London (another, named after the persecuted Jewish industrialist Arthur von Weinberg—see page 222—is located further upstream), in one key respect its bridges are similar: they have grown ever more numerous, punctuate today's city centre and are used by locals for orientation. Just like London Bridge, the Alte Brücke (Old Bridge) is to be found on the site of Frankfurt's oldest crossing, and is yet one of its newest. Erected in wood near the city's eponymous ford in the early eleventh century, it was first recorded as a stone crossing in 1222, whence it evolved continuously on the basis of the original structure until 1914, when it was dismantled while a new bridge was built next to it: one Mr. Heymann, resident at Heidestraße, and the pub landlord Effelsberger were the last two Frankfurters to use the seven-century-old crossing. The new structure was delayed by the onset of the First World War, however, and was not completed until 1926 after an association had been founded to raise money for the work; twenty years later, the bridge was in ruins, and was not reopened until 1947. Increasing car traffic led to it being extended—this time at record speed in order to be ready for the 1965 Motor Show—but by the mid-1990s the bridge was once again in need of repair work and has recently been refitted to match the Neuer Portikus, a small exhibition hall on the tiny island crossed by the southern portion of the bridge, the Maininsel.

The old Alte Brücke was once home to a gatehouse on the island section, as well as housing and water mills, towers at either end and a chapel through the centuries. The historicizing Neuer Portikus in red Main sandstone was completed in 2006 and can be seen in the context of the attempts to re-establish a more traditional style and scale of architecture in the city centre. A further, and far cheekier nod to the history of the bridge is the *Brickegickel*, Frankfurter dialect for *Brückenhahn*, or "bridge-cock". In a fairy-tale recorded by the Brothers Grimm, the master builder was behind with construction work on the bridge and entered into a Faustian pact with the devil by which the dark prince would make sure the bridge was ready overnight, but would in return receive the life of the first living being to cross it as tribute. Spotting a loophole, the sly workman sent a chicken across the bridge as soon as it was finished, which the devil tore to pieces and, in his fury, sent flying through the structure, puncturing the stones at two points at which they could never be closed (perhaps this myth explains the continuous need for repairs?). The bridge has always carried a gilded bronze statue of a cock—originally by way of marking the deepest point in the river and symbolizing the alertness of the city's watchmen, and then as a reference to the self-same myth it helped to create—the first of which was blown into the Main by a hurricane in 1434. Version 2 was shot off by Swedish canon fire in 1635, while no. 3 bit the water when a portion of the bridge collapsed in 1739. The great-grandson of the original made it through until 1945, despite sustaining several bullet wounds from French and Bavarian troops in 1813 and switching bridges in 1914, and can today be seen at the Historisches Museum after it was pulled from the river following its plunge during the Wehrmacht's destructive retreat. Bridge-cock no. 5, however, suffered a more mysterious fate, being stolen without trace in 1992, and the city is currently on rooster no. 6, who celebrated his tenth birthday in September 2014.

Some 140 years earlier, in 1874, the Untermainbrücke was opened, the third bridge over the Main in Frankfurt, and the second accessible to vehicle traffic; today's bridge is a completely new structure inaugurated, along with the Holbeinstieg and the Museumsufer, in 1990. It was followed in 1878 by the corresponding Obermainbrücke, today Ignatz-Bubis-Brücke in memory of a prominent city councillor who also headed the Central Council of Jews in Germany (Zentralrat der Juden in Deutschland, see pages 194 and 208).

Further bridges for railway lines to the east and west of the centre were built in the early 1900s, with the most recent road bridge, the Osthafenbrücke, completed in 2013. Today Frankfurt counts 21 bridges across the Main, nine of which are in the city centre.

Finance and Patronage in Frankfurt

Even more than its bridges, Frankfurt's defining landmarks are its temples to money, which form—quite literally—two sides of the same coin: especially outside the immediate centre, many of Frankfurt's major buildings can be categorized into places where money is created and places where that money is donated.

The Frankfurt Stock Exchange, the Börse is, when times are good, the number one address in the city for money creation. While breakfasting Britons are fed the figures from the FTSE with their toast and Americans digest the Dow Jones, German television viewers and radio listeners are given the lowdown on the DAX, widely used as *pars pro toto* for the exchange itself; newspaper readers are especially familiar with the 1985 sculpture of a bull and a bear, keenly used as a photographic metonym in stories about the market. Commissioned from Frankfurt sculptor Reinhard Dachlauer by the Exchange to celebrate its 400th anniversary, the sculpture's year of birth was also the 140th anniversary of the very short-lived antecedent to today's Börse. Opened in 1845 across from the Paulskirche, the Alte Börse was built just before an unprecedented expansion both in the size of Frankfurt and of the German economy (see Chapters 2 and 4); it soon proved woefully inadequate and was replaced by its imposing successor to the north of Hauptwache in 1879, forming a trio of Romanesque sandstone structures along with the station and the Städel gallery.

The building began business following the bursting of the post-Franco-Prussian-War bubble, and was to experience a series of travails, including the loss of international trade during the First World War, the chaotic hyperinflation of the early 1920s and the limitations placed on it by the Nazis, for whom investments in stocks were best replaced by the financing of tanks. Nevertheless, trading went on—during air raids in the cellars—and although the building sustained serious damage, it reopened in September 1945, barely five months after Germany's total collapse. The *Wirtschaftswunder* ("economic miracle") was driven by capital from—and led to unimagined successes at—the Exchange, where foreign trading was reopened in 1956, cementing Frankfurt's leading role in the global financial system.

Traders looking for a quiet place for their sandwiches are within shouting distance of the city's inner green ring on the site of the former walls, and on summer evenings some like to stroll the short distance under the trees around to the Alte Oper, the Old Opera of 1880, similar in style to Paris' opera house and undoubtedly Frankfurt's finest cultural landmark. Nowhere is the city's history of patronage more beautifully illustrated than in this link-up between big finance and big ladies: the Opera was financed primarily by the good burghers of Frankfurt from the start, and after the destruction of the Second World War its reconstruction, too, would have been impossible without donations from the city's big spenders. Yet the broader population has always had a difficult relationship with the prestigious cultural institution: when it was unveiled with its engraved dedication to *Dem Wahren Schoenen Guten* ("true, beautiful goodness"), city poet Stoltze translated into dialect with a sarcastic addition regarding the lack of state support: *Dem Wahren, Scheene, Gute, die Berjerschaft muss blute* ("the citizens must bleed").

Gutted following an air raid on 23 March 1944, the building was not prioritized in the immediate aftermath of war. A new Opera opened in 1951 (see below) and the burned out shell seemed destined to share the fate of churches in Berlin and Hamburg, left in ruins as what Germany calls *Mahnmale*, memorials with a cautionary message. In the 1960s, however, the city authorities published plans to knock the Opera down and replace it with a municipal office block, provoking a decade-long tug-of-war between planners and a newly-founded preservation group: eventually the restored building was reopened as a concert space in 1981 thanks to funds collected by what had by this stage become Germany's largest ever popular initiative. Another round of the battle between modern planners and heritage conservation was settled.

The city's actual Opera is now further round the green belt at Willy-Brandt-Platz, another location familiar to viewers of breakfast television or readers of financial pages thanks to the oversized sculpture of the €-sign in front of the former headquarters of the European Central Bank, the 1977 Eurotower (which, oddly enough, looks like an inverted $-sign from above). Between its 1902 creation on the site of the old Gallustor station square and 1992, the open piazza was known as Theaterplatz, featuring as it did the Schauspielhaus, which soon became the centre of a theatre scene second only to Berlin (see Chapter 7) until the ascent of the Nazis extinguished the creative scene. Following the destruction of the war, the theatre was rebuilt, but it soon became too small for the municipal players and was replaced with an ultra-modern structure in 1951 featuring a sleek glass frontage 100 metres in length. The building houses several theatre auditoriums (one in a small glass box in the foyer offering just sixty seats) and the city Opera. Renamed after Germany's beloved *détente* chancellor in 1992, this bustling square is the most visual representation of how Apollo and Mammon have always gone hand in hand in Frankfurt, bounded as it is on one side by prestigious nineteenth-century Fürstenhof banking house, on another by the city's premier theatre and on a third by a building in which, until recently, Euros were being feverishly created at the click of a mouse to plug holes in the finances of the continent's banks and governments. Those inclined to over-interpretation might see, in the square's elaborate Märchenbrunnen—the fairy-tale fountain—an analogy with money going down the drain.

Higher and Higher

At the very least, the continuous splashing is a reminder that Frankfurt is a city in which money is spent like water by people who are swimming in it. Those people are principally to be found in the nearby banks, the towers of which loom over the fountain, the square and the strip of green between them. Their sheer height alone makes the bank headquarters to the west of the city centre Frankfurt's most instantly recognizable landmarks: they are the first thing travellers approaching either by land or by air see, are visible from all over the city and are in their scale and density both unique in Germany and rare in Europe as a whole. In fact, at 148m (485ft), the Eurotower cuts a relatively low-profile figure and is only the fifteenth tallest building in the city, and is indeed dwarfed by the instantly recognisable triple-pillars of the Commerzbank Tower behind it, standing a full 259m (849ft) tall. Designed by Norman Foster, from completion in 1997 to 2003 it was the continent's tallest tower, remaining at the top of the EU rankings until 2012 and still leading lists in Germany. The two buildings stand staggered at the southern end of Neue Mainzer Straße, Frankfurt's "New York alley" lined from top to bottom with skyscrapers. Opposite the Commerzbank complex (which includes two smaller office blocks from the 1970s) just past Eurotower comes the brand new gleam of the 170m (557ft) Taunusturm, opened with a smaller set of luxury flats next to it in early 2014.

The new tower backs directly onto one of Frankfurt's oddest towers, the Japan Centre. At a diminutive 115m (377ft), it should not be much to write home about in a downtown of Frankfurt dimensions, but its bulky homage to the classic principles of Japanese design marks it out: the building is rigidly square and rectangular, carrying a terracotta-coloured cladding of natural stone. With its roof jutting outwards and its ground-level dimensions based on an aspect ratio of 2:1 like a tatami mat, it is in essence a giant Japanese lantern.

Across the road, the Garden Tower awaits: with twelve winter gardens spread across its polygon form, the 127m (416ft) building makes up for in extravagance what it lacks in exceptional height. Originally erected as the headquarters for the Hesse and Thuringia regional investment bank in the mid-1970s and kitted out with little more than the average pot-bound office plant, it was refitted (and cleared of asbestos) in the early 2000s, at which point the Babylonian features were added and it was re-let to several banks ranging from Société Générale to the city building society, Frankfurter Sparkasse.

The Hesse-Thuringia bank moved to the next skyscraper up the road—and into the one which is of most interest to tourists, housing as it does the city's only public skyscraper viewing gallery. At a proud and precise 200m (656ft), the Main Tower of 1999 is, depending on who you talk to, the joint-fourth or the fifth tallest of the city (see below). Its core tower is entirely cylindrical in shape and the panoramic deck offers the city's best view not just to paying tourists, but also to restaurant-goers and the local public service television channel, Hessischer Rundfunk. The neighbouring tower, built in tandem, also hosts overnight guests in a suite of short-term rental hotel apartments. This busy strip of skyscrapers peters out across the intersection at the workmanlike Bürohaus an der Alten Oper, or "office at the old Opera", a squatter and grimmer affair which, with its flat white façade, seems to do justice to its year of completion, 1984.

On the other side of the green belt (this section is called Taunusanlage) stand Frankfurt's very own twin towers: the jagged, reflective Gotham City-style Deutsche Bank Towers, beloved of the visual media for the way in which, on the numerous cloudy days, their inscrutable grey bulk symbolizes so well the impenetrable cynicism of Germany's most Anglo-American bank. With its aggressive bid for a slice of the investment banking markets in London and New York, Deutsche Bank got its fingers burned in the 2008 crash and has a been the object of much *Schadenfreude* at home ever since.

At this point, another spur of towers peels off down Mainzer Landstraße in a curving line up towards the Messe. First comes the somewhat unremarkable Trianon, proving the old development adage that the fancier the name, the more uninspiring the architecture. It is nevertheless the city's sixth tallest building (186m, 610ft) and has the footprint of an equilateral triangle. Next up is the 142m (465ft) Frankfurt Büro Center of 1981, equally unworthy of note, except perhaps for the astonishing way with which it really could be an office tower anywhere in the world. At the crossing with Westendstraße, however, an altogether more exciting prospect shoots up to 208m (682ft) and into third place in the citywide rankings. Semicircular in its cross-section and covered in gleaming white granite, Westendstraße 1 culminates in an overhanging crowning platform pointing towards the Dom in which the coronations of the Holy Roman Emperors took place. Unfortunately, the steel framework juts out over the footprint of the building at ground level, meaning that, in harsh winters, the front entrance and—in extreme cases—Savingystraße have to be closed off due to the danger posed by giant falling icicles.

The city's fourth-tallest building, Tower 185, is nearby as the parade of skyscrapers swings north onto the broad Friedrich-Ebert-Anlage boulevard: at 200m or 656ft, it is again either the joint-fourth of the fifth tallest building in Frankfurt (see above), but was very close to coming in far lower down the rankings: the name Tower185 refers to an earlier plan to build to 185 metres. At ground level, the building is striking for its horse-shoe-shaped entrance courtyard—and for the corporate drudgery the faceless and clinical exterior so successfully projects.

Trade Fairs and Trains

By comparison, the neighbouring Messeturm (Trade Fair Tower), marking the entrance to the trade fair area, is of more interest: shaped like an immense crayon, it looks like the kind of building Godzilla's kids could have fun with. From 1991 until the Commerzbank Tower went up, it was Europe's tallest building, and is at 257m (843ft) still Frankfurt and Germany's second tallest to this day. With distinctly art-deco elements and a daring postmodern mix of geometric forms, it is perhaps Frankfurt's best-loved and most eccentric tower: other oddities include the fact that, along with two other Frankfurt skyscrapers, it has its own post-code (60308) and also houses one of the highest consulates on the planet: in 2009 the Japanese consulate had to leave the Japan Center when it was re-let *en bloc* to the ECB, taking refuge in the 34th floor of the Messeturm.

While its tower may be its most visible element, the Frankfurt Trade Fair or Messe is famous in its own right. Frankfurt's history is so intertwined with its role as a trading city that the Messe area could only ever become a place of superlatives: with a surface area of over half a million square metres, it is beaten only by that other German Messe town, Hanover, in the worldwide rankings for expo areas. The quirky Torhaus office block at the centre of the site between the bright white halls has been likened both to a falling guillotine and, from the side and perhaps more fittingly for this site, to books on a bookshelf, while the baroque revival charm of the 1909 Festhalle, the Messe's oldest building, belies its dark past. Intended as an exhibition hall, its size, capacity and proximity to the city's railway infrastructure made it the logical choice for the Nazis to hold the Jewish population while readying it for deportation. A memorial plaque on the outside of the building reminds visitors to the various fairs held here of its key role in destroying one of pre-War Europe's liveliest Jewish communities.

From the Messe, Jewish victims could be sent to the once-extensive goods sidings nearby (disused since the 1980s and recently redeveloped into offices and flats as the Europaviertel), leaving Hauptbahnhof, the Main Station, to continue its day-to-day business. The enormous neo-Renaissance structure, opened in 1888 and the last in the prestigious Wilhelmine trio of Städel, Stock Exchange and station, is one of the very few landmark buildings in Frankfurt to have survived the air raids without serious structural damage—a fact all the odder when its status as a primary target and its sheer size are taken into account. It was, until the 1915 opening of the Hauptbahnhof in Frankfurt's rival book fair city Leipzig, the largest in Europe (an honour which Leipzig still retains) and remains one of the three largest stations on the continent today. Its dimensions were, from its inception onwards, enormous, and have only got bigger since: upon opening the station counted three vaulted train-sheds, each over 27m (90ft) high at the peak of the support arches; another two, slightly smaller, sheds were added—one to each side—in 1924; the roofing alone now covers an area of around 42,000m^2 or more than ten acres. Originally housing 18 platforms, Frankfurt Main Station's latest count is 25, not including the stations below ground level added in the 1970s as part of a gigantic, warren-like extension to allow suburban trains to run into a new tunnel under the city and out the other side. In between these two suburban service platforms (S-Bahn) and ground level, an intermediate level was added for the new underground metro (U-Bahn), and—in view of the atomic threat in the Cold War years—the city's largest known bunker was built into the bargain to keep railway staff alive and telephone infrastructure intact in the event of nuclear war (it remains operational, although the stockpiled tins of food have reportedly been removed).

Indeed, throughout the years of the German division, the German national railways (Deutsche Bundesbahn) were headquartered in Frankfurt, which lay at a convenient half-way point between Bavaria in the south of the country and Hamburg in the north. Even since reunification and the move of its semi-privatized successor Deutsche Bahn to Berlin, Frankfurt has retained a large portion of the rail company's operational and administrative activities—a role that increasing cross-border high-speed services look set to cement (at just under four hours average journey time, it now takes just as long to get to Berlin as it does to Paris; Brussels is closer at three hours).

The scale of rail operations at Frankfurt has led to several schemes for a German railways tower at Frankfurt, both to gain adequate office space and to keep up with banking and consulting counterparts by making a mark on the skyline. Budget and planning constraints have always put paid to such ideas, however, and the expensive move to Berlin with a prestigious tower at Potsdamer Platz seems to have given the current generation of railway managers a satisfactory skyscraper. Furthermore, Deutsche Bahn in Frankfurt is now the proud tenant of the striking Silberturm, Germany's tallest building between 1978 and 1990 and currently Frankfurt's tenth-tallest at 166m (546ft): at once monolithic and lithe, clumsy and sleek, this aluminium colossus stands in the Bahnhofsviertel, conveniently located between the main station itself and the two principal axes of skyscrapers in the west of the city.

The Rising East and the Sedate South

One organization that was simply not satisfied with tenancy was the European Central Bank (ECB, EZB in German), which moved out of the central Eurotower (see above, page 52) in 2014 to its own purpose-built offices in the east of the city. Observers have variously

seen this as a sign that the ECB, as a key European political institution, wished to demonstrate its aloofness from the commercial
banks surrounding it, or as a shrewd move to acquire cheaper land
and laxer planning restrictions in an area under redevelopment. At
185m (606ft), the deconstructivist split towers, which seem to turn
into one another, now rank as the city's seventh-tallest building, and
it is expected that the new headquarters will kick off a wave of vertical development around the now disused Osthafen (east harbour)
and the wide, flat expanse of the former wholesale market halls
(which have been renovated as part of the ECB plans).

The silver-blue of the ECB currently stands alone on the
northern side of the river, but forms an interesting duo with the red-
brick, art-deco-quoting Main Plaza on the south side. Although
only 88m (288ft) tall, the intricate detail on the upper portions of
this hotel and apartment complex—and the lack of any other towers of comparable height on the Sachsenhausen bank—draw the
eye to it from all along the river. Completed just weeks after 9/11 in
2001, it pays open homage to the early skyscrapers of New York and
houses Harry's New York Bar, where smoking is permitted—and
the smoking of cigars actively encouraged.

Back along towards the city centre on the south bank of the
Main is the Dreikönigskirche, the Church of the Magi. Built in the
high gothic-revival style of the late nineteenth century, the church
survived the Second World War more or less untouched, a fact that
some more devout members of the congregation may well have
ascribed to the church's early and unusually decisive stance against
the National Socialists. In 1934 the Dreikönigskirche parish was
the first in Frankfurt to affiliate itself to the *bekennende Kirche* movement, a group of Protestant congregations which openly positioned
itself against Nazi attempts to co-opt them as part of a semi-State
religion (see Chapters 8 and 11). This brave decision stands in
marked contrast to the position taken by the Paulskirche parish (see
page 38). A more curious aspect of the church's history is a panel
of the *Allgemeinen Almosenkasten*, a charitable organization dating
back to 1531 (the name means "general alms box"). The organization dispensed eagle markings for city beggars to wear on their

arms so that the populace could distinguish them from outsiders who came in during the day to beg, and the panel reminds members of the congregation to donate into the box rather than give to potentially duplicitous destitutes. It is the only reminder of this institution left in Frankfurt's churches today. The medieval church was also known as the Sachsenhäuser Dom because throughout the Middle Ages it was second in height only to the Kaiserdom itself: Frankfurt's obsession with height may be said to have started early.

Gates and Towers

Alongside ecclesiastical buildings, the defensive towers of the Middle Ages were then among the tallest buildings of the city. Medieval Frankfurt's fortifications were composed of two concentric rings: the inner ring of the city walls (the second, enlarged set of the 1300s) and the outer ring of fortresses linked by mounds, ditches and moats, all planted with thorny bushes. (As an interesting side-note: both lofty towers and thorny barriers feature in that prototypical German fairy tale, *Sleeping Beauty*, as recorded by the Brothers Grimm, who took many of their myths and stories from the towns and villages of the Hessian countryside north of Frankfurt.) Both the inner and outer ring featured towers from which city forces could survey the surrounding countryside for approaching threats and fire on enemy armies in times of war.

While the walls of the inner ring and the earthworks of the outer ring had all but disappeared by the end of the nineteenth century, several of their towers have survived to this day: three stand along the course of the city wall, while four of the fortresses also remain. A little to the east of the Dreikönigskirche in Sachsenhausen, a small part of which was enclosed in the city walls, stands the bucolically named Kuhhirtenturm: the cattle herdsmen's tower. Now part of the Frankfurt youth hostel complex and featuring an apartment in the fourth storey, this typically Central European tower, square and pitched-roofed, has in fact served as digs for a broad range of Frankfurters since losing its original purpose: the famed Frankfurt composer Paul Hindemith (1895-1963) lived in it in the 1920s before moving to Berlin, and although it was damaged badly in the bombing raids, it served as shelter for those who were bombed out. Today, the first two storeys offer an exhibition about Hindemith, who worked with luminaries such as Kurt Weill and Berthold Brecht and—everyone has a dirty secret—played model railways with Gottfried Benn (the layout is also on display).

The Rententurm (see above) is another survivor of the inner ring, as is the splendid gothic Eschenheimer Tor to the north of the Innenstadt. Today surrounded by several lanes of traffic and dwarfed by the bulk of the new cluster of mini-skyscrapers at Palaisquartier behind it, this tower straight out of *Rumpelstiltskin* looks perhaps all the more poetic for it. It was built in the early fifteenth century and at 50m (164ft) was a colossus in its day: topped with four smaller towers and culminating in a central spire, its intricate detail belies its deadliness in medieval warfare. The weather vane on the roof alludes to the legend of Hans Winkelsee, a poacher who had been condemned to death and was being held in the tower. He wagered the city that he would be able to shoot nine holes in the iron vane over nine days of captivity—and proceeded to puncture not only nine holes, but to make these holes form the figure nine. Winkelsee is said to have walked free at the end.

The outer ring of earthen defences was punctuated by fortresses known as *Warten* of which four survive as integral parts of city geography today. The best known is the northwestern Bockenheimer Warte of the 1430s, which once marked the end of Frankfurt and is now taken as the border between the districts of Westend and Bockenheim—both of which claim both the picture-book medieval round tower with its wooden-framed deck and the lively farmers' market on the square below. Below the tower, three of the city's underground lines converge, while around it, the hurly-burly of the university quarter begins.

In contrast, the fifteenth century Friedberger Warte to the north of the city and the Sachsenhäuser Warte to the direct south are further out and in sleepier parts of town. With no competing demands on the space around them, the two towers have also retained the fortifications that were built at their base (the Bockenheimer Warte stands in glorious isolation), which have been turned into restaurants and are popular weekend destinations.

The same cannot be claimed of the Galluswarte, the fourth remaining outer tower. Hemmed in by the railway trunk routes out of the main station and set on a traffic island on what has become a busy roundabout, the lone-standing Gallus tower received an interesting addition in the 1950s in the shape of a tobacconist's kiosk and off-licence—known in Frankfurt as a *Trinkhalle*—rounded off by a public toilet. With the tower's 600th anniversary approaching in 2014, the city set up a prize competition for a fitting re-design in 2011. As yet, however, the tower still remains a fortress of late-hours alcohol and nicotine provision.

Landmark Offices

For all its prowess in building upwards over centuries, several of Frankfurt's most interesting landmarks are far more horizontal. Within sight of the Galluswarte is the long, elegant and almost imperceptibly curving façade of the 1950s low-rise headquarters of the Frankfurter Societät, a publishing and printing company (fittingly enough, the side-street next to it is named after Gutenberg). In the modern glass and brick building next door, Germany's leading conservative daily *Frankfurter Allgemeine Zeitung* is produced (see Chapter 5).

Meanwhile, near the Bockenheimer Warte, the Palmengarten is laid out, featuring both a broad range of palms and other tropical or exotic plants and a gloriously incongruous administrative building from 1929 in immaculate white with all the curves and verve of a cruise liner. The Palmengarten runs straight into the University's botanical gardens, which in turn meld into the Grüneburgpark, creating the city centre's largest expanse of green space. It is in this latter that the city's most impressive and most infamous office block is located.

The IG-Farben-Haus, now officially referred to as the Poelzig-Bau after its architect, was built in record time between 1928 and 1931 and was the largest single construction project in the Weimar Republic. Hans Poelzig (1869-1936) was commissioned to build this gigantic office complex by IG Farben, an omnipotent chemistry conglomerate controlling hundreds of companies both in Germany and abroad. Interestingly enough, he was the only architect who did not propose a tower block, but a broad horizontal concave 250m in length and curving towards the south to maximize natural light; every single office room has a at least one window (there are 2,500 in the building). Poelzig was inspired by the Baushaus movement, focussing on how to distribute space ideally and to ease movement through and access to the building, and although the exterior style is classicizing and monumental, the steel-framed construction method was resolutely modern. Until the 1950s the building was widely considered one of the most advanced workspaces in the world.

It was in these bright, airy rooms that the management and staff of IG Farben joined the National Socialist government in pushing the boundaries of depravity in the modern world. The conglomerate was the archetypal wicked corporation, seizing every chance not just to profit from, but to help drive the Nazi efforts at war and extermination to new levels of barbarity. To benefit from slave labour, IG Farben decided to build a factory at Auschwitz, working with the SS to select forced workers for its own mini-concentration camp, Lager Buna, where conditions were just as appalling as on the neighbouring site: the death toll from exhaustion, disease, and murder is reckoned to be around 25,000—not counting those who were no longer fit for work, who were simply thrown, half-dead, into the gas chambers next door. In these chambers, more than one million were killed using Zyklon B, the product of an IG Farben subsidiary, Degesch. Immediately following the capitulation, IG Farben was placed under Allied control and its managers put in the dock at Nuremberg, yet plans to completely dismantle the giant company were soon put on the back-burner and some of Germany's largest chemicals companies today such as BASF and Bayer are direct successors of the concern, which was split up in 1952 (see Chapter 11).

The fact that the IG Farben-Haus survived the bombing raids so intact is the subject of many a conspiracy theory, the most harmless of which is that the American forces had already identified it as the best location for their headquarters (other more prosaic minds point to its isolation in a large park). Nevertheless, the Americans did very swiftly set up in the building, fencing it off and administering their occupation zone from it. Dwight D. Eisenhower placed his office in the former IG Farben directors' room and proclaimed the federal states of Hesse, Bavaria and—as it was then—Württemberg-Baden from it. It was also the room in which the presidents of these and other newly-founded states were given the task of writing a constitution for the new Federal Republic of Germany in 1948; the new "Deutsche Mark" was also unveiled here.

Although the city bought the complex in 1955, it gave the American forces continued rights of use. The building became the centre of the United States Army in Europe, USAEUR, and as such attracted no shortage of demonstrations from students, especially after 1968. In 1972 the radical Red Army Faction (RAF) terrorists set off bombs in the foyer, killing one soldier and injuring a dozen staff, and the building was hermetically sealed off from the city for some time to come (see Chapter 11).

As Allied military presence in Germany declined in the 1990s, so did the American requirements in Frankfurt: in 1995, USAEUR moved out of the building. Following emotional public debate about what to do with the building and ignominious initiatives—including a scheme to lodge the ECB there (which caused umbrage across the Euro states) and a proposed sell-off to a private estate agent—a suitable solution was eventually found: the Goethe Universität, having grown too big for its (aesthetically unimpressive) locations in Westend and Bockenheim, agreed to move into the building and make it the centre of its new campus. It set the tone by establishing a Holocaust documentation centre in the building named after Fritz Bauer, the Frankfurt prosecutor behind the Auschwitz trials of the 1960s (see page 224). Today, the building is open not just to students, but to the public, who can go in and marvel at the elegant sweep of its corridors and its timeless proportions, and at how modern Germany managed to become what it is today, an exemplarily tolerant and democratic country. There is perhaps no other building in the country in which past evil and present normality coexist so closely: with the decision to place an institution of learning in this environment—to look the demons of history in the face—the city has created a true landmark.

Francis I, one of the many Holy Roman Emperors to be crowned
in Frankfurt's Kaiserdom: a portrait by Leopold Kupelwieser
(Heeresgeschichtliches Museum/Wikimedia Commons)

4 | The Rulers and the Ruled
A Brief Social and Political History

The Secret Capital

Every now and then, when high-end German newspapers are casting around for a good waffling page-filler, the decades-old topic of "Germany's secret capital" will be dusted off and examined anew. The theory is always that the current capital of Germany is not actually in charge of the country, and springs from the post-war years, when—with Berlin out of action—Bonn was made the capital city of the fledgling Federal Republic, usurping much larger candidates such as Hamburg, Cologne, Munich and indeed Frankfurt, which it pipped to the post by a small parliamentary majority in 1949.

The gist of such pieces was always that, for all Bonn might on paper have the seat of government housed in expensive ministerial buildings, the genuine political, economic and societal agenda was being set elsewhere. Oddly enough, the transfer of the capital in the 1990s to Berlin—a city which, unlike Bonn, is both a metropolis in its own right and had previously spent almost a century at the head of a united German state—did little to put paid to this speculation that really, as the German phrasing would have it, "the music is playing elsewhere". In such Sunday-supplement conspiracy theories, suspicion of being the *de facto* capital almost always falls on either Munich (due primarily to its astonishing wealth, industrial might and a powerful regional political party) or on Frankfurt.

The preferred argument for Frankfurt-as-actual-capital is, as might be expected, finance: not only does the city's top earner bankroll German industry and government debt, but Frankfurt institutions also implement economic policy—functions which in many other countries are located in the same city as central government. In Deutschemark days, Frankfurt's almighty Bundesbank, responsible for Europe's strongest currency, was often considered more powerful than the German chancellor, and still sets the economic tone in Germany to this day, despite its function as the currency regulator having been passed up to the European Central Bank. In any case, this institution at the helm of the Euro is also located in Frankfurt, so the modern-day supplement musings often make Frankfurt the "secret capital" of all of Europe, not just Germany.

Given that measures implemented in Frankfurt have immediate, real-world effects everywhere from Helsinki to Thessaloniki, these theories contain more than just a grain of truth. Yet for all the financial decision-making power concentrated in Frankfurt, the city itself is no capital in the way that Paris, London or Washington DC are capitals. Frankfurt's banks may well rule Germany and much of Europe, but Frankfurt itself is ruled from elsewhere. Throughout its history, in fact, Frankfurt has been a city of great importance, but without a corresponding deal of say in its own affairs—a city through which rulers from elsewhere have always passed, and which has consequently been at their mercy. As such, Frankfurt's social and political history is one of the Emperors and kings who ruled it and used it as a base to rule, the vassals and townsfolk they ruled and those who actually ran the city. Right through to today, the differences between the rulers in Frankfurt and the people of Frankfurt have remained defining, with those running the city seeking to mediate between these two groups. Each of these factions has experienced several cycles of ascendency and retreat, usually when the others have been consumed by their own internal conflicts.

Yet at the same time, Frankfurt's importance to the rulers, combined with its sheer age, have always guaranteed it a special position: for roughly 1,000 years until 1866, Frankfurt was essentially an independent state in the same way that Monaco, Andorra or the Vatican still are today. Despite its geographically diminutive extent, the city was able to hold its own because it was of more use to the larger, more powerful territories around it as an independent space. This heritage is still tangible: even over a century and half after first being subsumed first into a German nation state, those who run Frankfurt and Frankfurters themselves still see their city as one which can and must set its own agenda, using every option available in a way that other cities of comparable size and identical constitutional positioning do not. Frankfurt may or may not be the secret capital of Germany or Europe, but it certainly sees itself as being in a class with Berlin and Brussels.

Founded and Abandoned: the Carolingian Centuries

It is characteristic of Frankfurt's role as a city that the first recorded historical evidence of it is as a location in which the great ruler Charlemagne held a Europe-wide synod in 794 AD. Many neighbouring towns such as Hanau and Rödelsheim had already made a far earlier entry into the annals, while others such as Mainz and Worms were long-standing market towns of Roman origin, and so the Frankfurt mentioned in the late eighth century can be assumed to have been considerably smaller and less developed than its neighbours.

Yet the synod of 794 was no small event. Charlemagne was the most powerful man Europe had seen since the Roman Emperors of the second century, ruling unchallenged over large swathes of what are today France, Germany and Italy. The synod was visited by clergyman from all over Christendom, with delegates from as far afield as the British Isles and southern Spain, and its decisions were far-reaching, regarding matters as varied as iconodulism and iconoclasm (the veneration and destruction of Orthodox icons, respectively), the persecution of witches (which, perhaps to the later advantage of the Brothers Grimm, it forbade) and the price of grain across western Europe. There is, however, no clear reason given in any of the recorded deliberations of the Synod of Frankfurt as to why it was held in a place which at the time was still made of wood (the first royal palace of stone, the Königspfalz, not being erected until the ninth century), while other cities with far more impressive Carolingian infrastructure were not chosen.

A further mystery is why Charlemagne then decided to spend eight months there, before leaving the settlement never to return. The best bet to date is that several poor harvests in the western part of the Carolingian Empire drove its court east and that Frankfurt was a logistically convenient place in which to benefit from a comparative glut of produce elsewhere, but a definitive answer is unlikely to be discovered; that Charlemagne never went back to this place at which such important decisions had been taken may have something to do with the death of his wife there during his stay; but once again, this remains speculation. Quite probably, the hamlet had served its purpose and was simply not important enough for another royal visit from a hard-pressed, fast-moving ruler. Having been put on the map by Charlemagne, Frankfurt was left by him to its own devices.

Perhaps it was the religious fervour of Charlemagne's son Louis the Pious which drove him to return to the site of the 794 synod: in 815 Louis is recorded as having stayed in Frankfurt and is assumed to have ordered the construction of the first royal palace (whose remains were recently reburied, see page 35), which was ready for his second visit to the city in December 822, when he stayed for six months as he desperately tried to keep the gigantic Carolingian Empire from disintegrating. Louis spent much of his reign crisscrossing his territory, ranging from Brittany to Bohemia, from Barcelona (which had reconquered from the Moors in 801) to Bingen on the Rhine, and this punishing peripatetic lifestyle might explain why he stopped in the conveniently located Frankfurt nine times during his reign. When his son Louis the German rose up against him, he occupied his father's favourite Frankfurt, showing that it had become a place of strategic importance.

Frankfurt's fortunes rose with those of Louis the German who, although defeated by his father, received the largest part of the Empire when it was divided between three successors after his death. Louis the German's name was given to him because much of the territory he received had been part of the Roman province of Germania, and as such he might be considered the first ruler of a kingdom called Germany: Frankfurt was his chief place of residence, supplanting the ancient Regensburg to the east, from where he had exercised his power during his father's day. It was Louis the German who had the first church built in the city (the Salvatorkirche, later the Kaiserdom, see Chapter 3), and it was during his reign that what had been a settlement with a palace attached began to grow into a market town in its own right. By the time he died in

Frankfurt in 876, the chroniclers were referring to it as *prinicipalis sedes orientalis regni,* or the principal seat of the king of the eastern Frankish empire, East Francia. In this way, Frankfurt can lay a very legitimate claim to being the first capital of Germany.

Louis' three sons, splendidly recorded in history as Carloman, Louis the Younger and Charles the Fat, received different portions of this German kingdom: Carloman ruled Bavaria, Charles the Fat was given Alemannia and Louis the Younger remained in Frankfurt as King of Franconia, Thuringia and Saxony. With this division, Frankfurt's sphere of influence waned, and when the three kingdoms—as well as much of the rest of Charlemagne's former empire—were briefly reunited under the considerable bulk of Charles the Fat as the only surviving successor in the 880s, power was exercised from elsewhere. It is possible that Arnulf of Carinthia, who rebelled against Charles in 887, had himself proclaimed King of East Francia in Frankfurt, which would make him the first King of Germany to *begin* his rule there, but his exact location at the moment of his usurping the throne is unknown. His son, Louis the Child (so-called because he succeeded his father at the tender age of six), died aged 17 or 18 in Frankfurt, bringing to an end the Carolingian dynasty and Frankfurt's first period as a capital city. For several centuries to come, kings in the lands around Frankfurt would come from elsewhere, and the city's royal buildings fell into neglect.

Abeyance and Renaissance: the Early Middle Ages

Although Frankfurt had been dependent on royal stays for its existence, and thus sank swiftly into decline after they ceased, its century at the centre of the eastern kingdom of the Carolingian Empire had left it an established market town nonetheless. Its riverside location and the fertile arable surroundings, as well as the church Louis the German had built and endowed with land, assured it of survival during the turbulent years around the turn of the first millennium. Yet the neighbouring Rhenish city of Mainz retained its role as the region's premier commercial and religious centre, and Frankfurt's secondary character as a city of royal residence left it entirely at the mercy of regal favour: Otto the Great, crowned (not yet Holy) Roman Emperor by the pope in 962 after adding Italy to his East Frankish possessions, was said to be fond of Frankfurt, and yet at some point after his death the royal palace burned down and its original location was forgotten, not to be exposed until one thousand years later by the bombs of the Second World War.

Frankfurt's very own Dark Ages persisted until the 1100s, when the city—and by now its importance in trade had made it one—once again took centre stage in the life of what would become the Holy Roman Empire. The first Hohenstaufen king, Conrad III, held court in Frankfurt, now described as an *oppidum* or market town in Church chronicles, regularly between 1140 and 1149. Here he organized his crusades to conquer the Slavs to the east and north and had his son Henry Berengar elected as his successor to prevent chaos breaking out should he not return from the Second Crusade to the Holy Land. He ordered the construction of a new palace on the river, the chapel of which has survived and is part of today's Saalhof complex. It was also during this period that work begun on turning the wooden crossing at the ford into a stone bridge, parts of which would survive as the Alte Brücke until 1914 (see Chapter 3 for both).

The city's increasing importance in royal power politics was now cemented by the fact that rulers of the German lands were being elected there, and this was due to three factors: firstly, it was centrally located for several of the electors—the Archbishops of Trier, Mainz and Cologne and the Princes of the Palatinate could all reach it by road or water within a few days; secondly, with its synodic history it enjoyed religious prestige; thirdly, it was an increasingly attractive place to raise funds. Under Frederick Barbarossa, elected King of Germany in Frankfurt in 1152 and Roman Emperor in 1155 (also the first to be called "Holy"), Central Europe was in the middle of a conversion to a monetary economy, and with the wealth of products passing through it Frankfurt was a logical location for a royal mint (founded around 1170) and for the targeted development of the financial expertise needed to fund an empire. Thus Barbarossa gave royal privileges to city merchants and encouraged the settlement of

Jews, who owed loyalty and taxes only to himself, bypassing both the town and Church coffers.

Despite such unholy motives, by the turn of the thirteenth century Frankfurt was the acknowledged location at which rulers would be elected with a Christian stamp of approval. The precedent set under Conrad soon became self-perpetuating. By the mid-1200s six elections had been held in the city. Yet often parallel elections were held elsewhere and there would be two competing candidates struggling for the German and Roman crowns. The issue of *where* the votes for them had been cast, however, showed the importance of Frankfurt as what Alfonso X of Castile called *locus debitus et consuetus*, "the place of duty and usage": his argument against competitor Richard of Cornwall (second son of King John) was that although this latter had four of the seven electors behind him, he himself had been elected by the other three in Frankfurt. Although he was not strong enough to carry the day, his insistence on the city is telling: competing elections elsewhere became rarer and the convention was set in stone by the Golden Bull of 1356.

While the geopolitical struggles of early medieval Central Europe were being played out in the city by powerful rulers, those who lived there as their vassals also began their own struggle—for citizens' rights. With the growing importance of the city to the rulers, those ruled by them had both direct contact with their overlords and a strong bargaining position: in 1219 the citizens (the merchants, tradesmen and Jewish financiers—not its overall population) negotiated for the first time as a collective with their king and gained a town charter, signing it alongside the ruler himself and his designated sheriff and magistrates and confirming their signature with the first ever use of the city seal.

In the course of the thirteenth century another source of power in the city arose: Frankfurt's first monasteries and nunneries were founded in the 1220s with royal support, as the magistrates nominated by the king simply donated land to religious orders. Indeed, the ruler's power remained almost absolute, as every concession won by the Frankfurt citizenry shows: in 1232, for example, Emperor Henry VII was gracious enough to deprive himself of his right to arrange the marriage of its daughters to members of his court. The tug of war continued through the century. Three years later, Henry agreed to give Frankfurt control of half the income generated by the mint and access to wood from his forest on the condition that the city would be responsible for maintaining the strategically crucial bridge over the Main. Yet internal divisions between those who counted as citizens weakened their bargaining power: the first Frankfurt pogrom took place in 1241, and the king claimed damages against the perpetrators for murdering the Jews, who were of course directly subordinate to him alone, and thus depriving him of tax income.

Despite this early flare-up of anti-Semitism (see Chapter 8), by the 1280s Frankfurt's Jewish community was larger and (measured in taxes paid) wealthier than ever before. A defining moment came during another bout of confusion between two competing Emperors of the 1250s, in which the city was besieged by Count William of Holland, pretender to the throne of Conrad IV, the last Hohenstaufen, in 1254. Unable to enter through the gates but unwilling to lay waste to this important place, William agreed to make Frankfurt a Free City of the Empire, confirming many of the rights granted over preceding decades.

Yet Frankfurt was considerably less militant that many other such *Freistädte*: its first councillors, citizens' representatives to the king's sheriffs, were elected later than in other Imperial cities and had fewer powers. The councillors only nominated their own mayor as a counterweight to the royal sheriff after Henry VII, strapped for cash as he waged war in northern Italy, pawned off his right to install the sheriff to noblemen from outside the city in 1311. The city would then adhere to this status quo for 250 years until the upheavals of the Reformation. Part of Frankfurt's reticence was undoubtedly its interest in preserving kingly favour in one important matter: its trade fairs.

Trading and Trade-offs: the Late Middle Ages

In the fourteenth, fifteenth and sixteenth centuries Frankfurt had a population of roughly 10,000. In medieval terms, this made it a medium-sized city at best: the metropolises of the time—Venice, Genoa, Milan, Florence, Paris, Bruges and Ghent—counted over 50,000 inhabitants, while second-tier cities such as London, Prague, Hamburg or Cologne were all at least three times the size of Frankfurt.

Yet Frankfurt could boast one superlative: the size and importance of its trade fairs. The beginnings of the fairs lay in the market held after the autumn harvest at which surpluses were sold off; Church holy days were selected to maximize turnout (the German word for trade fair, *Messe*, is related to mass). With the crusades of the thirteenth century having extended Christendom deep into eastern Europe, the much larger annual markets of Champagne and Lorraine suddenly found themselves a several hundred kilometres away from the geographical centre of European trade routes; at the same time, the rise of the Hanseatic League in the north and of the Italian city-states in the south increased the need for a Central European place of exchange. Frankfurt was in the right place at the right time, and had the right patrons: in 1240 Emperor Frederick II extended the official protection of the Empire to everyone travelling to and from the Frankfurt fair. In an era in which any journey of any length put travellers, especially wealthy ones, at risk of falling victim to robbers, bandits and often marauding mercenaries or armies of war, the protection of the continent's most powerful man was a crucial factor.

In the early 1300s crafted products started to overtake agricultural produce at the Frankfurt autumn fair. Besides raw materials such as wool, bales of yarn were now on offer, while crop surpluses were increasingly replaced by products made from them such as wine or flour. The Frankfurt toll decree of 1329, a reliable indicator of what was passing through the city, lists a veritable panoply from livestock, meat and butter to preserved herrings, glass and earthenware, as well as pitch, hemp and flax. In 1330, partly in return for the city's support during yet another round of double elections for the Holy Roman Emperor which pitted the Wittelsbachs against the Hapsburgs, the winning Wittelsbach Louis IV granted Frankfurt permission to hold a spring fair for products made during the winter months such as wine and wool. With yet more turmoil in the following decade, Louis even went on to grant Frankfurt exclusive Messe privileges, effectively banning neighbours such as Mainz from setting up competing fairs; in Frankfurt the usual rules and regulations applying to tradesmen and private persons in the feudal system were lifted for the fairs, allowing anyone and everyone to offer, sell and buy all types of goods and services.

Further Imperial proclamations throughout the prosperous fourteenth and fifteenth century continued to strengthen the Messe. In 1360, 1376 and 1465, for example, the level of protection from ongoing legal proceedings applied to trade fair visitors was progressively extended: in a time in which populations of whole cities could be made the subject of claims for damages or debt repayment suits, this temporary amnesty fostered trade between towns and cities which would otherwise have been impossible. In 1495 the Empire's high court (*Reichskammergericht*) was opened in the city by Emperor Maximilian I, the first of the Hapsburgs, giving the city one of the two most prestigious legal institutions of the Empire.

The commercial advantage of such decrees was obvious to Frankfurt's merchants, and explains their willingness to submit to interference from royal rulers in a way which other trading city-states such as Hamburg and Lübeck, Genoa and Venice, did not. It also underlines the importance of picking the winner whenever there were rival Emperors, a burden which was lessened by the Golden Bull of 1367, the papal decree which brought constitutional clarity to the Holy Roman Empire and put paid to the continued squabbles and double elections. It regulated the details of how the Holy Roman Emperor was to be elected and crowned in such detail that there could be no argument about the process; and crucially for Frankfurt, it was finally set down in writing as the city in which the elections were to be held (the coronations were to take place in Aachen). The Bull also placed a maximum on the number of armed guards and other members of court each elector could bring into the city, in return for which Frankfurt as a city would guarantee peace and good order within its walls; the danger of civil war within the Empire was banished until the Reformation.

The Imperial elections became something a third trade fair for the city, another event in which money from outside came flowing in and which Frankfurt tradesmen were not shy to take advantage of: the city council was often forced to regulate the prices for basic foodstuffs, drinks and lodgings in order to stop its own townsfolk from overplaying their hand and making powerful enemies among the entourages of the assembled electors.

This was the age in which another force arose among the ruled of Frankfurt besides the councillors: the patrician families who had accumulated great fortunes through trade. Buying paintings, prints and engravings from the likes of Dürer and Grünewald, families such as Limpurg or Holzhausen began a tradition of artistic patronage that has continued through the centuries in Frankfurt. They also began to club together and demand a greater say in the affairs of the city. The city council's front bench, composed of ancient aristocratic families, was often pitted against the second and back benches, on which the *parvenu* patricians sat with guild representatives. Yet throughout the prosperous fifteenth century, the distinctions between these benches progressively faded as the patrician families sought to distance themselves from the next wave of social-climbing tradesmen.

The council as a whole, meanwhile, was involved in a continuous struggle with the Church, which was in effect another ruler alongside the Emperor and was thus exempt from taxation. As the years went by, Frankfurt's councillors and wealthy taxpayers became less and less willing to tolerate this state of affairs, and started to press their case. In the late 1300s, the city's churches and monastic orders went to Mainz and then to Rome seeking protection from Frankfurt's exchequer, but were forced to concede defeat in the early 1400s after the city essentially bought the (temporarily broke) Archbishop of Mainz off. Yet the Church had been building up another stream of income by investing in property: ecclesiastical law at the time stated that houses, once acquired by the Church, would forever be saddled with interest payments to the ecclesiastical authorities, regardless of who acquired them at sale. On the face of it, this was a lucrative deal for the Church; but buyers were frightened off by the prospect of what amounted to mortgage payments in perpetuity, and by the late fifteenth century hundreds of houses in the otherwise crowded city were derelict due to Church intransigence, much to the annoyance of the city.

The Reformation and the Coronations: the Sixteenth Century

Developments in Frankfurt's nearby rival, Mainz, would soon indirectly lead to a situation in which the city had all the excuse it needed to lay its hands on Church property. In the 1450s Johannes Gutenberg invented the modern printing press and started printing bibles in Mainz, creating the technology and the distribution system which would, just over fifty years later, help to spread the revolutionary religious ideas of another German, Martin Luther, with previously unparalleled rapidity. Gutenberg's original press was reliant on paper purchased at Frankfurt's trade fairs, and Gutenberg himself earned income from copies sold at the fair; by his death on the cusp of the dawning sixteenth century, the city had already become the centre of the book trade. As Luther's ideas were disseminated in the early 1520s, Frankfurt had a fast-growing printers' quarter—ironically enough, based around the Catholic Leonhardkirche (see Chapter 3)—and as such, Reformation ideas were in circulation in Frankfurt from their inception.

Indeed, when Luther passed through Frankfurt on his return from the Diet of Worms in 1521, he was cheered by poor and rich alike; Protestant clerics such as Hartmann Ibach were allowed entrance to preach in the city in 1522, the city council and the patricians seeing Luther's ideas a welcome critique of a kleptocratic Catholic Church. Yet soon the Reformation threatened to meld with the proto-communist German Peasants' Revolt of 1524: whole church congregations in Bornheim near Frankfurt and Sachsenhausen within the city walls started demanding the right to choose their own priests as pitchfork armies marched through the surrounding countryside. A few hundred years ahead of schedule, another class of Frankfurt's ruled had reared its head: the general population. On Easter Monday 1525 the Mainz populace showed what is was capable of by force of numbers when it broke into a church compound to wine and dine on the clergy's stock of fine foodstuffs. Just weeks later, Frankfurt's tradesmen, radicalized by an Anabaptist preacher from Cologne, presented the city council with a list of demands similar to those being fought for by the peasants, one of which was explicit permission for Protestant clergyman to preach. Faced with a mounting crisis in the surrounding region, the city council was forced to concede, albeit welcoming the prospect of the land-grab of Church property it was then able to carry out.

Yet for all the city council's attempts to ride the wave, the Reformation (officially proclaimed in Frankfurt ten years later in 1535) had taken on a momentum of its own, bringing the city into direct conflict with the Emperor and ending the political balancing and bartering act of previous centuries in which powers and concessions were gained in exchange for the city's support. Now Frankfurt found itself facing Charles V, King of Spain, Holy Roman Emperor and one of the most rabid opponents of the Reformation. In 1536 the city joined several other Free Imperial Cities and a wealth of Reformationist German princedoms and duchies in a defensive alliance founded in 1530 to protect its members from counter-Reformation forces: the Schmalkadic League. Soon its ambition became not only to defend itself, but to replace the Holy Roman Empire with its own Protestant construct. Yet despite being militarily well-equipped and—thanks to Frankfurt—financially sound, the alliance could not compete with the overwhelming power of Charles V, ruler not only of half of Europe, but of a rapidly expanding overseas empire in the Americas. In 1547 Charles' army occupied the city and reparations were imposed; five years later, a rebellion by the Protestant Saxons saw Frankfurt besieged by the other side for weeks on end. Throughout the Middle Ages Frankfurt had faced attack from enemies—most often the jealous princes of neighbouring Hanau—but had either paid them off or relied on their common ruler, the Emperor, to intervene: the Reformation laid bare the city's vulnerability when it could rely neither on Imperial support nor financial incentives.

It was not until the Peace of Augsburg in 1555, which formalized the schism in Christendom between the Catholic and Protestant Churches and allowed the existence of both within the Holy Roman Empire, that some form of social, political and economic stability returned to Frankfurt. The city itself was unusual inasmuch as it remained officially Lutheran, but was forced to accept the return of Catholic clergy to its largest church, the Kaiserdom, as it was here that the Catholic Holy Roman Emperor was elected. Furthermore, the ever widening ripples from the religious earthquake of the Reformation, whose epicentre had been close to the city, made for choppy waters: the continuing conflict in the Low Countries and the bloody persecutions under Mary I in England sent wave after wave of Calvinist refugees into Germany. While most of the English returned after Bloody Mary's death in 1558, many of the Dutch stayed, creating the city's next religious conflict with their refusal to convert to Lutheran Protestantism, an issue stoked further by the steady stream of French Huguenots (also Calvinists) until the Edict of Nantes in 1598.

Yet the city had seen enough religious conflict and the spirit of pragmatism now prevailed. Calvinist services were held in Bockenheim, then just outside the city bounds in Hanau (and would continue to be for two hundred years, until the Frankfurt Protestant clergy were forced by the Imperial court in Vienna to accept Calvinist congregations on city territory but a few short years before the Empire's demise). The overcrowded ghetto, erected as one of the first in Germany in the 1430s after a century of tension within the city—the Jews having suffered another pogrom following the Black Death in 1349—was also allowed to expand twice in 1552 and 1579: the city council was fully aware of the Jews' usefulness (with all other trades closed to them, they were money-lenders by definition) and had profited whenever they were expelled from other cities.

The effect of the Dutch immigrants on the city's economy—many of them gifted craftsmen (see Chapter 6) and traders—and of the growing Jewish community following a wave of expulsions, starting in Trier in 1418 and culminating in Regensburg in 1519, was stark. Trade with Britain and the Netherlands, especially in cloth, blossomed and led directly to the founding of Frankfurt's stock exchange, set up as a bourse in 1585 to fix rates for the various currencies now in regular circulation. The city's growing prosperity was matched by an increase in prestige as in 1562 Emperor Maximilian II became the first Holy Roman Emperor to be not just elected, but also crowned in Frankfurt. While the Golden Bull was not altered and Aachen retained its official right to be the city of coronation, it chose to waive that right indefinitely and, until the ascension of the last Emperor in 1792, Frankfurt would be the location of both election and coronation.

Revolt and War: the Seventeenth Century

Yet all was not well in the city. The growing importance of trade and finance had put many a nose out of joint: the guilds, especially, feared competition from the stream of foreign wares coming into the city and began to demand protectionist measures and a greater say in municipal affairs, while price inflation driven by the city's financial muscle led to general discontent. Many struggling craftsmen were also indebted to the Jews, and the upheavals and influxes of the late 1500s had caused a general rise in xenophobia and racism in the general population. At the same time, those who had enjoyed newfound financial success as well as a nascent educated middle class composed of lawyers and book merchants demanded representation on the city council. So while business was good for the patrician families, money-lenders and traders, much of the rest of the city felt itself left behind. Tensions mounted, and the guilds and other citizens started to openly question the authority of the council.

This festering discontent exploded during the coronation of Emperor Matthias in the summer of 1612. The city council, worried by the tense atmosphere, asked the guilds and other citizens to swear the customary oath specified in the Golden Bull to protect the electors during their presence in the city: they refused to do so until concessions were made, demanding among other things limits to the interest rates the Jews could charge and a weekly public corn market to combat price rises. Yet in contrast to its stance during the near-revolution a century earlier, the council dug its heels in, refusing to compromise and leaving written petitions unanswered. The Emperor hurried away from the city almost as soon as the crown was on his head as armed gangs started stalking the streets and a group of the dissatisfied, led by Vinzenz Fettmilch, a gingerbread baker in Töngesgasse, broke into the Römer town hall to demand a fair hearing.

Rather than negotiate, however, the stubborn council members handed the keys to the city to the assembled malcontents and announced that they would refer the case to the recently-fled Emperor. He in turn sent in a commission of bishops and princes from neighbouring cities and states such as Hessen, Mainz and Nuremberg to mediate between the two parties: with concerns about the approaching autumn trade fair being cancelled (by now, even rival Mainz had become a supporter of the Frankfurt Messe rather than a competitor), a compromise was rapidly hammered out in the shape of a citizens' charter or *Bürgervertrag* by which the number of hereditary seats in the council would be reduced and auditors would be sent in to create financial transparency; limitations on the number of Jews and their rates of interest were also promised.

Yet the agreement, signed just before Christmas 1612, was implemented half-heartedly at best and the civil disobedience spread rapidly: taxes remained unpaid, municipal property went missing, law and order broke down. A year later, continued discontent culminated in an uprising, led once again by Fettmilch (and which therefore takes his name) when it became known that the city had heaped up extensive debts and that the council had misappropriated tax revenues from the Jews (which, since the late 1300s, had gone to the city rather than to the Emperor). The councillors were held captive in the Römer for three days by an angry mob as Fettmilch and his supporters seized control of the city, declaring its council deposed. When a herald from the Emperor arrived in August 1614 threatening an Imperial interdiction if the city council were not returned to office, the mob turned its anger on the Jews, storming the gates of the ghetto and plundering its main street Judengasse while it rounded up the scapegoats in the Jewish cemetery, from where they were expelled the following day. This was the final straw for the Emperor: despite their taxes going to city coffers, Frankfurt Jews still enjoyed direct Imperial protection and, as such, the ransacking of the ghetto could only be seen as a personal affront.

Chaos reigned until the Emperor, who had issued a death warrant against Fettmilch and his followers, was able to regain control of the city in late September using troops from Mainz, reinstating the city council and returning a measure of calm. Fettmilch was arrested and tried in Mainz for sedition and persecution of the Jews. In early 1616 he and two others were beheaded and quartered on Roßmarkt square before their heads were impaled on the north towers of the Main bridge: Goethe recalled his bleached skull hanging there more than a hundred years later in the autobiographical *Poetry and Truth* (see page 215). On the same day the Jews were led back into the city by the Emperor's soldiers, and so ended one of Germany's last pogroms until the Nazi years and Frankfurt's most damaging unrest to date. The rulers and those who ran the city had seen the destructive potential of those whom they ruled: yet soon, they all would have a common foe.

In 1619, following several years of intermittent religiously charged skirmishes around Europe and within the Empire, the ailing and childless Emperor Matthias sought to secure his family line by defying convention and having his cousin Ferdinand elected as his successor while he was still alive. Ferdinand, crowned in Frankfurt ten days before Matthias' death, was, however, a zealous Catholic and a fearlessly absolutist monarch who quickly upset the delicate balance of the Holy Roman Empire as set at the Peace of Augsburg seventy years before. Soon the Empire was in a state of civil war along religious fault lines and other European powers were fielding armies either in support of the breakaway Protestants or to prop up the official Catholic Empire in what became a tri-decade conflagration of apocalyptic proportions.

The burned child fears the fire: having seen in the sixteenth century the consequences both of religious unrest and of ending up on the wrong side of the wrong Emperor, Frankfurt resolved to remain decidedly neutral. In the first skirmish to take place near the city in 622, the Count of Tilly led Imperial forces to victory over the fanatical Protestant Christian of Brunswick at Höchst (today part of the Frankfurt municipality, see Chapter 12); in order to avoid the burden of an occupying army, Frankfurt simply paid off Tilly's forces, and even managed to secure continued Imperial protection for trade fair travellers from the Catholic generals into the bargain.

Yet Frankfurt was a considerable prize, both financially and symbolically, and passing armies could only bought off for so long. By 1630 the whole continent was at war and the Protestant Swedish King Gustavus Adolphus was in the middle of a stunning advance through Germany, rolling back Imperial forces and reaching Frankfurt in October 1631. Threatened with siege, Frankfurt opened the city gates to the monarch, who immediately blackmailed the council into swearing an oath of allegiance to him.

Frankfurt's position was now precarious: on the one hand, the city had to try to maintain neutrality in case Adolphus was repelled and the Catholic Ferdinand returned; on the other hand, Adolphus had to be appeased. His lightning campaign from the north having taken the whole of Europe by surprise (and having left its lasting mark in German slang: *Alter Schwede!*—"Old Swede!"—is an expression of shock), there seemed a very real chance that he would become the Emperor of a new, Protestant empire in Central Europe, using a reformed Frankfurt cathedral to crown himself in a highly symbolic manner. The latter solution was made all the more attractive by Adolphus' carrot-and-stick occupation: one the one hand, he ordered that the city keep his garrison or face plunder; on the other, he transferred all Church property to the city council with the exception of one monastery in Sachsenhausen, which he kept for himself.

Gustavus' death at Lützen brought a change in fortune for the Swedish occupiers, driven from their garrison in Sachsenhausen by advancing Imperial forces in 1635, who secured the bridge over the Main for the push back north. The city was "liberated" and immediately filled with soldiers and refugees from the surrounding countryside, who brought with them ravenous appetites and the bubonic plague. The coronation of Ferdinand III, who succeeded his father on 30 December 1636, was a subdued affair. Nonetheless, the focus of the war soon moved away from Frankfurt, and the city was spared the fate of other Protestant towns such as Magdeburg, sacked in 1631 by Catholic forces with such brutality that a new verb was coined, *magdeburgisieren*, for "to totally destroy". Since the most famous engraving of this barbarity was produced by the Swiss-born Frankfurter Matthäus Merian (see Chapter 6), it is safe to say the city was aware of its lucky escape.

Indeed, the Imperial coronation of Leopold I in 1657, barely a decade after the Peace of Westphalia in 1648, was a return to Hapsburg pomp and circumstance in a city benefiting from a post-war economic upswing: oxen were roasted once again on the Römer, wine was piped into its fountain and the citizens of Frankfurt gathered to swear their allegiance to the newly-crowned Emperor, who would reign until his death in 1705.

The Last of the Imperial Wine: the Eighteenth Century

Although the coronation of Joseph I in 1705 was not celebrated due to the threat of war, Frankfurt itself would not see actual military action until the end of the century. Instead, the 1700s were a time of peace and prosperity for the city, and with a lack of external threats as well as increasing disparities in wealth, the tensions between groups in the city which had led to the uprising of 1612 began to resurface.

The bone of contention was the almost century-old charter of 1612, most of which had been unceremoniously dumped by the reinstated city council. The structure of Frankfurt's government remained oligarchical, with the council still drawn almost entirely from the aristocratic and patrician families and able to rule almost completely unchecked: the promise of auditors for city finances had remained unfulfilled, and mismanagement, embezzlement and nepotism were thus rife. The only notable element of the *Bürger-vertrag* to have been implemented was the setting up of fourteen district constabularies in which men from the lower orders were obliged to serve; their regular street patrols were intended to lower crime and guard against any future revolutionary upheavals. Yet in contrast to the early 1600s, the general discontent did not coalesce around a demagogue, but around the former head of one such constabulary, Johann Wilhelm Fritsch of Sachsenhausen, who had been dispensed of by the mayor due to a personal disagreement. In contrast with Fettmilch before him, Fritsch decided to play by the rules: since the Middle Ages the Imperial elections, and eventually the coronations, had always represented opportunities for the Frankfurt city council to bend the ear of the new ruler of the Empire, and the city's citizens saw no reason not to make use of the event in the same manner.

At the perfunctory 1705 coronation, from which Leopold himself was absent, several heads of the city's constabulary presented the Emperor's deputy with a written demand for the conditions of the 1612 charter to be upheld. In the ensuing years, the Emperor's delegate to Frankfurt, by no means deaf to the citizens' cause, sent regular reports back to Leopold in Vienna detailing the city council's obstinacy. This steady drip had its effect at court and, after the coronation of the deceased Joseph's brother Charles VI in 1712, at which he was presented with another list of demands from the citizenry, the Archbishop of Mainz and the Duke of Hessen-Darmstadt were sent in by Imperial decree to acts as judges in what became a twenty-year-long legal battle between the citizens and the council. After several victories for the citizens, the "Frankfurt vs. Frankfurt" case was closed in 1732: not only were auditors to have access to the municipal books, but an advisory board of 51 citizens' representatives was empowered to sign off on all legislation passed by the city council. While this new system of checks and balances would remain in place until the end of Frankfurt as an independent city-state over a century later, the frequency with which both the council and the new board directly petitioned the Emperor during the 1700s shows that old conflicts died hard—and that in contrast to other German city-states such as Hamburg or Bremen, whose elected senates resisted external interference and preferred to integrate social climbers and new money into their existing systems, Frankfurt was a city which continued to defer to a strong ruler from outside.

Indeed, during the 1740s Frankfurt's relationship to the Holy Roman Empire was closer than ever before. Charles VI died without a male heir, provoking the War of the Austrian Succession and a two-year Imperial interregnum. The next Emperor was the Bavarian Charles VII, the first non-Hapsburg to be elected in over three centuries, from the house of Wittelsbach and thus a direct descendant of Louis IV, who had granted Frankfurt so many important Messe privileges in the 1300s. Hopes were thus high in the city that the new Emperor would, in contrast to the Hapsburgs who had been so focussed on Austria, take an active interest in the Imperial capital. Frankfurt pulled out all the stops, and the coronation in February 1742 was the most ceremonious and pompous to date. By December, Charles VII had returned to Frankfurt to make it his seat of government—although not out of love for the city, but because his Kingdom of Bavaria had been overrun by Austria. He resided in a splendid baroque villa on Zeil and became very popular with the Frankfurters during his three-year reign, but his inability to regain his territory before his death showed just how little actual power was now invested in the Holy Roman Emperor. Following the catastrophic wars of the previous century and the rise of large and increasingly unified nation-states such as Britain, France and Prussia, the flaws within the piecemeal, anarchic construction of the Holy Roman Empire were becoming clear, and the Emperor—in name also the ruler of Austria—had neither the political authority nor muscle to assert his authority.

Yet the less coherent and important it became, the more Frankfurt seemed to become attached to the institutions of the Empire. The 1745 coronation of Francis I was yet another show of Imperial pomp and circumstance, and although the city could—due mainly to brisk trade with France, the Low Countries and Britain—easily afford such extensive celebrations, its comfortable deference to the Emperor was becoming both increasingly passé and even economically limiting. As Enlightenment ideas spread, for instance,

Frankfurt's book fair, coupled to its annual Messe and Europe's oldest, was overtaken in size and importance by that of Leipzig, where Imperial censorship was implemented with a much lighter touch. In its overall look and feel, too, the city seemed stuck in previous centuries. Despite damaging fires in the Jewish quarter (1711 and 1721) and within the walls (1719) of the kind which other cities took as a cue to apply new principles of building, little was done to correct the narrow road layouts or to change regulations. While the 1700s saw many new buildings in the city, especially private houses for the upper classes and new wealthy bourgeois, they were stylistically and in terms of scale hopelessly outdated when compared to what was being constructed elsewhere in other German and European cities.

The Seven Years' War, starting in 1756, saw France and Austria line up against Britain, Prussia, Saxony and several smaller northern German states; the states of the Holy Roman Empire were, however, obliged to fight with Austria, and Frankfurt supplied a regiment to the Imperial forces. This did not prevent allied France, however, from occupying the city in 1759: with its important mint, currency exchanges and powerful banks, the city was strategically far too important to be left to its own devices, and French troops remained quartered in Frankfurt until 1763. Although trade suffered and the city's population had to house and feed billeted soldiers, the occupation was generally peaceful and brought some notable improvements and a breath of fresh air to what had become a sleepy city: the French introduced innovations such as house numbers, street signs and lanterns (previously, Frankfurters had been legally obliged to carry candles with them at night—one for a commoner, two for a citizen and three for a councillor); they also shielded the city's banks from a series of decrees from Emperor Francis limiting the production of coins in an effort to combat rampant inflation.

In fact, with its congenital obedience to rulers, satiating economic growth and the spectre of latent internal strife, only through outside impetus was Frankfurt willing or able to make changes. After the war, with the city's now outmoded defences having been of no use in protecting it from French occupation, the outlying

ditches and moats were filled in and turned into parks and prom-
enades. And while the coronation of Joseph II in 1765 was held
in the ornate and pompous style of old, the spread of Enlightenment ideas, particularly from France, through the city's increasingly
diverse range of newspapers—which, in contrast to books, were
exempt from censorship (see Chapter 5)—and the intellectual artic-
ulacy of the city's new middle class led to the first public criticism of
the expensive, anachronistic rigmarole. Nevertheless, it was repeated
in 1790 for Leopold II and again on 5 July 1792 for Francis II, who
became the last Holy Roman Emperor just three months before
French Revolutionary forces crossed the Rhine.

Between France, Freedom and Prussia: from 1797 to 1866

On 22 October 1792 the first French forces arrived at Frankfurt,
entering the city five days later to demand that it join the Republic; yet within days the Revolutionary troops were chased away by
the approaching Hessian and Prussian forces. There was a renewed
French attack in early December, but the inner city walls, despite
their antiquated nature, were well manned and the assault was
repelled (the Hessendenkmal at Friedberger Tor is a monument to
this victory). A truce followed in 1795, but when French forces surged
back across the Rhine in the summer of 1796, the tide turned: after
Frankfurt had come under fire—the Judengasse was burned down
for the third time in one century, and for the last time ever—the
Imperial army was forced to withdraw and the city was occupied.
Around twenty councillors were taken to France as hostages, and
by the time the French were pushed back out by approaching relief,
Frankfurt had already been blackmailed into issuing them with four
million *Livres* of bonds. Negotiations ensued and Frankfurt made
peace with France, declaring neutrality; the weakened Empire, also
desperate to make peace, soon followed suit, awarding all of its territory to the west of the Rhine to the rampant revolutionary nation.

The threat to the relative peace and tranquillity in which Frankfurt had spent the century thus far—a time of lawsuits rather than
uprisings, of trade and finance rather than religious conflict—was

THE RULERS AND THE RULED

clear, yet the city remained hopeful that the status quo could some-how be maintained, or deluded itself into believing that it could be. Goethe's mother wrote to him following the peace treaty in 1797 that, as far as she was concerned, "the left and right banks of the Rhine can belong to whom they like—I still eat and sleep as well as I ever have." When Goethe himself visited a few months later, he wrote to the Duke of Weimar that the eye-watering sums of money the city was being forced to pay every time a marauding French army passed by had only served to create "a general foolishness", noting to Schiller that the city was living "in a maelstrom of pur-chasing and consuming". The population of Frankfurt was in denial.

War returned in 1799—in a far more radical form. With Napoleon having made himself consul, the Free Imperial City of Frankfurt sent an official letter of congratulation, only to receive a curt reply stating that Frankfurt would not become "truly free" until the French had liberated it through force of arms. Yet despite the deep inequality in the city—only one quarter of the population was even considered as citizens—and the continuous bickering between the council and the advisory, when French Revolutionary troops once again occupied the city in 1800, they were not welcomed as liberators (as they were in many other parts of feudal Germany). The threat from outside held the city together, while the habit of defer-ring to authority meant that in the absence of a strong Emperor much of the population was more inclined to support reactionary *ancien régime* Prussia than Revolutionary France.

Yet it was the French who were dictating the terms of the new Europe, and Frankfurt had little choice but to try and preserve both its neutrality and its independence. In 1803 the last proper diet of the Holy Roman Empire consolidated its remaining territory right of the Rhine, secularizing the Empire so that it could compensate the hereditary princes with Church lands and incorporating almost all of the city-states into neighbouring territories. Frankfurt, along with a handful of other Free Imperial Cities and the three remain-ing Hanseatics, escaped being swallowed up, and received most of the remaining Church lands in the city into the bargain.

The reprieve, however, was temporary. When the city once again made efforts to cosy up to Europe's strongman Napoleon—and to get him to cancel the mountain of bonds it had been forced to issue to French armies—by sending a deputation to meet him at Mainz in autumn 1804, the rebuff was brutal: "How was your trade fair?" asked Napoleon sarcastically: "Do you do well? Have you not received many cloisters and church properties?" Working himself into a rage, he accused the city of mercenary neutrality: "You hide English agents and *agents provocateurs*, your bankers are always going off somewhere or other," closing with a threat to "give you a real beating and pass you on to the nearest local prince" during the next war.

A year later the next war was being fought and Frankfurt was again under French occupation. Far worse: on 16 July 1806 Frankfurt's deputation in Paris was informed that the city would become part of the Confederation of the Rhine, Napoleon's group of client states cajoled together to provide him with a buffer against Austria. On 6 August 1806, defeated by Napoleon at the Battle of Austerlitz, Emperor Francis II dissolved the Holy Roman Empire, and Frankfurt's new ruler was no longer the Holy Roman Emperor, but a lowly "Prince-Primate", Karl von Dalberg, the former Archbishop of Mainz (on Napoleon's orders, thenceforth "Mayence", and part of France), who was to lead the Confederation and chose Frankfurt as his residence.

For those who had run Frankfurt, especially the patrician families, becoming mere subjects of a prince as opposed to free citizens of an empire was an unwelcome climb-down; and although the council remained in place, the centre of power became the prince's own private commission. Yet for much of the general population of Frankfurt, the seven years of his rule until the disintegration of the Napoleonic order brought welcome changes. Although he reigned as an absolutist monarch, Dalberg followed Enlightenment principles, separating the judiciary from the administration and introducing the Napoleonic Code in 1811, abolishing the existing city laws with their feudal hangovers and opening up large swathes of the economy to everyman. In the same year, all religious groups were given equal rights, allowing Catholics, Calvinists and above all Jews to become citizens: the Jews, however, were made to pay the princely sum of 440,000 Guilders before they were fully emancipated and officially allowed to leave the remains of the Judengasse ghetto (since its destruction, most had been living in the city temporarily). In 1808 Dalberg set up a chamber of commerce on the French model, Germany's second after Mainz's. The year 1808 also saw the completion of the dismantling of Frankfurt's walls and towers begun by the French occupiers; Dalberg had the green belt around the city laid out and crowned the project with a set of building regulations which laid the foundations for less crowded quarters around the Old Town.

Nevertheless, the upheaval was not all for the better: the Continental Blockade meant swingeing cuts to the city's trade (a substantial portion of which was carried out with Britain) and forced previously legitimate merchants into illicit practices, while Dalberg's absolutist convictions led to a devastation of the city's beloved newspapers, of which only one was allowed to go to print, and heavily censored, during his reign. As such, Frankfurters wealthy and poor were united in welcoming France's change in fortunes: retreating through Germany in 1813, Napoleon spent Halloween night in Frankfurt, now run by his stepson Eugène de Beauharnais after Dalberg had fled to Switzerland earlier in the year, and on 6 November, an Austrian army liberated Frankfurt from French rule.

A period of uncertainty now began. The allies, meeting in the city, issued Napoleon with the Frankfurt Proposals, by which he would have remained Emperor of France in a peace settlement: but he refused, and the war dragged on into 1814. Even before the Congress of Vienna started that autumn, there was jostling for what had, in another Napoleonic reorganization in 1810, become the Duchy of Frankfurt: Hesse and Bavaria had both lost territory to this small state around Frankfurt and wanted not just their former lands back, but the former Imperial city itself into the bargain. Yet the city had a powerful ally in the form of Freiherr von Stein, the Prussian statesmen who was administrating the liberated German territories and who argued that, of all the former Free Cities, Frankfurt could lay the greatest claim to being reinstated as such in the new German Confederation. His official logic was that Frankfurt had the best geographical location for the members of the new group of states to meet and should thus remain neutral (in private, he pointed out that Frankfurt would make Prussian rival Bavaria far too powerful, giving it a territorial link to its possessions in the Palatinate that would cut Germany in two).

Thus started on 9 July 1815 Frankfurt's fifty-year period as a *truly* free city, which owed allegiance to no-one: with the Holy Roman Empire consigned to history, in terms of international law, the city's mayor was a sovereign of the same rank as the King of Prussia or the Emperor of Austria. Never before had those who ran the city also been its rulers, and never before had they been able—on paper—to do so freely. Yet those over whom they ruled were as powerless as ever: despite the city council being renamed a senate and being expanded to take on more citizens' representatives, the new constitution was one in name only, rolling back Dalberg's reforms on a broad front as it set the sum needed to purchase voting rights at 5,000 Guilders. It also emasculated Jews, Catholics and Reformists: although they were allowed to remain in the city and practise their religions, these groups were once again excluded from citizenship. Despite some progressive alterations over the decades (the Jews, for example, were made "Israelite citizens" in 1824 and finally full citizens in 1864), Frankfurt's social conflicts from previous centuries remained essentially unresolved—and looked increasingly quaint as the pace of the ongoing political and industrial revolutions picked up.

A rather light-hearted episode shows just how behind the times the city and its legislation were. Although the city walls had been removed, there were toll gates along the borders with the Duchy of Hesse-Darmstadt to the south and the Electorate of Hesse to the north, which were shut at night and would usually only be opened on payment of a tardiness fine. However, given that several wineries and *Appelwoi* cider yards were located in the surrounding countryside and were popular for evening or weekend excursions, the city had long allowed its residents free entry through the late gates. In 1831, with the July revolution in Paris underway, the Senate felt it was time to ramp up policing and re-imposed the toll; a mob of angry (and possibly drunken) residents refused to pay and broke through the gates, upon which the police ordered that everyone would have to carry a lantern with them after dark so that they could be identified. Fed up with this kind of positively medieval imposition, the population of Frankfurt took to the streets—all armed with every single lantern, lamp, and candle they had in their homes. The city was turned into a sea of lights.

Just a few years later, the toll gates were dismantled: yet the Frankfurters' protest had had little to do with it. Rather, it was in the interest of trade, which had suffered heavily during the Napoleonic years and never really recovered: as the industrial revolution gathered speed and the pace of economic life in Europe quickened, the myriad of customs checks between the patchwork of German states became a competitive disadvantage and by the early 1830s plans for a customs union under Prussian leadership were taking shape. Hesse-Darmstadt joined early in 1828, followed by the Electorate in 1831, potentially allowing products of all kind to bypass Frankfurt toll-free as long as they were not transported by river. The city's Messe had already become soporific, and when even a trade and shipping agreement with Britain in 1832 did little to combat Frankfurt's increasing isolation, it joined the customs union in 1836.

Not just economic but political influences came from outside. The principal argument at the Congress of Vienna for keeping Frankfurt as an independent city-state had been its usefulness as a neutral capital for the German Confederation, whose remit was to mediate between the interests of all its members, from the Hanseatic minnow of Lübeck, proud but past its prime, to the young and hungry piranha Prussia. Yet for disappointed revolutionaries and democratic activists, the *Bundesversammlung*, the Federal Congress composed of the rulers of the German, Austrian and Eastern European member states, was an instrument of autocratic oppression. Disquiet grew.

In 1833 student radicals from nearby Gießen tried to storm the Congress, leading to an increased military presence in Frankfurt (and the city's first taste of a police state thanks to the Austrian founder of modern snooping, Metternich). This was, however, just a foretaste of the 1848 revolution, Germany's first widespread popular movement for democracy, which saw tumultuous popular uprisings across the land. On 5 March a group of opposition politicians, seizing the moment, convened in Frankfurt to set up the *Vorparlament*, or "pre-Parliament", as a competing institution to the Congress. Their aim was to write a democratic constitution with an elected parliament for all German states. As the civil unrest gathered pace, smaller princes and dukes cowered in their castles; and after proletarian masses barricaded the streets of Berlin, even Germany's most autocratic rulers such as the King of Prussia cracked and agreed to hold elections for the national constitutional assembly.

The *Nationalversammlung* gathered in the Paulskirche (see Chapter 3) for its constituting session on 18 May, making Frankfurt the city in which Germany's first genuinely democratic parliament was situated. The general population, downtrodden and deprived of rights as it was, welcomed the deputies, yet events elsewhere soon led to the disintegration of this united democratic front: the Schleswig-Holstein question—which, according to a *bon mot* accredited to contemporaneous diplomat Lord Palmerston, had only ever been understood by three people: Prince Albert, who was dead, a German professor, who had gone mad, and himself, who had forgotten all about it—reared its head.

The Duchies of Schleswig and Holstein had long been protectorates under the Danish crown, yet Holstein had been a member of the Holy Roman Empire and, thus, the German Confederation. The new parliament, however, wanted German-speaking Schleswig admitted and the Confederation occupied the two territories, leading to a short war with Denmark which was settled by the Malmö Treaty of 26 August 1848; the Parliament at first condemned the arrangement, which entailed the withdrawal of all German forces, but then, on 16 September, agreed to it by a narrow majority.

THE RULERS AND THE RULED

Condemning the truce as an anti-democratic stitch-up, the left wing of the Parliament rebelled, refusing to recognize the assembly any longer and accusing it of being little more than a talking shop; this captured the mood of the increasingly impatient population, who rioted, manning barricades and murdering two conservative Prussian parliamentarians, Felix von Lichnowsky and General von Auerswald, as they rode out to meet Confederation troops coming into to quell the civil unrest; Auerswald was shot and Lichnowsky beaten so badly that he died of his wounds the following day in the Bethmann villa in which Napoleon had spent Halloween fifty years before.

The violence provided the sceptical conservatives, led by the Prussian and Austrian monarchs, with all the arguments they needed to move against democratic forces. Troops occupied the city and the Parliament, increasingly discredited, harassed and forgotten, limped on into 1849 before moving to Stuttgart and political oblivion. Meanwhile, the presence of Confederation troops, both Austrian and Prussian, in and around the city meant a *de facto* end to Frankfurt's independence, turning it into a pawn between these two powers set on a course for collision in their efforts to dominate the German Confederation.

Frankfurt became a place of diplomatic intrigue; Bismarck arrived as Prussian ambassador in 1851 and spent the next eight years there planning Austria's demise. It also become one in which freedom of expression was increasingly risky: the light-touch press censorship reintroduced after the Napoleonic interlude was a thorn in the flesh of the resurgent autocrats and, along with the symbolic importance of the city, became the justification for tightening control in the early 1860s, as both Austria and Prussia began to make threatening noises about ending Frankfurt's special status as a city-state.

With its historic affinity to the Hapsburg Emperors, Frankfurt's government was generally in favour of Austrian domination in the German Confederation, and it was this positioning as much as anything that led to its final downfall. In 1863 Bismarck successfully countered an attempt by the Austro-Hungarian Emperor

Franz Josef to have himself made German Emperor in Frankfurt; the press published unflattering cartoons of the Iron Chancellor and although his time in the city had taught him to value its inhabitants' witty humour this, combined with the presence of an increasingly strong socialist party in the rapidly industrializing city, made him determined to strengthen the Prussian grip on it. When war with Austria finally came in summer 1866, rendering the German Confederation asunder, Frankfurt's leaders hurriedly declared neutrality—only for a Prussian army to march in and demand unrealistically large sums from the city government under the threat of execution. The history of previous Swedish and French occupations seemed to be repeating itself: unable to find the money, Mayor Viktor Fellner hung himself. Yet it became clear to his successors that joining Prussia was unavoidable—and would perhaps even be beneficial to the city—and that the sky-high ransom demands were little more than an announcement of the end of the city's independence, a piece of the *Realpolitik* for which Bismarck became so famed. On 8 October 1866, one thousand years after the city was first recorded in the annals as the seat of an Emperor, it was swallowed up by an expanding Prussia; the three remaining Imperial city-states of Hamburg, Bremen and Lübeck would soon follow. Speaking to the city elders during negotiations about which parts of state property would become Prussian and which would remain in city hands, Bismarck, however, was at pains to underline the city's special role: "Prussia will do all in its power for Frankfurt, which it sees as a jewel in its crown. Its position at the border to southern Germany is of extreme importance and when it is no longer a border city—it will not remain one forever—it will become twice as important."

From Imperial to Radical: the Wilhelmine Years and the Weimar Republic

Although Frankfurt's absorption into Prussia marked the point at which its position and role within Germany changed irrevocably, it was as much a sign of the times as a cause of great change. With the removal of the walls in the early 1800s and the arrival of the railways in the 1840s, by the time Frankfurt became part of Prussia, the city's population had already doubled from its stable early-modern figure of 40,000. Just forty years later, Frankfurt would be home to over 400,000 inhabitants and one of the ten largest cities in Germany. As 1848 had shown, for all its outdated baroque architecture and lack of heavy industry, the city housed the same new class of precarious proletarian worker as other large towns—and faced the same overcrowding, disease and poverty as were causing political instability elsewhere.

These social ills and the revolutionary potential they brought with them were only set to get worse. Not hemmed in by state borders, the villages around Frankfurt such as Bornheim and Bockenheim had already become industrial towns and were slowly expanding towards Frankfurt, which was itself growing outwards, swallowing the former in the 1877 boundary reform and the latter in 1895. The edge-of-town villas of the bankers and aristocrats were soon surrounded by the suburbs of what was fast becoming a conurbation. The character of the city changed: while the old business of finance grew at a faster pace than ever after 1867—particularly on Prussian government borrowing up to and during the Franco-Prussian War—industry, above all metalworking and chemicals, expanded even more rapidly. The banks and financiers of Frankfurt had never made more money, and yet had never been less dominant.

While on the outside the absorption of 1867 had left the structure of municipal government in Frankfurt almost untouched (only its name changed from the Imperial *Senat* to a simple *Stadtversammlung*, or city assembly), the changes were actually far-reaching: voting restrictions were loosened to Prussian standards, allowing most men in regular work to cast a ballot; the assembly had to nominate a mayor who would be given royal approval; furthermore, the electorate now also voted for members of the North German Assembly, and after 1871, for the Reichstag.

With increased suffrage, Frankfurt was soon regularly returning left-wing and social-democratic candidates both to the city assembly and to Berlin, while the city's mayors, now elected for 12-year periods, had to be politically acceptable to the reactionary Prussian rulers: a rift thus opened up between the mayors and the elected representatives. Moreover, before 1867 only those with Frankfurt citizenship rights had been eligible for office: the integration with Prussia opened up opportunities to candidates from across the new German Empire. The mayors were thus frequently unpopular, both among the city's established families as geographical outsiders, and with the man on the street as autocratic imposters.

Yet with some historical perspective, the four mayors Heinrich Mumm (governed 1868-80), Johannes Miquel (1880-91), Franz Adickes (1891-1912) and Georg Voigt (1912-24) can be said to have made a good fist of navigating these murky, semi-democratic waters. The only mayor of what is referred to as the Wilhelmine period (of Emperor Wilhelm II) to actually come from Frankfurt, the energetic Mumm, initiated a veritable slew of grand schemes to give his hometown the necessary infrastructure for its expansion and the architectural wherewithal to compete with Europe's established great cities—the gigantic new railway station being the most prominent example. At the same time, his weakness for grandeur brought him into frequent conflict with both the rising proletariat and the city assembly: the wildly overpriced Opera, finished late and over budget, ruined his reputation among both the political classes and general population. His efforts to improve the city's water supply were forgotten and credited to his slightly more hesitant successor, Miquel, whose period in office was less ambitious and—perhaps due to this—viewed as more successful: besides strict financial discipline, Miquel's principal interest was in the new methods of transport and energy distribution, on which he tried to exercise his authority to the greatest possible extent.

Adickes, too, was well aware of the importance of municipal policy in questions of infrastructure: during his term of office the tram network and the city's power stations were brought entirely under municipal control, starting a long tradition of public provision in Frankfurt. Beyond this, Adickes' economic ambition for the city was boundless. Captured by the vision of a canal connecting the Main to the Danube, which would put Frankfurt at the centre of a cross-European waterway, he had the Osthafen built (the canal, however, would only be completed in 1992). Adickes was also the driving force behind the city's university, opened in 1914 in honour of Goethe, at a time when the colleges of sedate towns such as Heidelberg and Tübingen were considered completely sufficient and big city industrialists were suspicious of tertiary education.

Voigt, meanwhile, was the most left-leaning and socially engaged of the mayors, and also the most hamstrung by external circumstances: while his three predecessors governed in a period of unparalleled expansion during which Germany overtook Britain in terms of industrial might and established the world's first national social and health insurances, Voigt's term of office was beset by the catastrophe of the First World War and ended a year after hyperinflation had wrecked the Weimer Republic.

Indeed, until the war years Frankfurt had seen little by way of social unrest: in the decades of peace following the proclamation of the Second German Empire, the whole country was economically dynamic but politically stable. Despite the lack of genuine democracy (women were not allowed to vote; the Reichstag was limited in its power by the authoritarian Prussian rulers) and seething tensions among the working class (especially after discriminatory laws were passed against Social Democrats in the 1880s), incomes and standards of living had been rising rapidly enough to head off any serious questioning of the status quo. With the increasing hardships towards the end of the First World War, however, and the national chaos following Imperial Germany's surrender, this unspoken socio-economic contract was ruptured and suppressed conflicts rose to the surface.

Although the mobilization of 1914 was first greeted in Frankfurt—as it was elsewhere in Germany and Europe generally—with a surge in nationalist enthusiasm, the city began to suffer under the wartime strain early on. The increased demand for metal and chemicals production led to longer working hours, while food was soon in short supply. Even before what became known across Germany as the "turnip winter" of 1916-17, rationing was tight in Frankfurt due more than anything to its history: arable land surrounding the city was traditionally Hessian and Bavarian and, even within the united German Empire, the old states had retained their territorial boundaries and control of local government. Agricultural produce from the fertile Main valley was thus requisitioned in Munich or Wiesbaden and distributed elsewhere, while Frankfurt was territorially Prussian and had to be supplied from that state's northern heartlands. By 1916 the population was severely demoralized and the city saw two of wartime Germany's largest peace marches; in by-elections to the city assembly the Social Democrats, who had profiled themselves as a party of peace throughout the Wilhelmine years, surged, while both the absence of men at the front and increasingly vocal calls for women's rights led to the first high-profile appointments of female candidates to municipal positions.

Mayor Voigt, although not deaf to left-wing causes, was the Kaiser's man and national legislation prevented Social Democrats from being included in government at any level: with the defeat of 1918, dissatisfaction and disillusionment with the discredited, disintegrating old order were just as strong in Frankfurt as elsewhere and the city was a fertile ground for revolution. When the first mutinying Navy sailors, whose uprising was a clarion call to revolutionaries across the country, arrived by train in Frankfurt on 7 November, the power vacuum in the city had already been filled by revolutionary committees of Social Democrat workers who took control of public buildings and factories. Although they left the mayor and city assembly in place, Frankfurt descended rapidly into ungovernable chaos: declared a demilitarized zone by the allied victors, the city faced anarchy as the police force was woefully inadequate in the face of bands of militant revolutionaries, soon joined by disaffected and armed soldiers. Law and order broke down, giving way to mob rule and vigilante justice until well into 1919. In June of that year, in a scene reminiscent of the Fettmilch Uprising, unemployed workers stormed the Römer and strong-armed the terrified civil servants into paying out their jobless benefits early.

While in 1614 Imperial troops had been sent in to restore order, the young Weimar Republic was more or less powerless. In September police reinforcements from the surrounding provinces were finally able to disarm the Naval police and several other vigilante groups, but state authority was fragile at best, while increasingly deep rifts ran between various wings of the Social Democrats and the increasingly militant Communist Party. With the reactionary Kapp putsch against the Weimar Republic of March 1920, another revolution seemed imminent as the bickering left-wing factions called a general strike which quickly turned into a riot: Weimar troops, lightly armed under the terms of the Versailles Treaty, were called in. Three weeks later, with civil unrest spreading across Germany, the occupying French Army of the Rhine took control of the industrial cities of the Ruhr and Rhine valleys and of Frankfurt, sending in tanks and imposing martial law. Following several bloody encounters with the occupiers, the revolutionaries slowly began to melt back into the population and, with the spring trade fair approaching in May, the French forces were able to withdraw, leaving a pacified and thoroughly exhausted city behind them.

Yet while Frankfurt as a whole, desperate for a return to normality, now settled down, the radicalism of the revolutionary years remained latent. The left-wing workers' movements did not disband, while the chaos and shame of the defeat gave birth to the first far-right political groupings: among the city's lower classes the left held sway, but Frankfurt's proximity to right-wing Bavaria and its central location in Germany made it a popular meeting point for nationalist and fascist groups from all across the country.

Throughout the Weimar years the first city government elected by universal suffrage—a coalition of moderate Social Democrats and Catholic liberals—became increasingly active. The old city elite, which had provided poor relief to those ineligible for national insurance benefits and had financed artistic and cultural life through charitable giving, had been weakened by the war and the tumultuous interregnum. Faced with an impoverished population counting numerous war invalids, the city government realized that the only way to keep Frankfurt from renewed social conflict was the use taxes and city property—two constants immune from the increasingly ruinous inflation—to fill in the gaps still left by the national social welfare schemes. Taking the policies of previous mayors further,

Voigt authorized municipal takeovers of veterans' homes, financed free school meals and even set up what would today be called "drop-in centres" for those suffering from alcoholism and drug addiction.

The trend was only strengthened by the next wave of chaos to sweep over the city: the 1923 hyperinflation. By the highpoint of the crisis in November, a ride on Frankfurt's tramways cost ninety billion Marks. With the Republic no longer able to print money as fast as it was becoming useless, cities themselves took to issuing rudimentary emergency notes. Several decades ahead of its role as the centre of Germany's financial policy, Frankfurt printed three rounds of such *Notgeld*, the first of which totalled 5 quintillions; the second and third rounds were slightly less extravagant, running to 211 quadrillions and 500 trillions respectively. A full fifty per cent of the companies registered in the city were forced to close, while unemployment rocketed to 20,000, with a further 60,000 workers on short hours.

By the time the Rentenmark currency reform took effect and the situation stabilized in 1924, the city's middle class had been all but destroyed. Anyone relying on savings, bonds or anything other than property or paid work for their income, was destitute and reliant on municipal hand-outs. As such, the city government saw little choice but to continue down its path of progressive social policy; at the same time, the rebound in economic growth, as well as new taxes on property aimed at redistributing the wealth preserved through the crisis, provided Frankfurt with the funds it needed for its plans. As the roaring half of the 1920s finally began, schemes became more ambitious, especially after the election of 1926, which put the Social Democrats at the helm of the city government.

A golden period in Frankfurt's history set in under Mayor Ludwig Landmann (1868-1945), whose clear and far-thinking plans gave the city an entirely new direction: Landmann's big idea was to decrease the number of Frankfurters living in the overcrowded Altstadt and the dilapidated Wilhelmine tenements surrounding it by moving them out to purpose-built greenfield estates; space in the centre would be used to create civic infrastructure, while the riverside would be reserved for industry. He ordered a ring of new settlements around the centre, drafting in Frankfurt native Ernst May (see page 231) to plan them. May, a cosmopolitan proponent of Bauhaus standardization, had worked on and been inspired by the Edwardian garden cities around London, and now designed districts of mass-produced terraced houses and low-rise apartments with gardens, interspersed by green space. Using a systematic pre-fab approach, he was able to provide 8,000 new homes in just three years, all with fitted kitchens and bathrooms, electricity and hot running water.

Industry, too, was part of the plan: Landmann set up not only Germany's first motorway-building consortium for the first ever autobahn, envisioned to run from Hamburg to Basel, but also worked with bankers to found an airport company: not only was Frankfurt ahead of other cities nearby in developing its aerodrome into a civilian airport, but public works such as this provided jobs for the city's unemployed. At the same time, Landmann was an opera-lover and former theatre manager who encouraged the development of the city's artistic institutions. His culture secretary, Max Michel, decreed it his goal to turn the city's "masses into Maecenas", to use municipal funds gathered through taxation to support the arts and wrest control of high culture from the traditional patrons in the banks. On 16 November 1930, for example, the Messe festival hall was filled with 100 musicians and 700 singers from the *Kulturkartell*, a workers' cultural association, who sang Beethoven's Ninth Symphony to an audience of 18,000. It was a highpoint of the reformist, democratic Frankfurt that had been created during the Weimar Republic. Yet, statistically speaking, around 4,000 people present in the hall that night had voted for the National Socialist Workers' Party (NSDAP) just two months previously.

From Progressive to Destructive: the Hitler Years

For all his decisiveness and ambition, Mayor Landmann was no uncontroversial figure. Many traditional liberals and reactionary forces, including several in the city's industrial and financial dynasties, felt put out or even threatened by the way in which he expanded the role of the municipal government. Against the frightening backdrop of the Wall Street Crash, and with liberal and right-wing party organs agitating about supposedly excessive municipal spending and what they called the "Landmann system", his coalition fell in the local elections of 1929. The Nazis doubled their share of the vote to ten per cent, and doubled it again in the nationwide elections of September 1930, suddenly becoming a political force to be reckoned with in the city.

The Brownshirts were, in any case, no strangers to Frankfurt: as in other German cities, they had well-organized district gangs who had honed their street-fighting skills against communists in continual low-level violence throughout the 1920s. Although small, the local party was ready when, in the late 1920s, the national party began its ascension: six weeks before the 1930 election—and three months prior to the *Kulturkartell* concert there—Hitler had managed to fill the Messe hall, giving the Frankfurt NSDAP a surge in membership as he denounced the progressive city as a "town of democrats and Jews".

In the early 1930s, mass unemployment spread throughout Germany, hitting Frankfurt particularly hard: 70,000 people were unemployed, half of them with no right to state unemployment benefits and therefore dependent on the municipality. Meanwhile, the Nazis in the city assembly brought local government to a standstill, bombarding Landmann's fragile new coalition with useless enquiries, questions and objections, helping to create the situation of parliamentary logjam which they attacked in election propaganda. Following the seizure of power in Berlin in January 1933, the city assembly was dissolved in February by Göring's decree; he also replaced the head of the city police, a member of the Social Democrats, with his own man. New local elections were scheduled for 13 March, and Mayor Landmann, of Jewish descent, was top of the hit-list handed out to the Nazi thugs now roaming the streets. Landmann, visiting friends in the country, got wind of the death threats and fled into anonymity in Berlin (and thence onto Holland, where he died in penury just before the end of the war, see page 219). Despite their grip on the city, the Nazis did not quite manage an absolute majority in the local elections, but a coalition with the willing German Nationalists gave them 51.8 per cent of the assembly and the appearance of upholding constitutional government.

Landmann was replaced as mayor by long-time Nazi activist Friedrich Krebs, but from now on, the real power lay with former post office clerk Jakob Sprenger, who had led the Hessen-Nassau district NSDAP and would now go on as *Gauleiter* to rule Frankfurt and its surroundings as his private fiefdom until the fall of the Third Reich. Under his leadership, the paramilitary Storm Troops began a year-long reign of terror in city hall, courts, museums, libraries and the university, forcing Jews, Social Democrats and other "undesirables" out of office. Throughout the summer, the city bled academics such as Max Horkheimer and Theodor Adorno, and a veritable army of painters, musicians, judges and lawyers.

While they were ridding the city of their enemies, the Nazis began to implement the very same large-scale projects they had so criticized as part of the "Landmann system" in order to get unemployment down. In a bitter irony, it was Sprenger who turned the first spadeful of earth on Germany's first autobahn, while Landmann and May's plans for slum clearance in the old town—fought against tooth and nail by the Nazis in opposition as a "destruction of German culture"—were put back into motion. In addition, grandiloquent schemes were devised for the Gutleut district along the Main which would give Frankfurt its very own set of National Socialist monuments on the same scale as the Nuremberg rally arena.

The plans were never realized: although it was an important industrial and logistical centre, and as such crucial to Nazi war planning, the upper echelons of the party hierarchy remained suspicious of Frankfurt and preferred to concentrate resources on the more fanatical cities of Munich and Nuremberg—and on the new capital, Germania, which was to replace Berlin and much of its equally suspect population. Although the persecution and extermination of the Nazi years led to the complete destruction of its age-old Jewish community (see Chapters 8 and 11) and its nascent democratic tradition, for all the enthusiasm of Frankfurt's party leaders and the compliance of its population with National Socialism, the city never quite found its cultural role in Hitler's Reich: nevertheless, it would be engulfed in flames like the rest of it.

The Almost-Capital, the Secret Capital: 1945 to 1990

When American forces liberated Frankfurt on 29 March 1945, over half of the city's dwellings had been completely destroyed; the pre-war population of over half a million had sunk to 270,000. One year before, the heaviest raids of 18, 22 and 24 March had destroyed the Old Town and wrecked much of the remaining city centre. Sporadic air attacks had continued since, and the German commanders refused to surrender the city to General Patton without a fight: the bridges in the city centre were blown up and American forces had to battle their way into the city, finally knocking out the German field headquarters near the station with artillery after five days of fighting.

The material and political destitution of the city and the country in early 1945 make the facts of the post-war reconstruction and democratization—both of Germany as a whole and of Frankfurt itself—all the more astonishing. The American occupying forces moved fast to rebuild something approaching a constitutional order: in the absence of a German state, they created the Federal State of Hesse, of which Frankfurt was a part, and the city's first post-war local elections were held in May 1946. Those Social Democrats who had survived the Nazi years were rewarded with a majority and elected Walter Kolb, a lawyer and local politician from Düsseldorf, as mayor.

Faced with a population at the limits of physical and mental exhaustion, a city in ruins, and an economic state of limbo without a currency or any available resources, Kolb had little to work with except personal charisma: the portly, bespectacled man appealed to citizens to help clear away rubble, having himself photographed with a pneumatic drill outside the Römer and making frequent personal appearances at the *Trümmerbahnen*, human chains along which rubble was passed to be sorted at the newly founded *Trümmerverwertungsgesellschaft* (see page 23). Slowly, confidence, and

Frankfurters, returned: the city's population was already approaching the 500,000 mark again by 1947.

The indefatigable Kolb was soon a national celebrity in a nation which still did not exist: with no *Führer*, no Emperor and no Chancellor, Germany looked to the mayors of the largest cities for political orientation. Frankfurt's Kolb was soon mentioned alongside Berlin's legendary Ernst Reuter and Hamburg's beloved Max Brauer as embodying a new and better Germany as, in the vacuum of occupation, the city soon began to take on tasks which had previously been part of Berlin's role as capital: the *de facto* ruler of the whole of southern Germany, General Patton, had taken up residence at the IG Farben headquarters in the city, and decisive discussions about the country's fate were being held there. As Marshall Plan dollars flowed into Germany from 1947 on, they were allocated across the Western Allies' zones from a central board in Frankfurt; the new Deutsche Mark, introduced on 21 June 1948, was prepared by the Bank deutscher Länder, set up in the city by the Americans on the model of the Federal Reserve (and which would go on, in 1957, to become the mighty Bundesbank); that summer, the heads of the new German federal states were called to Frankfurt and told by the Allies to produce a constitution.

The timing could not have been more poignant—and more promising—for the city. On 18 May 1948, the centenary of the first democratic National Assembly had been celebrated in the frantically reconstructed Paulskirche, and many now assumed that the new constitution would be hammered out in the city, which would then be a natural choice as the new capital—out of historical symbolism, due to the tri-zonal institutions already established there, and with a view to its central location, with Berlin already blockaded by the Soviets and thus out of the running for the foreseeable future. The city began to build: in Dornbusch to the north—named after the thickets once part of the city's medieval defences and home to the Frank family until they left for Dutch exile—a round plenary was started which would function as a parliamentary chamber.

Yet the constitutional committee left Frankfurt that summer for a hunting lodge in nearby Rüdesheim: the city was still largely in ruins and the dust of demolition, clearance and rebuilding filled the air; legend has it that, into the bargain, Frankfurt hotels were unfriendly to the German delegates—preferring Americans with their hard currency and inexhaustible supplies of cigarettes—and that the city government gave off a generally arrogant and entitled impression. In any case, the committee decided to relocate to Bonn, and the first parliamentary sessions were held there that autumn.

Frankfurt was unruffled. With all the administrative apparatus settled in the city, its leaders assumed that once the first national elections had been held, one of the parliament's first decisions would be to select Frankfurt as the new republic's capital. The Basic Law for the Federal Republic of Germany was enacted on 23 May 1949 and the new nation's first elections held in August. By autumn the fledgling parliament, in which the conservative CDU under Konrad Adenauer held the majority was ready to vote on the capital city, and on 3 November, in a secret ballot, Bonn beat Frankfurt by 200 votes to 176. While rumours abounded for many years to come that the geriatric Adenauer, a Rhineland native who lived within spitting distance of Bonn, had twisted arms in favour of the provincial town so that he could take afternoon naps at home, the simple fact was that a majority of the elected members also lived closer to Bonn than they did to Frankfurt. The plenary chamber at Dornbusch, now ready but lacking plenaries, was given to the Hessian public service broadcaster in 1950, and Frankfurt's city council concentrated on running the nation's capital in all but name—and on continuing where the Social Democrats of the 1920s left off.

Up until 1977, when the post-war Social Democrat majority in the city assembly ended, the city pursued a two-pronged strategy of business-friendly, finance-friendly policy on the one hand and heavy investment in social infrastructure on the other. While the industrial concerns in and around Frankfurt—many of them successors of the IG Farben conglomerate—were showered with cash, and banks, investment funds and federal agencies were tempted into settling in the city, social housing went up at an unparalleled pace. Often, the two sides of municipal policy were in competition with one another: while new apartments were being built just south of the Römer and around the Dom (the unmistakable 1950s pre-fab buildings still provide centrally located, if aesthetically question-able, homes today), the first corporate and government tenants were already complaining about the lack of space in the city centre. The snowball effect had set in: a critical mass of banks and economic institutions had made the city into the undisputed financial centre of Germany. Foreign banks looking to set up in the country as it returned to the fold in the late 1950s went to Frankfurt without exception.

The problems were solved with money. The *Wirtschaftswunder* was in full swing, with the German economy growing at record pace, and Frankfurt at the forefront. By the mid-1950s the city was taking in more corporation tax than any other in the country; unem-ployment remained at less than one per cent until the late 1960s. Municipal funds were plentiful, and the Social Democratic signa-ture was clearly visible as new homes went predominantly to the elderly, war invalids, refugees from former German territories and Frankfurt residents who had suffered under Nazi rule. Meanwhile, the banks and federal offices, also able to invest heavily, started to build upwards to escape the pressure on space: the 1960s saw the first skyscrapers go up (albeit at comparatively modest heights). As well as with the meteoric rise in commuting, the undisputed pre-dominance of the airport—the city assembly had been far-sighted enough to give planning permission for new runways in the city for-est back in 1949—and the renaissance of the Frankfurt trade fairs as a series of industry-specific expos (the International Motor Show, the Book Fair, the ACHEMA chemicals meet) were clogging the city's roads and railways. In 1963 the ground-breaking ceremony for the city's first underground out to the new town Nordweststadt was held.

On the surface, the city was running like a well-oiled machine: after twenty years of solid, Western democracy and uninterrupted economic growth, Frankfurt in the late 1960s was a freer and wealthier place than it had ever been before, its patches of rubble successively replaced by modern housing and offices. And yet not everyone in the city was satisfied. Hessian state prosecutor Fritz

Bauer, persecuted by the Nazis and appalled at the veil of silence laid over their crimes, catapulted the Holocaust into the national discussion with the Auschwitz trials. Although judicially of mixed success in achieving convictions, the trials put painstaking reconstructions of the Nazi extermination system into the public domain and were a crucial first step in what modern Germany calls *Aufarbeitung*—coming to terms with the crimes of the past (see Chapter 11).

The controversy came just as a growing intellectual counter-culture based around the city's university was beginning to question the silence of its parents' generation with regard to recent history, and thus the legitimacy of the both the socio-economic and political order of post-war Germany; the more radical began to reject the Western model of democratic capitalism as a whole. Just weeks before the Paris student revolt of May 1968, the hard-left Baader-Meinhof militants burned down two department stores in Frankfurt, choosing the city for their attack over Berlin due both to its symbolic power as the centre of capitalism in Germany and its practical location (fleeing from West Berlin was always somewhat difficult). Soon the students at the Goethe University were following those at the Sorbonne, occupying the university and renaming it Karl-Marx-Universität: their protest was Germany's first, its longest and its most radical.

After the students' specific demands for a greater say in running university affairs had been satisfied by state lawmakers in 1970—and their more general critique regarding the ignorance and bigotry of plastic-fantastic post-war German society had started to gain acceptance—general unrest died down, only to be replaced by terrorism as the Baader-Meinhof group mutated into the "Red Army Faction" (*Rote-Armee-Fraktion*), targeting high-powered industry and banking bosses as well as American forces. In 1972, and in 1976 again, they carried out bomb attacks on the US military headquarters in the former IG Farben building; in autumn 1977 there was a spate of kidnappings across the country, and the chairman of the Dresdner Bank board, Jürgen Ponto, was murdered in his villa just outside Frankfurt. Despite a successful government crackdown and the imprisonment, shooting or suicide of almost all of its members, the group limped on into the 1980s: in 1985 RAF terrorists planted a bomb on the Rhein-Main Air Base, an airfield directly to the south of Frankfurt airport used by the US Air Force. In 1989 the chairman of Deutsche Bank, Alfred Herrhausen, was killed in the last high-profile terrorist attack claimed by the group (see Chapter 11).

Meanwhile, a far less violent but immeasurably more effective offshoot of the 1968 mentality was making headway in the city: the German green movement. The oil crises of the 1970s and the end of the *Wirtschaftswunder* had done more than the student demonstrations to spread criticism of the post-war economic model into the mainstream: for the first time since the war, the German economy experienced recessions and unemployment grew. Meanwhile, the consequences of pollution were becoming clearer every day, and nowhere more than in Frankfurt, now at the centre of an urban conurbation of more than two million inhabitants, with a booming chemicals industry and one of Europe's largest airports in the middle of its extensive woodlands. In 1977 local elections put the conservative CDU in charge of the city for the first time, a sign of growing dissatisfaction with the status quo: the fifth post-war SPD mayor, Rudi Arndt, already unpopular due to his investor-friendly redevelopment plans for the area around the university campus, had suggested blowing up the derelict Alte Oper (see Chapter 3). Known thenceforth as "Dynamite Rudi", he lost in a landslide to the CDU. Yet the real revolution came with the 1981 election, in which six *Grünen im Römer*, a local forerunner of the national green party, were elected to the city assembly.

1981 was the year in which Germany became the first democratic country with an established green party, and Frankfurt was at the centre of the movement. Since the late 1960s plans to add a second runway at the airport had become the focus of a nationwide ecological debate: a suit brought by a residents' initiative against the plans, beginning in 1972, ran until 1978, when the expansion was finally given legal approval. By this stage, activists from across Germany had coalesced and, as the first trees were felled in 1981, rushed to occupy the site. Politically very similar to the Greenham Common Peace Camp (there were fears that the new runway would lead to increase in nuclear armaments stocked by the US Air Force), the protest became one of the largest citizens' movements in Europe to date: in November, a petition with 220,000 signatures against the plans was submitted to the Hesse state government after an eight-kilometre-long march had encircled the city centre. For over a week, demonstrations continued, blocking off much of Frankfurt, the airport and several surrounding towns. The petition was refused, the demonstrations broken up and the runway built. Yet the controversy surrounding the issue gave the Greens the momentum they needed.

In the city assembly, the first radical Greens drove their colleagues to distraction: everything from their sometimes questionable personal hygiene to their over-ambitious motions ("Let's make Frankfurt a nuclear-weapons-free city!") was completely unheard of—and Frankfurters could not get enough it, voting along with the rest of Hessen to put them into state government for the first time ever with the SPD in 1985: the first national coalition between the SPD and the Greens came thirteen years later in 1998 under Gerhard Schröder, and since the 1977 landslide towards the CDU had preceded the replacement of the SPD Chancellor Helmut Schmidt with the CDU Helmut Kohl by several years too, political pundits have been keeping a close eye both on the Frankfurt city assembly and the Hessen state parliament ever since as a sign of things to come.

Since 1990

As Germany celebrated Reunification in 1990, both Frankfurt's political classes and its population were less enthusiastic. Not only was the financial burden of integrating the former East Germany detrimental both to public and private finances—the state of Hessen had to contribute surpluses to the new states in the East, while wage earners began paying a tax supplement on their personal income—but the city's role as the *de facto* capital of the country was in question; all the more so once the parliamentary decision to move to Berlin had ruled out an American solution in which a sleepy governmental city houses the legislature while other cities function as cultural and economic magnets. Would the Bundesbank move to Berlin and start an avalanche, especially given the newly reunited city's abundance of cheap space?

These fears were unfounded: with the investments the banks had made in the second generation of skyscrapers during the 1980s boom years, there could be no question of relocating soon. Yet other elements of the city's economy had no such qualms: with the Cold War over, the US High Command moved out of the city in 1995, taking with it thousands of well-paid staff. Municipal debt, which had been creeping up during the 1980s, started to soar. Pessimism was rife: the German economy generally had been sluggish since the oil crises and every recession added percentage points to baseline unemployment that refused to disappear in the next upswing. While Frankfurt's banks had enjoyed the preceding decade's boom years, the lower and middle classes were, as elsewhere in Europe, beginning to feel the pinch. Social problems became increasingly visible: in the run-down Bahnhofsviertel, heroin junkies shot up on the streets as bankers with briefcases and brick-sized mobile phones walked on by; the gigantic underground transport system conceived in the 1960s and 1970s offered plenty of dark corners and protection from the elements for petty criminals.

Voters turned back to the SPD: governing with the Greens, the two left-wing mayors of the 1990s tackled the city's drugs problem with radical solutions: the city piloted modern Germany's first drop-in centres and legal dispensing of methadone, increasing police presence in public spaces to drive drug users into treatment; in Germany, it became known as the "Frankfurt model". At the same time, the necessity of repositioning the city became clear: with the Maastricht Treaty of 1992 and preparations for the European single currency afoot, Frankfurt started lobbying for the European Central Bank. At the same time, planning permission for new towers was given and the international profile of the city's trade fairs strengthened. The turbulent coalition shattered in 1995—the old-fashioned SPD politicians simply did not get along with the radical, yet politically flexible Greens—clearing the way for CDU Mayor Petra Roth, who would run the city for the coming 17 years.

Focussing on reducing the city's debt, Roth was helped by the arrival of the ECB and the two finance booms of the late 1990s and mid-2000s: cooperation tax, raised by her predecessors, filled the city coffers, while unemployment dropped. At the same time, her *laissez-faire* attitude to social issues and closeness to business paved the way for a transformation of the city. New towers went up, large-scale redevelopment projects such as the Westhafen development were given the rubber stamp, municipal housing was privatized. The issues thrown up by gentrification—the decreasing amount of genuinely public space, the unaffordability of central areas, the replacement of lived-in housing with investment properties—are nowhere more visible in Germany today than in Frankfurt.

Yet Roth was no ideologue austerity politician who sold off the city silver for the sake of it: Frankfurt today still retains a far greater number of pockets of social housing or municipal infrastructure near its centre than many comparable cities, partly due to the sheer extent of city building in the post-war years and partly due to an unspoken cross-party agreement in Frankfurt politics that the city must remain active in preserving spaces for the vulnerable. When set against the astronomical figures of its finance industry, the city's comparatively petite geographical scale makes its banking sector look wildly outsized and dictate that, if city hall does not have an active agenda, the entire city will be swallowed up by the banks: second only to London in Europe in banking, Frankfurt is less than one tenth the size of the British capital.

Hopes are high that Roth's successor, the Social Democrat Peter Feldmann, will be able to help Frankfurt keep the mix of bankers and benefits claimants, of financiers and students, that developed in the 1950s and 1960s and which is now under threat: plans have been announced to start building new social housing in the neighbouring problem-city of Offenbach, where land is cheaper. Municipal finances, although good compared to many other parts of Germany, are not what they were in the 1950s and the German state has put itself into a legislative straightjacket of no more debt after 2016. As a result, the city's hands are tied. New development projects in the city have the same interchangeably expensive look as in London, New York or Paris—because Frankfurt is subject to the same forces as they are. The rulers of today are the Masters of the Universe: "the markets" dictate to what extent countries and cities can invest—and in what—while market forces gain entry into ever more areas.

Yet the city of Frankfurt still sees itself as something of an exception, as a community that can and must take responsibility for itself: like other ancient German cities such as Hamburg, Bremen or Cologne, Frankfurt has over a millennium of history behind it, 800 years of which it spent ruled from elsewhere—but running itself. This may explain the city authorities' enthusiasm for reconstructing the Old Town on the site of its former Technical Offices: the city both owns the land and has the opportunity to create an architectural homage to its glorious past. To what degree the independence of city policy today is an illusion, and to what extent the city can shape its own destiny in the coming years, is the big question—not just for Frankfurt, but of our time.

5 | **The Written Word**
Literature, Publishing and Ideas

I t would be hard to overstate Frankfurt's role in the spread of the written word. Not only as a centre of the nascent printing industry in the fifteenth century, but later as an early hotbed of newspaper journalism and as the home to one of the world's most influential schools of academic thought, the city has been the site of revolutions in the way the written word is produced, distributed and received. Yet its importance as a subject of literature—while by no means negligible—somehow lags behind this pivotal intellectual role. Every Germanist can easily cite several "Berlin novels", from Fontane's *Poggenpuhls* to Döblin's *Alexanderplatz*, or name a wealth of settings immortalized by the language's greats: Munich as described in Mann's *Doktor Faustus* and Lübeck as the backdrop for his *Buddenbrooks*; the Prague glimpsed in Kafka's halls of mirrors; or the Danzig of Grass' eponymous trilogy. Yet Frankfurt remains something of a blind spot: even Goethe, the city's most prominent literary son and the German language's most famous author, no less, describes his hometown only as part of his autobiography *Dichtung und Wahrheit* (*Poetry and Truth*), not within his far more widely read fictional work.

Yet while the city may be lacking the kind of *opus magnus* whose existence its crucial role might seem to merit, Frankfurt is nonetheless a recurring setting in literature and an object of description in works of travel writing. Given its prominence as a centre of publishing and its history as a European crossroads, it would be highly unusual if this were otherwise, and this range of writing gives us a varied and lively view of the city from the sixteenth century onwards.

Descriptions of Frankfurt

One of the oldest surviving written descriptions of Frankfurt in any language is drawn from Fynes Moryson's *Itinerary*, considered by many scholars to be the first piece of travel literature in English.

Das Göthe Monument [Frankfurt] Le Monument de Göthe
am Main

C. Jügel.

An 1845 engraving of the Goethe Monument, now to be found on
Hauptwache near the bard's childhood home (Wikimedia Commons)

Moryson (1566-1630) left England in 1591 to spend several years travelling around Europe, noting information about sights, customs and business as he went. He first sailed to Stade, near Hamburg in northern Germany, reaching Frankfurt in 1592 after passing through Saxony, Bohemia, Bavaria and northern Switzerland; from there he travelled via Strasbourg and Heidelberg to what was then the flourishing Free Imperial City of Frankfurt.

Frankfurt is a free City of the Empire, famous for the Electors meeting there to choose the Emperour, and for two yeerely Faires, as also for the many Parliaments of the Empire held there, and it is called Franckfort upon the Mæne, to distinguish it from another City of the same name, built upon the Brooke Odera, and named thereof.

Moryson goes on to give a brief sketch of the local geography and to explain the two etymologies he finds plausible for the word "Frankfurt".

For the River Mæne running from the East to the West, divideth the great City from the lesse called the Saxons House, vulgarly Sachsen-hausse, and betweene them is a bridge of stone upon foure narrow Arches. Both the Cities are governed by the same Senate and Law, and have the same name, either of Francus re-building it, or of a Foord for passage of the Franckes or French.

The liveliest part of Moryson's description concerns the lay-out of the city. With a dash of period anti-Semitism, he mentions the Jewish ghetto, and the western Welschtor gate: in old Germanic languages, "Welsh" meant "strangers from the West" (in modern German "gobbledygook" or the Greek in the sense of "it's all Greek to me" is referred to as *Kauderwelsch*). Moryson also highlights the intriguing possibility of enjoying sanctuary in the Deutscherrenhaus, the old monastery on the site granted to the Order of the Teutonic Knights in the thirteenth century (see page 117).

The City is compassed strongly with a double wall, and upon the East side is the gate Heilegthore, where is the Jewes street, who are permitted to dwell in this famous Mart-towne, and sucke the blood of the Christians by extortion. There is another gate called Freydigthore: On the North side of the City is the gate Brickenport, and a large place for an Horse Faire. On the West side is the gate of the strangers, vulgarly Welsh-thore, so called because the French enter that way: it is very strong; and without the gate there is a very pleasant walk upon the banke of Mæne, among Vineyards and Meadowes, with sweet Groves. On the South side the Mæne runneth by, dividing (as I said) the new City from the old. In the new or lesse City called the Saxons-house, is a house of old belonging to the Teutonike order of Knights, which by old privildege is to this day a Sanctuary for banckrupts and manslaiers, so they be not wilful and malicious murtherers; but the enjoy this priviledge onely for foureteene daies, so as when the time is neere out, or upon any opportunity during the time, they use to steale out, and returning after an houre, begin a new to reckon againe the foureteene daies. A little before my coming thither, a certaine bankrupt of Colen entered the same for a debt of twenty thousand Guldens. On this side some ground without the wals belong to the City, but on the other sides it hath almost no Land without the wals. The City is of a round forme, seated in a large plaine, the streetes are narrow, and the houses built of timber and clay, the foundation of some being of stone.

He closes by documenting the price of a standard meal in an inn ("seven or eight batzen") and explaining that "at the times of the faires, Coaches are set dearer then any time els." For several decades, Moryson's work served as a reference for British travellers to the continent, due in no small part to the precise information he offers about money: with the proliferation of currencies in the Holy Roman Empire, his was a valuable, place-by-place record of prices, and several editions were complemented by tables of exchange rates. A few years after Moryson's visit, Frankfurt received another itinerant literary Englishman, Thomas Coryat (1577-1617), a *parvenu* court writer out on his travels around Europe as part of an attempt to improve his standing at home. He arrived in Frankfurt in autumn 1608 on the return leg of what became, based on his record of the trip, *Coryat's Crudities*, the route of the Grand Tour of the British nobility. Coryat's description of Frankfurt is not only longer, but livelier than Moryson's, going into far greater detail and giving us a more textured approach to the city as Coryat proffers lengthy descriptions mixed with his own feelings and opinions. He is soon very taken with the city skyline.

> The walles that do inviron the citie, and built with such admirable strength, being compacted all of hard stone, and beautified with a great company of towers, strong bulwarks, and faire gatehouses, that they yeeld a most singular grace to the city. Also the same walles are inclosed with deepe trenches and moates. The principall Church of the city, which was built by Pipin King of France . . . doth present a goodely shew a farre off.

While the interior of St. Bartholomew's Church disappoints him ("yet the inward matter of the Church is but ordinarie"), he is enraptured with the Messe, which is in full swing during his stay and where he meets the Earle of Essex, also abroad in Europe at the time.

> The riches I observed at this Mart were most infinite, especially in one place called Under Den Roemer, where the Goldsmithes kept their shoppes, which made the most glorious shew that ever I saw in my life (. . .) The wealth that I sawe here was incredible, so great that it was unpossible for a man to conveive in his his minde that hath not first seene it with his bodily eyes. The goodliest shew of ware that I sawe in all Franckford saving that of the Goldsmithes, was made by an Englishman one Thomas Sackfield a Dorsetshire man, once a servant of my father, who went out of England but in a meane estate, but after he had spent a few yeares at the Duke of Brunswicks Courte, hee so inriched himselfe of late, that his glittering shewe of ware in Franckford did farre excel all the Dutchmen, French, Italians, or whomsoever else.

Coryat also has trouble keeping his adjectives non-superlative when he visits Frankfurt's Buchgasse, where he sees the genesis of what is today the world-famous October Book Fair.

> For this street farre excelleth Paules Churchyard in London, Saint James streete in Paris, the Merceria in Venice and all whatsoever else that I sawe in my travels. In so much that it seemeth the very epitome of all the principall Libraries of Europe. Neither is that streete famous for selling books onely, and that of all manner of artes and disciplines whatsoever, but also for printing of them. For this city hath so flourished within these fewe yeares in the art of printing, that it is not inferior in that respect to any city in Christendome.

Unexpectedly perhaps, the only thing which Coryat seems to find underwhelming about Frankfurt is its commercial infrastructure. He is surprised to note that the city's merchants sell from the ground floors of their houses, "so that there is no common place either in the streetes or in any open yard or field". This, he observes, "maketh the Fayre seem but little, though indeed it be very great". The Exchange, too, set up on the Römer around twenty years before his visit, leaves him nonplussed: "nothing like to ours in London . . . For it is nothing but a part of the streete, under the open ayre."

In his journey upriver to Frankfurt, Coryat notices the "very fat soile" of the fertile Main valley, an attribute of the region that is noted a century and a half later by philosopher David Hume (1711-76), travelling along the Main and the Danube to Vienna in 1747.

> Betwixt Weis Baden & Frankfort we travel along the Banks of the Maine, & see one of the finest Plains in the World. I never saw such rich Soil, nor better cultivated; all in corn & sown Grass. For we have not met with any natural Grass in Germany. Frankfort is a very large Town, well built & of great Riches & Commerce. Around it, there are several little Country Houses of the Citizens the first of that kind we have seen in Germany: For every body except the Farmers, live here in Towns. And these dwell all in

Villages. Whether this be for Company, or Protection, or Devotion, I cannot tell: But it certainly has its Inconveniences. Princes have also Sears in the Country, & Monks have their Convents: But no private Gentleman ever dwells there.

By this period, with the Thirty Years' War having proven Frankfurt's defences essentially pointless, wealthy Frankfurt merchants had indeed started to build country houses outside the city walls. Moreover, with a few brief interjections, this part of Europe was at peace for much of the eighteenth century, and the protection offered by moats, ditches and walls seemed less necessary than ever. This time of growth and wealth is remembered by the city's literary pride and joy, Johann Wolfgang von Goethe (1749-1832) in his biography, *Dichtung und Wahrheit*, written in his final years about his youth and covering the period between 1749 and 1775.

Nowhere, however, does one enjoy such a pleasant time of peace in as much comfort as in cities which live according to their own laws, which are large enough to be composed of a fine number of citizens, and which are well situated so as to be enriched by trade and change.

His memoir from this golden era forms the most valuable written record of life in Frankfurt in these years, and perhaps the most enjoyable description of the city ever produced. With Goethe, we get to know the exquisite townhouse in which he spends his early years with his parents and sister Cornelia, receiving lessons from his father, a private scholar, and inspiration from an unexpected live-in guest in the form of French General Thoranc, who requisitions rooms in the house in 1759 when the French occupy Frankfurt during the Seven Years' War. We then accompany a teenage Goethe into Frankfurt's underworld, when he gets sucked into the shady doings of a group of friends and narrowly avoids disgrace, leaving the city for Leipzig to start a degree. Following a bout of unexplained internal bleeding, he returns to Frankfurt to convalesce, before continuing his studies in Strasbourg. Then, as a peripatetic lawyer and poet in several parts of southwest Germany, he frequently returns to his home city, where he writes his first play (*Götz von Berlichingen*, which starts the *Sturm und Drang* movement), experiences a turbulent engagement, and eventually leaves, following his old art tutor and good friend, Georg Melchior Kraus (1737-1806, see page 145) to Weimar.

With Goethe we experience everyday life in the city, from details such as the nocturnal obligation for those outside to carry lights befitting their status to extraordinary events such as the coronations of the Holy Roman Emperors. We learn about specific events in the city, too, such as General Thoranc's decree that there should be street lighting to replace the abovementioned lanterns, or how Goethe's grandfather, Johann Wolfgang Textor (1693-1771), in his capacity as city sheriff, ordered the reform of midwives' training after his grandson's birth had almost ended in disaster. We also learn something of the oppressive bourgeois atmosphere that drove young Goethe to settle elsewhere in Germany, of the inhabitants' all-consuming pursuit of money and unbudging cultural conservatism, of the sleepy and outmoded nature of the city in the twilight of the Holy Roman Empire. The coronation of Joseph II (1741-90, see page 87) as Holy Roman Emperor in 1764, for example, sharpens Goethe's awareness of the anachronisms of Frankfurt life.

> The young king, however, dragged himself along in this monstrous piece of attire with the relics from Charlemagne in such a way that he looked as if he were wearing a costume and, looking at his father from time to time, he could barely suppress a smile.

Goethe's life in Frankfurt before his reign as the master of German letters on the throne of Weimar Classicism is also a rich source of biographical detail, combed over by literary historians looking for the experiences that marked him and helped shape his writing. The most obvious influence—and the most exciting case—is that of Susanna Margaretha Brandt (1746-72), nicknamed "Magarethchen" and the blueprint for Gretchen in Goethe's *Faust*. Growing up an orphan, Brandt worked as a housemaid in the Frankfurt inn Zum Einhorn ("To the Unicorn"), where she was seduced (or possibly drugged) by a wandering goldsmith's apprentice and fell pregnant.

She hid her fate from the landlady, out of desperation killing her new-born child straight after its birth in the cellar of the inn: after an unsuccessful bid to flee to Mainz, she was tried and sentenced to death for murder. Goethe became mildly obsessed with her tragic fate, having minutes from the trial made and brought to him, and went on to weave her almost unchanged into *Faust*.

While Goethe's works were almost as instrumental as Martin Luther's translation of the bible in defining modern High German, another Frankfurt literary figure, Friedrich Stoltze (1816-91), is credited with being one of the first writers to document Hessian dialect and the specifically Frankfurt argot. In contrast to Goethe, who turned his back on the city once he had left, Stoltze was a patriotic Frankfurter who kept coming back. This is best illustrated by his best-known verse, *Frankfurt*:

> *Es is kaa Stadt uff der weite Welt,*
> *die so meer wie mei Frankfort gefällt,*
> *un es will meer net in mein Kopp enei:*
> *wie kann nor e Mensch net von Frankfort sei!*
>
> There is no city in the whole wide world
> that I like more than my Frankfurt,
> and one thing I cannot get into my head:
> how can anyone not come from Frankfurt?

The poem, which can be read painted on a building on the corner of Wolfgangstraße and Bremerplatz, close to Stoltze's last abode on Grüneburgweg, loses everything in translation, except perhaps its ironic undertone. For all Stoltze's love for the city and its culture, he was a man of the world, having been tutored by Goethe's cousin, Friedrich Karl Ludwig Textor (1775-1851, author of the first play in Frankfurt dialect), studied in Lyon and lived in Swiss exile when his satirical writing was banned by Prussian authorities in 1866; his poem is both a paean to Frankfurt and a joke at the expense of its more parochial inhabitants.

One British visitor to Frankfurt who spent several months there in the early 1800s, Henry Crabb Robinson (1775-1867), clearly found the city deeply provincial, sharing his dislike of it with Goethe, whom he met during his nine years of study and work as a newspaper correspondent in Germany: "Here are no literary Institutions—No public Libraries but one belonging to the City and which is more a matter of form and a collection of ancient books than a *useful* and *used* Library," he wrote back to England in 1800, and "there are no *Gentlemen* properly speaking—Indeed the remark might be extended to almost through Germany." He was unimpressed with the architecture and the economy of the city, too, contrasting the descriptions of it in newspapers and writing with his view:

The Gazatteers, too, call it an ancient, rich, free, commercial, imperial Stadt or Town, each of which phrases is by no means insignificant & forms an important Circumstance in the History of the place and they luckily affoard me a Number of Heads or Divisions . . . Imprimis, then it is ancient: That is the Streets are narrow & wretchedly paved the Houses lofty, & irregularly built, the Churches mean & the whole without either dignity or beauty excepting one broad place which is called Zeil or straight line, though it is unluckily rather crooked 2nd & 4th it is rich & commercial— And in this character it holds a distinguished Rank in the Cities of the Empire. From its situation so near the Confluence of the Rhine and Maine and the singularly good Roads which are kept up between it and the great Cities higher in the Empire it has become the great Mart of Commerce with france—and on each Side with Holland—and Switzerland even down to Italy—That even the length of Land carriage is not a sufficient Impediement to this Trade (...) As the balance of Trade is altogether against Germany— its exports being very inconsiderable—while it imports the Luxuries of politer france more industrious Holland & more enlightened England, the Patriots affect to consider the Town as carrying on an harmful and pernicious Trade—I leave to Economist to determine what the Effect of this is upon the Empire—It does not make the Town more agreeable to me—It takes away all the distinctness & pleasing peculiarities of a national character & gives it only the mean vices of wealth.

Fifty years later, however, the "narrow & wretchedly paved" streets would make an entirely more poetic impression on another English Germanist of note, finding their way into one of her most important works.

Frankfurt as a Literary Setting

In a letter to Charles Bray of August 1854, written from Weimar, one Mary Ann Evans comments perfunctorily on her visit to the city: "We went up the Rhine from Cologne to Mainz, Frankfurt being the main attraction to us for Goethe's sake." There is little further trace of the city in her private correspondence, yet under her pen-name George Eliot (1819-1880), she would go on in 1876 to include the city at a key juncture in one of her most important novels, *Daniel Deronda*. The hero, on a quest to understand Judaism and the Jewish people, stops off in Frankfurt on his way to the fictional German spa town of Leubronn:

> It was on this journey that he first entered a Jewish synagogue—at Frankfort—where his party rested on a Friday. In exploring the Juden-gasse, which he had seen long before, he remembered well enough its picturesque old houses; what his eyes chiefly dwelt on now were the human types there, and his thought, busily connecting them with the past phases of their race, stirred that fibre of historic sympathy which had helped to determine in him certain traits worth mentioning for those who are interested in his future.

At this point in the novel the eponymous protagonist Deronda begins to actively seek contact with Jewish people and to acquire literature about the faith, and the Judengasse functions as a kind of opening to the rabbit hole, a Jewish environment which, unlike that in London, he does not automatically avoid as befits his standing as a gentleman. After he has been bewitched by this romanticized ghetto, however, he will start frequenting the Jewish quarters of Victorian London:

> I have said that under his calm exterior he had a fervour which
> made him easily feel the presence of poetry in everyday events;
> and the forms of the Juden-gasse, rousing the sense of union with
> what is remote, set him musing on two elements of our historic life
> which that sense raises into the same region of poetry;—the faint
> beginnings of faiths and institutions, and their obscure lingering
> decay . . .

Nevertheless, Eliot's narrator is not without a sense of humour
and an eye for the prejudices of her time: the dreamy Deronda is
swindled by a smooth operator when he walks into a bookshop in
the Judengasse asking for directions to the orthodox synagogue,
walking out with a supposedly rare book he did not even intend to
buy:

> He was affectionately directed by a precocious Jewish youth, who
> entered cordially into his wanting not the fine new building of
> the Reformed but the old Rabbinical school of the orthodox; and
> then cheated him like a pure Teuton, only with more amenity, in
> his charge for a book quite out of request as one 'nicht so leicht zu
> bekommen'.

Another young hero who finds himself in the less salubrious
quarters of Frankfurt—albeit as the swindler rather than the unwitting victim—is Felix Krull, the hero of the unfinished final work of
Thomas Mann (1875-1955), *Confessions of Felix Krull* (in German
literally "Confessions of a Conman", *Bekenntnisse des Hochstaplers
Felix Krull*). Arriving in early 1900s Frankfurt on his way to begin
work in a Paris hotel, the wily young protagonist is deeply embar-
rassed by his family's poverty in a place of such wealth:

> I shall swiftly pass over the first, confusing days following our
> arrival in Frankfurt, as I am loath to remember the sorry role we
> were condemned to play in this trading city of such wealth and
> such finery, and would have cause to worry that too comprehensive

a description of our circumstances at that time might put the reader into an infelicitous state of mind. I shall remain silent about the dirty hostel, about the filthy quarters which had no claim to the name "hotel" to which they pretended . . . I shall remain silent, too, regarding our lengthy wanderings through this large, cold-hearted city so hostile to poverty, looking for an affordable abode.

The plan is for Krull's mother to open up a boarding house while Felix himself learns the trade in a fine Paris hotel: in this detail and many others in the book, Mann draws parallels to Goethe's *Dichtung und Wahrheit*, as Goethe's family fortune came from the Frankfurt inn his grandparents had run. *Felix Krull* was intended as a comedic parody of Goethe's autobiography, running on the supposition that jack-of-all-trades Goethe (poet, dramatist, statesman, scientist) had been something of a chancer himself, adopting many roles simply by stating that he was fit to carry them out, and then growing into them *post facto*.

Having tricked his way out of being conscripted for military service, the young Krull wanders again and again through the nocturnal city, waiting for his departure to Paris in the coming weeks, describing the richly attired and bejewelled wives of the city's bankers and industrialists—and a short, passionate liaison—as he satirizes polite society in the city. Yet for satire of Frankfurt's wealthy, there really is no writer better qualified than Siegfried Kracauer (1889-1966), the hero of whose first novel *Ginster* (1922) also tries to trick his way out of military service. Set during the First World War, the novel follows the fortunes of this sceptical young architect as he is repeatedly drafted by the army and manages to escape a tour of duty at the front, staying in Frankfurt and observing the lies and hypocrisy of the city's wealthy elite. Based on Kracauer's own experience working in the bureau of architect Max Seckbach (a renowned designer of synagogues), *Ginster* is, along with Kracauer's second novel *Georg* (published posthumously and parodying Weimar society in the city) perhaps as close as one can come to "a Frankfurt novel".

Anyone looking to find a more modern literary perspective on the city, however, will find that all roads lead to Jakob Arjouni (1964-2013), something of the Henning Mankell of Frankfurt in that he is the creator of a literary character who is famous in his own right among lovers of crime fiction: Kemal Kayankaya, a middle-aged, chronically directionless, low-achieving private detective of Turkish descent who was adopted by German parents and works his gritty Bahnhofsviertel beat in a bumbling but ultimately successful fashion. Set in the 1980s, 1990s and early 2000s, the five Kayankaya novels hang Germany's—and above all Frankfurt's—dirty linen out to dry. Arjouni's detective novels describe how ethnic tensions mount in the rundown area near the station as each new wave of immigrant criminals starts a war with the preceding group, while the police, under-informed and understaffed, leave them to their own devices. They also take us on excursions out to the white working-class suburbs full of neo-Nazi skinheads and biker gangs, or to the leafy stockbroker belt villages with their meticulously trimmed shrubbery and patronizing bankers' wives. In his final years, Frankfurt native Arjouni also produced a dystopian novel, *Chez Max*, set in a totalitarian society in Paris in the 2060s erected to counter terrorist attacks, and two critically acclaimed comedy romps.

Frankfurt and the Press

Champions of Arjouni's writing were to be found on the culture desks of Frankfurt's two most important newspapers, *Frankfurter Allgemeine Zeitung* and *Frankfurter Rundschau*; and indeed, Frankfurt has never been short of its own distinctive voice in the German-speaking media. Frankfurt's proximity to Mainz, the birthplace of printing, and its annual trade fairs made it a logical location for the production and dissemination of the printed page to develop, and by the mid-1600s the city was a key cultural site in the pre-Enlightenment world of European letters (see Thomas Coryate's description above).

The Enlightenment, however, brought a dip in Frankfurt's publishing fortunes. As the ideas being printed became more radical, the city's censorship became more conservative: in the 1700s Frankfurt city authorities saw themselves as the guardians of the old order of the moribund Holy Roman Empire and took their duties of Imperial (i.e. Catholic) censorship very seriously. The autumn book fair lost ground against that of Leipzig, which was under the considerably laxer rule of the Enlightened, Protestant Saxon monarchs and close to the new cultural hub of Weimar.

Yet at the same time, Frankfurt developed a broad and lively printed press for the very simple reason that until 1784 journals and newspapers were not subject to the censorship regime applied to books. Moreover, due to its commercial importance, the city was home to an educated, international readership which required information about goings-on in the wider world. The first newspaper appeared in 1722 under the title *Wöchentliche Frankfurter Frag- und Anzeigungs-Nachrichten*, or "weekly Frankfurt question and announcement news", later changing its name to the *Frankfurter Intelligenzblatt*, or "Frankfurt Intelligence Sheet". A series of such proto-newspapers followed, many with a clear concentration on trade and commerce: sheets such as *Handlungs-Avis-Comptoir-Zeitung*, or "Trade, Statement, and Bursary Paper" soon abounded, and were followed in the course of the century by increasingly political publications. The official city gazette, published since the 1600s by the principal post office, *Oberpostamtszeitung*, led the way, slowly spinning away from the authorities and publishing an increasing number of opinion pieces as it became more and more independent.

With its strong connections to nearby France and the pre-eminence of the French language in Enlightenment Europe, Frankfurt also had a vibrant French press, too, counting publications such as the *Courier Curieux*, *Mercure curieux*, and the very well read *Quintessence de Toutes les Gazettes*, a sort of early stringing service which collated news stories from a range of newspapers in several languages and repackaged them for a Frankfurt public. The most successful of the Frankfurt French titles was *L'Avant-Coureur*, which was read as far afield as London and Moscow; the German weekly *Frankfurter Staats-Ristretto*, famed not only for its political but for its literary and artistic reporting, even had subscribers in Scandinavia and America. There was no other German-speaking city with this spread of journalism at the time, and Frankfurt can therefore lay claim to the creation of lasting German press institutions such as the *Feuilleton*, a sort of cultural-philosophical desk which goes beyond the remit of the review pages of standard English-language quality papers and is a hallmark of the big-name German newspapers to this day.

Thus Frankfurt began the tradition of breadth and quality to which the city's press would compare itself in the centuries to come, a tradition which often appeared on the brink of being eradicated in periods of radical censorship and economic catastrophe, but which has always been remembered and resuscitated at key points in Germany's history. Under the Enlightened absolutism of Prince Karl von Dalberg during the Napoleonic Wars, for example, only one heavily censored newspaper was permitted, and one of the first developments following the restoration of Frankfurt's status as a free city in 1815 was the rebirth of many suspended publications: the first half of the nineteenth century was the golden age of papers such as the *Frankfurter Journal*, as well as the surviving *Oberpostamtszeitung* and the *Ristretto*. This latter became ever more radical under the stewardship of Ludwig Börne (1786-1837) in 1819, who then founded his own newspaper *Die Wage* in an attempt to establish a genuinely critical voice in the city. A son of the Frankfurt ghetto and a firebrand for the cause of democracy and civil rights whose refusal to temper his ardour or mince his words brought him into conflict with the city censorship office, Börne was despised then and is remembered today for pithy morsels such as: "A river of blood flows down the past eighteen centuries, its banks settled by Christendom." Harried by authoritarian forces in Frankfurt and Germany generally, Börne eventually settled in Paris, welcoming the 1830 revolution there and travelling to meet German democrats at the Hambacher Fest of 1832, considered as the first meeting of a movement for democracy in Germany. Despite having left the city, disgusted by its "philistinism, of which I am more afraid than of cholera", he retained high hopes for the future: "Frankfurt's destiny is to become the capital of the German Empire and the seat of its national parliament" (both from his

Above The iconic Frankfurt skyline shot from the Main river at Ostend, with Flößerbrücke in the foreground (Mylius/Wikimedia Commons)

Below The fountain on the Römerberg marketplace looking east to the picture-postcard row of reconstructed medieval houses (dontworry/Wikimedia Commons)

Above left The historic Salzhaus on the Römerberg as it was in the late nineteenth century (Mylius/Wikimedia Commons)

Above right The controversial 1950s reconstruction of the Salzhaus, mixing original stonework and modern outlines (Mylius/Wikimedia Commons)

Below The Kaiserdom — or simply Dom — where Holy Roman Emperors were crowned (Mylius/Wikimedia Commons)

Above Rebuilt as a matter of priority for the centenary of German parliamentary democracy in 1948, the Paulskirche's oval hall lacks its original domed roof to this day (Andreas Praefcke/Wikimedia Commons)

Below St. Leonhardskirche on the banks of the Main, Frankfurt's main Catholic church and the city's oldest fully intact structure (Mylius/Wikimedia Commons)

Above The Saalhof complex, now housing the Historisches Museum, consisting of the medieval Rententurm (left) and the baroque Bernusbau and Burnitzbau (right). The pitched roof behind the Burnitz building is what remains of the thirteenth-century Hohenstaufen chapel and is Frankfurt's oldest surviving building (Mylius/Wikimedia Commons)

Below The Alte Oper, completed in 1880, rebuilt a century later following citizens' protests against demolition (Felix König/Wikimedia Commons)

Above Topping the European skyscraper charts from completion in 1991 to 1997 (when it was superseded by the city-centre Commerzbank tower, the Messe tower remains Frankfurt and Germany's second-tallest building. Below it, the grand Messe Hall of 1909 sits, squat yet elegant (LSDSL/Wikimedia Commons)

Above The "Guillotine" Torhaus at the Messe
(Sebastian Kasten/Wikimedia Commons)

Right Frankfurt's most exotic tower, the Japan Center
(Jerry Fischer/Wikimedia Commons)

Below Besides the Messe, that other great Frankfurt institution, the Stock Exchange, with its trademark bull & bear statue representing the ups and downs of the market
(Vivimeri/Wikimedia Commons)

Above Deutsche Bank, or the "Two Towers", in all its inscrutable, tinted-glass glory (Epizentrum/Wikimedia Commons)

Below left The superbly gothic Eschenheimer Turm has survived nearly 600 years of war, demolition, traffic planning, and gentrification (Epizentrum/Wikimedia Commons)

Below right The Kuhhirtenturm has also made it through the centuries, today housing an appartment and forming part of the city's youth hostel in Sachsenhausen (Frank Behnsen/Wikimedia Commons)

Above The main entrance to what is not only one of Frankfurt's most important structures, but also one of its finest: the late nineteenth-century Main Station or Hauptbahnhof   (russavia/Wikimedia Commons)

Below Another piece of beloved transport infrastructure from the second half of the 1800s: Eisener Steg   (Mylius/Wikimedia Commons)

Above The Frankfurt National Assembly, Germany's first democratically elected parliament, meets in the Paulskirche in 1848
(Historisches Museum Frankfurt/Wikimedia Commons)

Below After the failure of the Parliament in autumn that year, chaos breaks out and Frankfurt is stormed by Prussian and Hessian troops, who restore order—and the old order   (*Frankfurt-Archiv*/Wikimedia Commons)

Above The northern bank of the Main River with Saalhof and Dom viewed from Sachsenhausen around 1900   (Library of Congress, Washington DC)

Below Kaiserstraße around the turn of the century, back when this thoroughfare through the Main Station was home to wealthy burghers rather than sleezy strip-joints   (Library of Congress, Washington DC)

10

Above The chaos of the hyperinflation in the 1920s finds its most concisely eloquent illustration in this *Notgeld* (emergency money) voucher for ten billion marks. When the crisis was at its most acute, nine such vouchers would have been required to purchase a tram ticket   (www.volksbank-offenburg)

Below right The recovery was swift. By 1925, the twenties were roaring and Frankfurt was displaying its progressive, proletarian credentials by hosting the International Workers' Olympics   (Wikimedia Commons)

Below left This memorial to the burning of books on the Römerberg is encircled by the prophetic words of Heinrich Heine: "That was but a prelude; wherever books are burned, in the end people will be burned too"   (ArtCan/Wikimedia Commons)

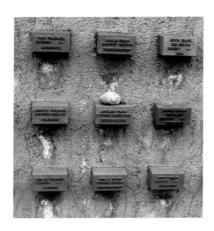

Above An 1885 view of the Hauptsynagoge, or Main Synagogue, on Börneplatz, built during the late nineteenth-century flourish in German-Jewish culture and burned to ruins in the pogrom of November 1938
(Wikimedia Commons)

Left Between 1996 and 2010, the walls of the Jewish cemetary near Börneplatz were studded with almost 12,000 stones bearing the names of the Frankfurt Jews murdered in the Holocaust. One stone stands for Anne Frank, who was born in the city
(Flibbertigibbet/Wikimedia Commons)

Above The IG Farben building, also known by the name of its architect Poelzig, was one of the places in which the Holocaust was devised. Today, it houses Frankfurt's Goethe University and a documentation centre for the genocide and war crimes of the 1940s (Daderot/Wikimedia Commons)

Below A view of Frankfurt's skyline in the mid-2000s. The Henniger-Turm in the foreground, once home to a brewer's grain silo and a rotating restaurant, was demolished in 2013 to make way for a new 400-foot residential tower (rupp.de/Wikimedia Commons)

Above left Goethe's Frankfurt home, where he was born in 1749
(Mylius/Wikimedia Commons)

Above right The interior of a typical Frankfurt patron of the arts, Johann Noë Gogel,
as painted in 1776 by Christian Stöcklin (Wikimedia Commons)

Below Frankfurt riverfront around 1760 as painted by Schütz   (Historisches Museum
Frankfurt/Wikimedia Commons)

Bottom Another riverfront view in 1850 by Carl Morgenstern
(Städel Frankfurt/Wikimedia Commons)

Below right Hans Christoffer von Königsmarck by Matthäus Merian the Younger
(Google Art Project/Wikimedia Commons)

14

Above A traditional Trinkhalle situated next to the Galluswarte tower
(Metroskop/Wikimedia Commons)

Below The Ebbelwei-Express streetcars ready for another Sunday ferrying drinkers
through Frankfurt (Labanex/Wikimedia Commons)

Left The Ernst May House in a suburban street of his prototypic Römerstadt estate features an almost entirely original Frankfurt kitchen and offers a range of information about this visionary urban planner and architect (Jürgen Heegmann/ Wikimedia Commons)

Below A late nineteenth-century view of Mainz and the Rhine (Library of Congress, Washington DC)

Bottom The Stadtschloss palace in the former spa town of Wiesbaden today houses the Hessian state parliament (Wolfgang Pehlemann/Wikimedia Commons)

letters to Jeanette). Today, his commitment to the causes of democracy and press freedom has been memorialized in the city of his birth: since 1993 the Ludwig Börne Prize has been awarded annually in the symbolic Paulskirche to journalists and publicists who produce thought-provoking critical essays and reportage.

Another Frankfurt writer whose relationship to the city censorship authorities was somewhat strained was poet Friedrich Stoltze (see above), who founded the *Frankfurter Laterne* satirical weekly in 1860. With its lampooning of authoritarian figures (most notably Bismarck), the publication was frequently closed by police decree, going through eight name changes until the tireless Stoltze's death in 1891. Its criticism of Prussian authoritarianism made it popular in the whole of Germany during the years of forced unification, but also made it a target of state repression, especially following the Prussian annexation of Frankfurt in 1866, when Stoltze briefly fled to Switzerland.

Censorship became far less rigorous as the century came to a close, however: *ante bellum* Prussian society remained authoritarian but became ever more tolerant of critical voices, which goes some way towards explaining how Stoltze managed to keep publishing the *Laterne*, albeit under different names after each closure. Another publication of crucial importance, both in Frankfurt and in the wider German-speaking world, which continually stretched the limits of what it was permitted to print was the *Frankfurter Zeitung*, founded in 1856 as the *Frankfurter Geschäftsbericht* by two bankers Heinrich Bernhard Rosenthal (1829-76) and Leopold Sonnemann (1831-1909). From its inception, the newspaper was politically and economically liberal, advocating the free movement of capital along with democratic freedoms. The Prussian police banned it immediately following annexation (the fact that Stoltze openly supported it was probably grounds enough) and it was only permitted to return after Sonnemann had demonstrated his determination and resources by fleeing to Stuttgart and producing the paper from there for three months.

During the Wilhelmine era, the paper became the centre of a nexus of political liberals and reformers, a role reflected in its very structures as it replaced an omnipresent editor-in-chief with a *primer-inter-pares* system of editorial conferences (a step unthinkable in most German papers at the time). The paper also pioneered the right of journalists to protect their sources, with several of its reporters spending time behind bars for refusing to pass on the details of those from whom they got their often explosive information. The paper's deeply honourable record continued through the First World War, it being one of the only publications in Germany both to condemn mobilization in 1914 and advocate the Peace of Versailles in 1919. During the Weimar years it continued to promote its liberal and democratic agenda in the increasingly fraught atmosphere of post-1929 Germany.

During these decades the paper took the *Feuilleton* format to new heights, establishing with its critical essays from Weimar intellectuals the standards to which newspapers aspire. Many of its editors and writers were part of the Jewish intelligentsia so detested by the Nazis, and were forced to leave in 1933 following the seizure of power: Siegfried Kracauer and his close friend and contributor Walter Benjamin (1892-1940) lost their positions and fled the city. On 17 June 1934 the remaining staff of the paper printed the transcript of the Marburger Speech delivered by Vice Chancellor von Papen, the last made by a politician in high office against the Nazi regime: the print run for that day was confiscated. The paper changed gears, writing in a more subversive way against the increasing madness of Hitler's dictatorship and limping on under intense scrutiny from censors and Josef Goebbels until it was finally banned on 31 August 1943.

In view of the newspaper's importance in the Weimar Republic and its tenacious fight to disseminate critical views during the Nazi years, in 1945 it seemed of the utmost importance to continue the paper. The company set up by Rosenthal and Sonneborn, Frankfurter Societäts-Druckerei, had survived the war and published *Die Gegenwart* (The Present), a paper established by several of the *Frankfurter Zeitung* veterans as soon as a licence could be procured from the Allies. Others, however, had grouped around the *Allgemeine Zeitung*, founded in Mainz in the tradition of an Enlightenment newspaper, and in 1949 the two were combined after the Allies lifted publishing restrictions, paving the way for a free press in the newly founded Federal Republic. The new *Frankfurter Allgemeine Zeitung* became the legal successor of the *Frankfurter Zeitung*, using the Societäts-Druckerei machines to print (and becoming the property of its charitable foundation Fazit in 1989).

Although it owns the rights to the name *Frankfurter Zeitung* and has continued its tradition of publishing the shamelessly intellectual *Feuilleton* today's *Frankfurter Allgemeine Zeitung*, referred to colloquially as FAZ, is politically only partially its heir. FAZ has consistently drifted towards the right-wing end of the political spectrum on social, law-and-order and cultural questions, and the economic liberalism it inherited from the old paper has in recent years become neo-liberalism. The German right-wing populist party Alternative für Deutschland (AfD), founded in the wake of the Euro crisis, is said to have been born of a meeting of minds among Eurosceptic commentators in the paper's internet forum. Today's FAZ competes on a national level with the more left-wing *Süddeutsche Zeitung* in Munich and *Die Welt* of Berlin (produced by *BILD*-owners Axel Springer and even further to the right) as Germany's daily paper of reference.

The heir to the *Frankfurter Zeitung* in political (although by no means in *Feuilleton* terms) is the *Frankfurter Rundschau*, permitted early by the American occupiers in 1946 and quickly attracting leading left-leaning journalists from across Germany. From the 1950s to the 1990s, the *Rundschau* was a leading voice in the Federal political debate, contributing to the liberalization of West German society in the wake of the 1968 student protests; one of its finest hours was research by its star reporter Thomas Gnielka (1928-65), a charismatic chain-smoking Berliner who had been forcibly conscripted in a battalion of child-soldiers used by the SS to man flak batteries around Auschwitz. His knowledge of the concentration camp system—and determination to prevent it slipping into historical oblivion—enabled him to recognize documents smuggled out by an Auschwitz survivor for what they were and pass them onto state prosecutor Fritz Bauer, who led the controversial Auschwitz trials of the 1960s (see Chapter 11). Throughout the early 2000s the *Frankfurter Rundschau* suffered more than many from the changes to the newspaper industry, going insolvent in 2012 and being saved at the last minute by Frankfurter Societät and by its conservative rival, FAZ. Its staff has been hollowed out and most of the content is either hurriedly rewritten agency copy or bought-in articles from its former competitor: an ignominious end for one of the most important papers in modern German history.

Frankfurt and the Book

The young Federal Republic offered not only the free press a second chance, but also encouraged publishing generally. Following its descent into irrelevance during the Enlightenment, the Frankfurt Book Fair had never recovered its position as Europe's leading publishing event from its rival Leipzig; yet in 1949, with a free and democratic German state proclaimed in the Western occupation zones while the future German Democratic Republic in the east sank ever further into Stalinist dictatorship, the time was ripe for Frankfurt to reclaim its crown. Some 205 exhibitors from around Germany thronged into the rebuilt Paulskirche for a week in September 1949; this first post-war Frankfurter Buchmesse/Frankfurt Book Fair was a resounding success, and within less than a decade it had become the largest international publishing exhibition in terms of the number of publishers and visitors, a title it has retained to this day. While the fair itself soon moved out of the crowded Paulskirche and has taken place at the expanding Messe premises since, every year since 1950 the former church has welcomed dignitaries for the Peace Prize of the German Book Trade during the fair; past laureates have come from all over the world, and since the late 1980s a guest country has been nominated annually as the focus of interest for the festival, underlining its global ambitions and worldwide relevance.

With Berlin's future uncertain in the immediate post-war period and Frankfurt's literary resurgence, the number of publishing houses in the city rose rapidly. Big names such as Fischer and Suhrkamp set up in Frankfurt, and it was in this city of such historic meaning for the book that a free Germany was once again given access to works from across the world and the world in turn was supplied with the best of German thought and writing. Fischer made its name in the 1950s with Tennessee Williams, Arthur Miller and Virginia Woolf in translation, as well as publishing Sigmund Freud's works in non-academic editions for a general readership. The German-language edition of *Doctor Zhivago*, published in 1958, remains one Fischer's biggest earners to this day, along with the perennial editions of Kafka. Its current authors include Florian Illies, who landed an international success in 2013 with his examination of the world as viewed from 1913. The Suhrkamp house, meanwhile, which grew out of Fischer after the war following disagreements over the management during the Nazi years, is now back in Berlin and weakened by an ongoing insolvency case; during its time in Frankfurt, however, Suhrkamp was one of the key literary and political publishers in Europe; with its *Reihe Theorie* ("Theory Series") from 1966, it played a key role in disseminating the thinking of the city's academic pioneers, the Frankfurt School.

The Frankfurt School

For all its international importance and its revolutionary effect on a range of academic disciplines, the history of the Frankfurt School began in a manner utterly typical of the city when wealthy father-son duo Hermann (1868-1927) and Felix Weil (1898-1975) donated a large sum of money to the University. Hermann Weil had made millions trading in grain—around 1910, his was considered the world's leading business in the agricultural sector—and inhabited a magnificent villa in Frankfurt with his son, a scholar of radical left-wing political convictions, from which he became increasingly active as a benefactor. Concerned by the rise of authoritarianism and anti-Semitism in the Weimar Republic (the assassination of foreign minister Rathenau, Jewish like the Weils, was the trigger), they financed the *Frankfurter Institut für Sozialforschung*, or Frankfurt Institute for Social Research. While the father wrote cheques, the son, working with dissident Marxists such as Friedrich Pollock (1894-1970) and the Hungarian Georg Lukács (1885-1971), gave the new institution its direction as a centre for neo-Marxist thought. With the overall political climate in Frankfurt favourable (these were the years of social housing and the democratization of municipal culture under Mayor Landmann), the institute rapidly established itself, cooperating with the Marx-Engels Institute in Moscow and housing an archive of the history of socialism and workers' rights.

Its first director Carl Grünberg (1861-1940) suffered a stroke in 1928 and was succeeded by Max Horkheimer (1895-1973); Horkheimer favoured a less narrowly-Marxist, more interdisciplinary approach to social research that became the hallmark of the Frankfurt School as we know it today and essentially founded both social sciences as a field of academic study and critical theory as a tool with which to work it. Horkheimer began to edit the *Zeitschrift für Sozialforschung* with contributions from staff members such as Leo Löwenthal (1900-93) and Erich Fromm (1900-80) as well as Frankfurt-based academics and authors including Theodor W. Adorno (1903-69) and Walter Benjamin; others such as Herbert Marcuse (1898-1979) contributed from other universities.

The journal was begun in 1932, but only one year later the institute had been closed and half of its personnel thrown out of the university by the new Nazi government. The climate was deeply hostile to what was branded "Bolshevik-Jewish academia", and the entire social environment in which the institute and journal had flourished disintegrated as authors such as Siegfried Kracauer and Walter Benjamin fled for France. Horkheimer and Pollock, however, aware of the growing totalitarian climate around them (this was, after all, the main subject of study of the institute in the early 1930s), had prepared for the eventuality and reopened the institute in Geneva as the Société Internationale de Recherches Sociales. From there Horkheimer and Pollock moved again to Colombia University in New York in 1935 after Swiss legislation regarding foreign asylum seekers proved too great an obstacle in running the institute as planned.

It was in this period of exile that the journal, now appearing in English as *Studies in Philosophy and Social Science*, began to attract a wide academic readership in the English-speaking universities. With most of the members and contributors now in the United States (Adorno came in 1938 after an interlude at Merton College, Oxford; Marcuse—originally at Freiburg with Heidegger—had joined him in Geneva), the institute, although plagued by financial problems, began to produce the work for which it is still renowned today. Pollock defined concepts such as totalitarian state capitalism, divorcing dictatorships from the inferior economic systems thus far considered inherent to them, while Horkheimer and Adorno produced *Dialectic of Enlightenment*, a masterpiece examining how societies can regress from technological and societal advancement into previous stages of development influenced by their experience of Germany's reversion into fascism. The chilling message of the work was that Positivism—the enduring Hegelian idea hung over from the nineteenth century that history can only, perhaps with the odd setback, move in the "right" direction—has no place in fact. Enlightenment and progress are not necessarily self-sustaining, and may even contain the seeds of their own destruction.

This decidedly pessimistic analysis may reveal why Horkheimer, Adorno, and Pollock chose to relocate back to Frankfurt following the war: in their final analysis, no democratic society was immune to dictatorial forces, so perhaps a new democracy in a former dictatorship appeared no riskier to them than more staid Western nations. Another factor in their returning the Institut für Sozialforschung to Frankfurt was the importance of the institute to the city—and of the city to the institute. Immediately following the end of Nazi rule, Mayor Kolb and the Rector of the Goethe University wrote to Horkheimer and Weil inviting them to come back, and the promise of financial support and new headquarters in the university district of Westend on Senckenberg-Anlage must have seemed tempting following years of foreign penury dependent on various American sponsors.

The institute's new premises (where it remains to this day at a crossing known colloquially as the "Adorno traffic light") saw several pioneering post-war studies, including a disheartening look into Germans' feelings of guilt following the Third Reich in which so many of them had participated: nobody seemed to feel any personal responsibility for what had happened at all. Yet the second wave of Frankfurt School scholarship would be instrumental in changing this. In 1956 a young doctor of philosophy, Jürgen Habermas (1926-), who had been living in Frankfurt writing for FAZ and several other *Feuilleton* desks and magazines, was accepted into the institute and began work on his seminal *Strukturwandel der Öffentlichkeit (The Structural Transformation of the Public Sphere)*, with which he founded Media Studies as an academic discipline by examining the role writing and arts play in creating a vibrant public discourse (he is credited with creating the concept of the "public sphere"). Eight years later, after earning a professorship at Marburg, Habermas returned to Frankfurt, turning down leadership of the institute to be able to concentrate more on research (Horkheimer was succeeded by Habermas' close colleague Ludwig von Friedeburg). With Habermas—trained not just in continental but in analytical philosophy—as its intellectual doyen, the Frankfurt School became internationally more relevant than ever before, refining the tools of critical theory to suit the Anglo-American academic tradition of pragmatism and coining "communicative action" as a way of talking about how societies define and uphold concepts of what may be considered rational and enlightened.

An inspiring speaker who filled lecture theatres, Habermas was friendly to the student revolt of 1968 and encouraged the widespread questioning of old authorities in the light of Germany's past crimes which came to revolutionize German society. His passion for debate with his students and unambiguous positioning helped to found the legend of the *Frankfurter Schule* in Germany and reintroduced its concepts, more widespread in America and Britain due to the exile of the 1930s and 1940s, to a generation of young German academics. Habermas has gone on to become the leading figure in post-war German philosophy and is still a much sought-after commentator today, especially on questions around the European public sphere and Germany's role in it, an area into which he grew as the European Union developed from the 1970s onwards.

Today, the Frankfurt Institute for Social Research retains a prestigious name in sociology and critical theory under the leadership of Axel Honneth (1949-), and the legend of its first wave lives on across academic disciplines—perhaps most eccentrically in the form of @NeinQuarterly, a Twitter account run by former academic Eric Jarosinksi. In recent years, the long-time researcher into German critical theory has managed to gather over 100,000 followers writing 140-character notes in the parodic persona of a grumpy cultural pessimist largely based on Adorno, making the Frankfurt School perhaps the only academic discipline so recognizable as to be a legitimate target for high-level satire. An apposite taste of NeinQuarterly's unique humour in the context of this work comes from the 2014 Frankfurt Book Fair: "You can tell the agents at the FBF by their jackets—and the authors by their dust."

FRANKFURT.

A bird's eye view of Frankfurt in the eighteenth century (Wikimedia Commons)

6 | **Visual Images**
Money, Models and Museums

M
any of Europe's medieval metropolises have survived
into the present day almost unchanged since their hey-
days: Venice, Toledo and Bruges are all—seen through
a squint that shuts out shop frontages and street signage—more
or less original. Frankfurt, of course, with its turbulent history and
continuing importance as a global city, has not had the luxury of
preservation: yet, due to the wealth of visual representations of
Frankfurt throughout the ages, there are very few medieval cities
about whose geography and appearance we know so much.

The importance of images to the city, and the considerable
resources that have always been present to help in their creation,
have also made Frankfurt into a centre for the visual arts in general:
many important artists have learned their craft or experimented
with new ideas in the city, which has—in view of its role as a trading
hub—also developed an important infrastructure for commercial
imagery. Frankfurt never runs short on images, both of itself and
more generally.

Views of the City

The fact that views of Frankfurt today are both dominated and
afforded by skyscrapers finds a clear echo in the earliest representations of the city recorded in the medieval *Bedebuch*, a municipal
chronicle which recorded taxes and tolls, births and deaths, and not
least architectural information—this latter in the form of sketches.
These early drawings show the old Main bridge in 1405, for example, with its towers at either end, while early woodcut engravings
often stress the tall towers of the city wall. In the 1485 Strasbourg
version of the Golden Bull, the 1356 document that secured Frankfurt its role in the Holy Roman Empire, we see the seven prince
electors arriving at the western city gates under the mighty Rententurm, which bears the imperial eagle.

The 1485 Strasbourg print is, however, quite crude, not only by today's standards, but even by those of the time: in that other great Imperial city to the east, Nuremburg, the 1400s saw an unsurpassed flourishing of woodcut artistry culminating in the engravings of Albrecht Dürer (1471-1528). Meanwhile, just to the west in Mainz, the invention of the movable-type printing press by Johannes Gutenberg (1398-1468) had created a new distribution channel for woodcut prints beyond one-off sheets: the book. As both moveable type-sets and wooden blocks are forms of relief printing, images could easily be integrated into the new medium; and Frankfurt— not only conveniently located between the home of the printing press and the centre of woodcut artistry, but also the undisputed trade fair capital of Europe—was best placed for this marriage. By the early 1500s, the city housed both book resellers and several early publishers who produced illustrated volumes; this in turn had attracted artists to set up shop in Frankfurt, many specializing in woodcutting.

For these early pioneers, the Reformation was an economic catastrophe: art in medieval Europe had been almost entirely an ecclesiastical affair, and the sudden end to Church demand for richly decorated iconography and scenes from the lives of holy men sent many into penury. One Frankfurt painter, Conrad Faber von Kreuznach (1500-52/3), spent the rest of his days in debt and was forced to search for other sources of income; together with fellow artist Hans Wurzgart, he became a toll officer, weighing iron that came into the city over the Main bridge. The job gave Faber not only a secure living until his death, but a house in Fahrgasse too, and allowed him to continue exercising his talents; and soon enough, the market was adapting from Church to secular demand, applying the illustrative and decorative skills developed for religious works and bibles to items of general interest. For the *Cosmographia* of 1550, for example, the earliest German-language encyclopaedia, Conrad produced a bird's-eye view of Frankfurt depicted during the siege of 1552 in the civil wars following the founding of the Schmalkaldic League. The work is both of painstaking geographical detail and of impressive artistic skill: despite his evident difficulty with perspective in some individual buildings, the overall impression of this view is convincingly realistic and, as such, exceptional for its time (and for its book, in which many cities are portrayed in a more or less interchangeable high-medieval fashion). Above all, it was physically impossible for Faber to achieve the view of the city, depicted from the southwest, which he recorded: Frankfurt, now so often seen from the top of a skyscraper or the window of a plane, was shown from this perspective before the means were available for the human eye to see it.

Meanwhile, with the technological transfer from woodcut printing to chalcography—the use of engraved copper plates, also pioneered by Dürer in the late 1400s—the level of detail that could be achieved in book illustrations increased further. A centre for copper engraving was Basel, a city with which Frankfurt had close trading connections and from which it attracted the man who would produce the best known portraits of it: Matthäus Merian (1593-1650). Following years of apprenticeship in southern Germany and the Netherlands, Merian arrived in Frankfurt in 1616 to work for publisher and engraver Johann Theodor de Bry, a Strasbourg Calvinist of Dutch origin whose family had fled to Frankfurt during the persecutions of the late 1570s and then settled in nearby Oppenheim, where their religious services were permitted. De Bry's publishing house specialized in the kind of secular geographic and scientific works the Reformation had opened the door to, and Merian, who swiftly married de Bry's daughter, continued this tradition after he inherited the business in 1623.

Despite his deep religious fervour and illustrations for a Lutheran bible that soon become eponymously known as the *Merian-Bibel*, Merian's real passion was for topography: his depictions of several European cities from hillside elevations or the bird's-eye perspective were of such quality—and distributed so widely through his successful publishing house and the Frankfurt book fairs—that he started a Europe-wide trend in pictorial representations of cities. His Bohemian apprentice Wenceslaus Hollar (1607-77), went on to settle in London and produce some of the finest depictions of the city both before and after the Great Fire. His opus magnum *Topographia Germaniae*, meanwhile—16 volumes of richly illustrated German geography produced between 1642 and 1654—inspired the Swedish etcher Erik Dahlberg (1625-1703) to produce *Suecia antiqua et hodierna*, the first detailed geographic representation of Scandinavia.

That Dahlberg acknowledged his debt to Merian is not without poignancy. He was the chief fortifications officer of the Swedish Army and, as a young man, spent the end of the Thirty Years' War surveying Sweden's military strongholds in northern Germany. Merian, however, had been in Frankfurt during the occupation by the Swedish Army in the 1630s, producing engravings both of the entry of Gustavus Adolphus into the city and of the fighting in Sachsenhausen as the Swedish forces were repulsed. Indeed, his first major topographical publication *Theatrum Europaeum*, on which he continued work until his death, was a series of volumes about the Thirty Year's War, showing many of its battles in all their brutality. The fact that Dahlberg was five years old when Sweden occupied Frankfurt and had had already had a career in the Swedish Army by the time the war finished is a reminder of just how long and grinding this conflict was. Matthäus Merian would only survive its end by two years.

His two sons, Matthäus the Younger (1621-87) and Caspar Merian (1627-86) continued the publishing house—and the two key works, *Topographia Germaniae* and *Theatrum Europaeum*. Matthäus, however, was more of a gifted portraitist, and gained recognition in his own right for his depiction of Leopold I during his coronation in the city; Caspar followed in his father's footsteps and continued his line of detailed city views, architectural elevations and geographical images, one of the finest of which shows the Römer square in 1658. The dynasty continued under Matthäus the Younger's son, Johann Matthäus Merian (1659-1716) and this latter's niece, Charlotte Maria (*von* Merian, the family having been ennobled in Mainz) until 1727, adding detailed street maps to the publications as surveying grew both in its possibilities and its importance. The "Merianplan" would be the document of reference for city planners for decades to come, and the lasting importance of the Merian clan to the city is evident today in the name Merianplatz given to a square between Nordend and Bornheim. What is more, anyone in one of the newsagents at Frankfurt station looking for some reading material for a long train journey will note that Merian is now a brand name for a range of *National Geographic*-style high-end glossies about various cities: across German-speaking Europe, Merian remains synonymous with geography.

The peaceful and prosperous 1700s allowed no shortage of artistic talent to develop in Frankfurt. The wealthy city provided a good living for both locals such as painter Christian Georg Schütz (1718-91) who left several warm, slightly idealized views of the city, and newcomers such as the Swiss artist Johann Caspar Zehender (1742-1805) who drew the city in detailed, intricate monochrome images. Of particular note in this generation of Frankfurt artists was Georg Melchior Kraus (1737-1806), born within the city walls— like Johann Wolfgang von Goethe twelve years later—into a family which had made its fortune by running an inn. Kraus, a one-time apprentice of Tischbein the Elder in nearby Kassel and a teacher in Frankfurt who gave the young Goethe drawing lessons, dreamt of setting up an academy of arts in Frankfurt, but could not secure permission from the city when he tried in 1767. A few years later, the Duke of Weimar proved a more willing patron, and Melchior upped sticks in 1775; in conversation with Goethe during a visit back to Frankfurt that year, he helped persuade the poet and playwright to join him in this up-and-coming centre of the German Enlightenment. Kraus died in Weimar many years later, leaving behind a range of landscapes and portraits which were incredibly popular in their day, including a still-iconic image of Goethe looking longingly at a paper silhouette.

Yet for all its artistic philistinism and Weimar's cultural attraction, Frankfurt did not bleed altogether dry of artists: Schütz' workshop, for example, attracted young painters such as the Thuringian Johann Ludwig Ernst Morgenstern (1738-1819), whose paintings and etchings of the city's religious architecture in the detailed style of the old Dutch masters are of particular historical value. The Morgensterns went on to become a Frankfurt artistic dynasty much in the same manner as the Merians: Johann Friedrich Morgenstern (1777-1844) followed in his father's footsteps, producing architectural paintings as well as panoramas (a 306m² or 3,300ft² view of the city as it was in 1811 was unfortunately lost to fire in 1817). He painted parts of the city in the early nineteenth century that would fast be disappearing by the 1840s and, due both to his choice of subjects and predictable, orthodox style, earned the family a place as the city patricians' painters of choice. His son, Carl Morgenstern (1811-93) would go on to be the artistically most important of the family, however: while maintaining the conservative clientele of the family workshop, he introduced brighter colour and a more Romantic atmosphere into his paintings. In 1850 he was even commissioned by the Senate to capture the city from the southern bank of the Main on a canvas which now hangs in the Städel gallery, built twenty years later close to the spot from which the view was painted.

The Städel gallery (see page 45) and art school were founded using the legacy of Frankfurt banker Johann Friedrich Städel (1728-1816), who stands alongside the Bethmann and Rothschild families in the tradition of artistic patronage which flourished in Frankfurt during the prosperous eighteenth century. With the establishment of the gallery and school in 1828 (following a lengthy court case brought by disappointed relatives), Frankfurt was finally anchored in the German art scene at a propitious moment just as other cultural centres such as Weimar were going into steep decline. The directors of the museum and of the school were able not only to acquire works for the collection and attract young artists, but actually influence the kind of art being produced: the director from 1830 to 1840, Philipp Veit (1793-1877) established the Nazarene movement which swept through Germany, making Frankfurt the second centre for this late Romantic, reactionary religious style after Munich. He was followed by Johann David Passavant (1787-1861), also a Nazarene, who went on a shopping spree through Europe and to whom the gallery today owes its important collection of medieval and Renaissance masters.

Indeed, as the century passed and the city collection grew, Frankfurters became less interested in depictions of their own city and more interested in acquiring prestigious works from abroad. Henry Thode (1857-1920), director from 1889 onwards, concentrated on buying in the Italian masters, and in 1899 the charitable Städelsche-Museums-Verein was founded to fund further big-ticket acquisitions. At the same time, the artistic scene in Frankfurt, marked by the Nazarene years, continued down a reactionary road: Thode used his influence to support the work of painters like Hans Thoma (1839-1924), who produced idyllic country scenes and pre-Raphaelite-style throwbacks to the old masters, and whom Thode stylized as a "national" painter with a purported "understanding of the German soul". Thode also led media campaigns against the modern artistic forms emanating from France and taking hold in the capital as part of the Berlin Secession. This type of tendentious publicity drive, combined with his friendship with Wagner and race-based approach to art criticism, made him a favourite with the Nazis and prefigured their own crusades against "degenerate" and "un-German" art.

Yet before these dark times, the considerable resources of the Städel were for several decades directed away from such ideologically suspect terrain, and Frankfurt turned from a stronghold of traditionalism to a fertile terrain for artistic experiments. The change came with the appointment of Ludwig Justi (1876-1957), whose one-year reign from 1904-1905 saw the museum acquire its first Monet. His successor, Georg Swarenski (also 1876-1957), had 26 years to continue down this new path, now backed up with municipal money: Mayor Adickes, and his successors Voigt and Landmann, ran ever more left-leaning administrations in which the aim of the city's culture administration progressively became to pluralize the funding of the arts in Frankfurt, allowing for a move away from the narrow tastes of the banking elite and towards a broader range of styles. In the years leading up to the First World War and again in the Roaring Twenties, Swarenksi was able to use municipal funds to buy up several paintings by old German masters such as Holbein along with a range of Impressionist and Expressionist works to be shown in a new wing of the museum, completed with some delay due to the war in 1921. At the school, too, Swarenski rang in the changes, bringing in the Modernist Max Beckmann (1884-1950) to lead a master-class.

Beckmann, returning to Germany traumatized from the western front in 1915, settled a stone's throw away from the Städel in Sachsenhausen. Having worked as a medical orderly rather than fight the French from whom, he professed, he had "learned so much about painting", Beckmann had seen enough butchery to fuel a lifetime of artistic darkness. The chaos of the war, its aftermath and the Nazi years hang like a pall over his work, characterized as Expressionist despite his own refusal of the term. Besides his disturbing, Boschian images such as *Die Nacht* (*The Night*) and his unsettling self-portraits, Beckmann also produced several depictions of Frankfurt which rank among the most atmospheric ever made of the city: a view over the Eisener Steg bridge to the city in 1922, crisscrossed by smoke and power-lines, shows Frankfurt in a gritty industrial palette of browns and greens, while the 1919 masterpiece *Die Synagoge in Frankfurt am Main* captures the vibrant, slightly chaotic Börneplatz and its place of worship, all surveyed by a black and white cat. A similar feline observer can be found in *Frankfurter Hauptbahnhof*, a peaceful crepuscular view of the main station from 1942. This latter canvas was painted in Amsterdam, to where Beckmann, stripped of his teaching office by the Nazis and his work included in the 1937 *Entartete Kunst* ("Degenerate Art") initiative, had fled: the beauty of the painting speaks eloquently of his longing for the city in which he had spent such a productive period—and in which his works had now been burnt.

Many Beckmann paintings, as well as those of his students (artists such as Theo Garve, Leo Maillet and Marie-Louise von Motesiczky), which were not thrown onto the shameful bonfire on the Römerberg were sold by the profit-hungry Nazi apparatchiks who took over at the Städel; following the war, the gallery, once again supported by private money from the city, was able to buy several back. In contrast to the previous charitable initiatives, however, donations in the 1960s and 1970s came not just from bankers and financiers, but from a wide range of Frankfurters. A city-wide appeal was launched to collect enough money to buy back Beckmann's iconic *Synagoge* in the early 1970s. With the building itself and the city's Jewish community entirely destroyed, the painting is one of the most painful reminders of what Nazi dictatorship cost not only in terms of human life and dignity, but in cultural and artistic achievement. In the coming years, the city may once again have the chance to reacquire Beckmann works: the spectacular emergence of the Gurlitt collection in 2012, which contained hundreds of paintings stolen and sold on by the Nazis, revealed the existence of several Beckmanns thought lost.

The theme of loss is also the key feature of one of the most exciting visual representations of Frankfurt: the *Altstadtmodell* by the brothers Hermann (1876-1962) and Robert Treuner (1877-1948). Their 1:200 scale model of Frankfurt's Old Town was begun in 1926 and completed in 1961, by which time one of the brothers, Robert, was dead and most of the buildings shown it the model had been either consumed by flames or knocked down by post-war planners. Hermann, who had learned his artistic craft at the Städel, was originally commissioned by the Frankfurt Historisches Museum in 1923 to produce a model of Löhergasse, an old set of tradesmen's houses on the Sachsenhausen bank of the Main which was about to be demolished. As the radically modern urban planning of the 1920s began to take shape and plans were afoot to demolish the Fahrgasse thoroughfare to make way for a wider road, the Museum's management, against the destruction of the old town (see Chapters 3 and 4), asked the brothers, who worked together, to start documenting this street too. With the financial support of the *Bund tätiger Alstadtfreunde*, a residents' preservation initiative, they began to measure up and model the entirety of Frankfurt's old town, street by street and house by house. The museum added each piece to their original models, although payment was often delayed or not forthcoming and the brothers were frequently forced to stop work on the project to take on other paid commissions; yet the location of the models in the museum meant that they, too, were put into safe storage and survived the war unscathed—in contrast to much of the original town. Realizing the documentary importance of this model, and of the drawings and measurements of other buildings made by the Treuners, the post-war city authorities supported the completion of the model, which Hermann eventually finished in 1961.

Visitors to Frankfurt's Historisches Museum can now see the old city as it was in the late 1920s, and the model can also be viewed on the internet using 3D imaging software as part of the virtual *Altstadtmodell*, which draws on watercolours, sketches and photos of the time to extend the area covered by the model and allows "visitors" to stroll through the lanes and alleys of the Old Town in a manner similar to the Google Street View application. This can be seen as both the most recent, most technological form of the seventy years' mourning for the buildings destroyed in the Second World War—and as a useful practical resource for a city planning department now looking to reconstruct several old streets between the Römer town hall and the Dom cathedral as part of a modern identity crisis.

A Metropolis for Modern Images

Yet for many in the city—and not just the ambitious urban planners who rubbed their hands at the *tabula rasa* of the late 1940s—lamenting the Altstadt has amounted to little more than crying over spilt milk. One of the things that has defined Frankfurt since the Second World War has been its relentless focus forward, its willingness to build bigger and higher than almost anywhere else in Europe in order to look the part of the financial metropolis it has become—and wants to stay. This pioneering spirit, present through to this day in the Westhafen and Osthafen redevelopment projects, has also been reflected in the city's role in the new mass visual media of the twentieth century.

In German photography, for example, Frankfurt, and above all its post-war skyline, has become an inexhaustible motif attracting the attention of countless camera lenses. For the same reason that New York is a popular destination for photographers, Frankfurt lures both beginners and masters of the craft with its contrasts between extreme vertical modernity and small-scale, brick-built houses, between shining glass and green parks, between briefcases and coffee mugs full of coins. Many photographers settle in the city, turning their cameras to portray places elsewhere once these contradictory motives have become trite, and with the Fotografie Forum Frankfurt, founded in 1984, the city has an exhibition space to underline the importance of this visual art form to the cultural life of the city, featuring up to 200 exhibitions annually. More recently, the revival of the run-down Bahnhofsviertel has precipitated a flood of high-profile photographic pilgrimages to capture the area's trademark mix of seedy dive-bars and shining skyscrapers, of bare-walled galleries and crack-smoking streetwalkers—a blend which so intoxicates trendy types in fashion, the media and advertising. Jürgen Teller is the most recent international photographer to have published a paean to the pimps, prostitutes, pubs and yuppies of the area.

For all the city has proved popular with photographers, film-makers have been far less attracted to it. Even within German cinema, the city has rarely featured in major film productions and is lacking pop-culture movies which define its sense of who and what it is (residents of cities such as Hamburg and Berlin have a wealth of cinema hits in which the city plays a defining role). At best, Frankfurt had a brief run as a setting for films about the glamour, grit and pitfalls of prostitution, starting with *Das Mädchen Rosemarie* (1958), a satirical and socially critical exploration of the life and death of a high-class escort girl and both the first and best of this subgenre. Despite the city's edgy and modern appearance, however, as well as the wealth of potential for exciting thrillers provided by rivalries between fabulously wealthy bankers, the city has seen few important film productions in recent years. A welcome exception was the deeply moving 2014 *Im Labyrinth des Schweigens* (released as *Labyrinth of Lies* in English-speaking countries) about the Auschwitz trials of the 1960s (see page 224). While it featured brief shots of the Römer and the IG Farben Building, it was by its very nature a film of (very authentic) *Wirtschaftswunder* period interiors.

Yet Frankfurt's role in the history of film in Germany is far more important than the paucity of films in which it is visible would suggest. In fact, the very first film material recorded in Germany was shot by the Lumière brothers in July 1896 in Frankfurt, showing the old marketplace and the arrival of Emperor William II to celebrate the 25th anniversary of the end of the Franco-Prussian War (the French visitors filmed in secret). Furthermore, with its range of theatres, Frankfurt was one of the first cities in Germany to show movies: the Orpheum theatre ran a short film made with the Edison camera in May of that year. In 1905 the city's first proper cinema opened at Kaiserstraße 60 in the Bahnhofsviertel, at that point a new and impressive district which linked the station and Theater-platz, the centre of Frankfurt's vibrant entertainment industry. Soon the Bahnhofsviertel, as well as the area around Konstablerwache at the other end of the city, had a large number of cinemas; by 1925 there were 35 in the city, several of which were *Kino-Paläste*—film palaces—with more than 1,000 seats. This gave Frankfurt the largest number of cinemas in Germany after the capital, Berlin, and quite possibly the highest density of movie theatre seats in the country.

Sigfried Kracauer (1889-1966), who was born and raised in Frankfurt and a two-time Berlin resident, was a regular at cinemas in both cities. While he wrote frequently about the exciting social mix of moviegoers in Berlin and analysed the cinemas themselves, he left little about Frankfurt's numerous movie theatres: however, in his eleven years writing for the leading left-wing liberal daily, *Frankfurter Zeitung* (see Chapter 5), he progressively broadened his remit as culture editor to include film criticism. Soon he was writing more about film than anything else, and it was in these articles that he first turned his attention at several points from the films he was watching to the political position of the films and even to the role of film criticism itself. Fleeing Germany in 1933 after the Reichstag fire, Kracauer—from a family of Jewish traders—escaped Europe in time, ending his days in New York, where he wrote his masterpiece *From Caligari to Hitler: A Psychological History of German Film* (1947), which essentially founded film criticism as an academic subject. In this way, too, Frankfurt had a role to play in modern visual arts.

Following the defeat of Germany, not only were Frankfurt's numerous cinemas in ruins, but the German film industry—discredited entirely after the Nazis' abuse of it for propaganda purposes and devoid of its most talented personnel, who were in exile—was at its lowest ebb. The Allied occupying armies were fully aware of how effective the Nazi use of film had been and kept a tight rein on both the production and distribution of films: after complete bans on both directly following the victory, restrictions were soon loosened (the Lichtburg was the first Frankfurt cinema to reopen in July 1945) but all films made or shown had to pass Allied censorship—and most were simply American films subtitled, and later dubbed, into German.

The result of this policy was that as the centre of American operations in post-war Germany and with its central position in what became Western Germany, Frankfurt became the centre of commercial film lending and distribution, too. Reels arrived fresh from Hollywood at Frankfurt airport, and throughout the 1950s, an industry grew up to receive, store and deliver the films to cinemas throughout the country. American film companies such as Metro Goldwyn Mayer and Columbia set up their German operations in the city, and as such, several national premieres and galas took place in Frankfurt in the 1950s, although other cities soon became more popular locations for such celebrations due to their successful studios.

As has always been the case in post-war Frankfurt, the strongly business-orientated environment of the city brought an equally strong reaction. While local companies grew wealthy on importing and distributing American blockbusters and the city's wealth of cinemas were as popular as ever, a growing counter-culture in the 1960s and 1970s began to demand a less commercialized, more artistic and experimental form of film. The culture secretary in the left-wing city government of the late 1960s, Hilmar Hoffmann, was a particular proponent of independent cinema, having been head of a short film competition in the Ruhr city of Oberhausen. Hoffmann's stated aim was to "democratize culture"—meaning that both the consumption and production of works of art should be kept away from monopolistic commercial structures—and in Frankfurt one of his key contributions was opening Germany's second publically funded cinema: the Kommunales Kino, or "KoKi", in 1971.

It was high time: the cinemas in the Bahnhofsviertel had already degenerated into showing little more than soft porn, while many of the city's art-house cinemas had gone bankrupt as city centre rents went up. The KoKi showed retrospectives, shorts and foreign films not picked up by commercial distributors and cinemas, and was integrated into a much larger project driven by Hoffmann during his twenty-year reign from 1970 to 1990: the Museumsufer (see Chapter 3). It is now part of the Deutsches Filmmuseum, opened in 1984 in a restored classical villa on the south bank of the Main. The villa also houses the Deutsches Filminstitut, founded in 1949 and the oldest film institute in the Federal Republic of Germany; in Fechenheim in the city's suburbs, it holds over 2,800 cameras, tripods, flatbeds and similar items as part of its archive of film production artefacts.

Frankfurt, it would seem, attaches importance not only to preserving images of itself as it changes through the ages, but to preserving the history of images itself.

7 | **Leisure and Pleasure**
Popular Culture and Pastimes

Due to the substantial financial resources both of the city itself and its inhabitants, residents of Frankfurt enjoy a cultural offering and choice of leisure activities easily on a par with cities of a much greater size. How many cities with a population of under one million can boast a 1.5km stretch of museums along their riverfront, a world class opera and a wealth of nightspots spanning everything from the gritty to the glitzy? Even taking into account the Main conurbation as a whole and its population of approaching two million, the area in and around Frankfurt is disproportionately provisioned with interesting ways for its inhabitants to spend their free time.

Nevertheless, not all of the activities concerned are of equal accessibility—or of equal appeal—to everyone. Frankfurt has to cater both for Germany's highest-earning employees and one of the country's most alternative artistic scenes, and the diminutive dimensions of the city mean that more often than not one group has to make way for the other. Yet by the same token, Frankfurt is no New York or London: high-rollers on the Main are still leagues behind the Gordon Gekkos and Nick Leesons of this world, and globetrotting oligarchs have to date shown remarkably little interest in the place. As such, the eye-watering extremes of other financial metropolises are somewhat toned down: blacked-out limousines are relatively rare, as are genuinely low-class drinking holes; neither the number of rhinestones at cheap discos nor the diamond quotient at the opera are, to an observer from Britain or America, particularly striking.

Opera, Theatre, Galleries
Frankfurt has had regular opera performances since the early 1700s, and by 1780 was building its first opera house on Roßmarkt. A century later, the small, somewhat plain building in a vaguely

Frankfurt's *Alte Oper* back in the late nineteenth century, when it was still the New Opera (Library of Congress, Washington DC)

neoclassical style was replaced by the colossal opera house at what was then Bockenheimer Tor, known since its opening in 1880 as Opernplatz. Today called the Alte Oper, the restored building (see Chapter 3) remains perhaps the most impressive testament to the city's dedication to high culture: ruinously expensive during its construction, it could only be completed thanks to donations from the city's great banking families; since then, opera in the city has always relied on public subsidies running into the millions per annum; and following its almost complete destruction in the bombing raids of the Second World War, the building was saved thanks to donations from private citizens totalling 15 million Marks.

The Alte Oper today, however, is a general purpose concert location used by the Frankfurt Symphony Orchestra and also featuring music, dance and stage performances with a broader commercial appeal, as well as conferences and smaller trade shows. Not reopened until 1981, the city's opera company had already found another abode. Indeed, operatic life returned to the city as quickly as any other form of entertainment: both the first film showings and the first opera performance following the Second World War took place in July 1945. With its premises in ruins, the opera company performed in the one large hall to have survived the bombing raids: the trading floor of the Frankfurt Stock Exchange.

This is just one way in which Frankfurt's financiers have supported opera in the city in recent history. While the German state is generous in its cultural subsidies by comparison to the United States or many other European nations, state hand-outs are not what they used to be and both the Deutsche Bank and DZ Bank Trusts now sponsor the operatic society, Oper Frankfurt. It is also the done thing for wealthy private individuals from the world of finance to become friends of the Frankfurt Opera, guaranteeing them entry to the premiere soirées and the publication of their name in the programmes and in the foyer of the Städtische Bühnen building, the 1950s theatre complex on Willy-Brandt-Platz (see page 52) which has housed the opera hall since 1951. In 1987 the new stage fell victim to arson and the Opera once again moved—this time to the neighbouring theatre—while the space was renovated. Despite its travails, however, with around 180 performances a year and over 11,000 subscribers, the Opera today is thriving.

Besides the Opera, the Städtische Bühnen Frankfurt am Main offer three stages for spoken performances: the grand theatre seats 700, while a smaller chamber space holds 185 and the "box" in the entrance hall, conceived for experimental items or lectures, holds sixty. The entrance hall, though, is worth visiting in its own right, featuring a painting by Marc Chagall (1887-1985) titled *Commedia dell'Arte*, a striking homage to the old Italian performances which so influenced modern Western drama, and the 100-metre-long copper ceiling sculpture running the length of the building.

Besides the official municipal stages, Frankfurt offers a varied theatrical landscape: the cosy Kellertheater, located in a city-centre arched cellar, runs a varied programme of comedy, classics and new plays, and stages children's performances, too. Meanwhile, the Volkstheater of Großer Hirschgraben, the street in which Germany's most famous playwright Goethe was born (see Chapter 5), has a special place in the heart of many a Frankfurter due to its founder, Liesel Christ (1919-96). Christ, a gifted stage presence who was performing in the ballet company at the Alte Oper before she was ten, became an ambassador for the city in her later years, opening the Volkstheater ("People's Theatre") to put on plays in Hessian and Frankfurt dialect in 1971. Christ's love for the patois of her native city even saw her work a telephone line called *Frehliche Frankfort-Telefon* ("Happy Frankfurt phone") a pre-internet way for those who had left the city to keep in touch with its news, culture and dialect by ringing up to hear pre-recorded anecdotes and accounts of life there; the line only survived Christ's death by two years.

Those who are new to Frankfurt and to Germany as a whole, however, will have enough trouble following drama in High German, let alone dialect. For the city's consistently high population of expats both English-speaking and international, performances in English are a more attractive option and can be found in the Commerzbank Galileo Tower, which houses a 300-seat auditorium, the largest permanent English-speaking drama premises in continental Europe. The thespians of the English Theatre Frankfurt, founded in

1979, are part of the third-oldest English-language drama company in Europe (Vienna and Hamburg are older) and are generally drawn directly from the West End or Broadway for the popular programme of musicals and modern drama. Meanwhile, the more rough-and-ready Ostend Internationales Theater offers a broader range of less commercial fare, ranging from art-house or experimental productions in English through Russian drama, French chansons and Portuguese dance; with over 150 performances a year, this institution offers something for almost every homesick nationality in the city—and plenty for residents curious about other languages and cultures.

The city's impressive theatrical range is rounded off by the Komödie, a light-hearted and comedy-focused company nestling in between the skyscrapers of Neue Mainzer Straße: bankers who simply cannot face another night in their tuxedos at the Opera at the end of the road can dive in here for cabaret and stand-up, while those who still value their reputations above their impulses can save their dignity and jump into a taxi out to the Fritz-Rémond-Theater, set in a stately pile at the zoo. Although originally founded to bring works by the likes of Ibsen, Anouilh and Schnitzler onto the stage, it is now owned by the Komödie, which bought it in the late 1970s to save it from closure, and generally shows plays with a broad appeal and the odd modern classic.

Art lovers can take their pick in Frankfurt, too. The central Schirn Kunsthalle is the city's premier gallery for modern classics with a collection including works by Matisse, Giacometti, Chagall and Seurat; it has made a name for itself by putting on sometimes daring contemporary exhibitions as well as taking unusual thematic approaches. A few streets to the north, the Museum für Moderne Kunst specializes in movements from the 1960s and onwards such as Pop Art and Minimalism, while the Kunstverein im Steinernen Haus offers a smaller, less formal forum for exhibitions and conferences. The Städel, of course (see Chapters 3, 4 and 6), has a formidable collection from throughout the history of art, while the Städel art school continues to train young painters and sculptors, whose work is frequently exhibited in the Portikus, the reconstructed gatehouse on Alte Brücke.

Conspicuous Consumption

Yet however broad the city's range of cultural pursuits and theatrical and musical entertainments may be, it cannot compete with the sheer breadth of opportunities to spend money on products. The city in which money is made at the click of a mouse or the swipe of a finger is an attractive market, and one in which luxury brands try out innovative approaches to bag high-net-worth customers. Some of its most exclusive shopping experiences are little more than rumours to most: Deutsche Bank headquarters is said to feature an outlet store run by shirt-makers Chef (*Chef* being the German for "boss") frequented by bankers pulling double all-nighters. German carmakers, too, have tested various sales concepts in the bank towers: if the clients with the cash for a Porsche do not have time to go to the dealership, then the dealership must go to them.

Other pricey bankers' accoutrements are sold in more visible situations. Central Frankfurt has, as one might expect, several expensive-looking jewellers as well as a vibrant tailoring scene, which is notable for a country as congenitally casual as Germany: Frankfurt is one of the only cities in Germany where, if you are wearing a suit, the person you are talking to may check your jacket sleeves to see if one of the buttons is undone and eye up your shirt-cuffs for discreetly expensive links. Several shops for the status-conscious are gathered in Westend, where they are close to their time-is-money clientele, or are located in the stockbroker belt at Bad Homburg, the leafy suburb of bankers' choice.

Bad Homburg and the patchwork of market towns and old bathing spas in the Taunus hills to the north of Frankfurt (see Chapter 12) are also noted for their density of Michelin-starred restaurants, which thrive in this landscape of bankers' villas and picturesque winding roads (along which driving sports cars is that much more fun). Yet within the city, high-end gastronomy is less developed and less adventurous than might be expected. While the streets of Westend are certainly home to expensive eateries, there is something almost touchingly provincial and outdated about them: there are steakhouses with private dining areas, cigar humidors and piles of wooden place-markers with the names of banking big-wigs embossed on metal plaques, or exclusive restaurants in the top floors of the towers with menus featuring caviar and champagne. It is easy to run up four-figure restaurant bills in Frankfurt, but the frenetic novelty of New York eating-out or the "next big thing" trendiness of London gastronomy are notable by their absence.

The city and its stockbroker belt also feature no shortage of five-star hotels—ten at the last count—with some spectacular properties. Bankers and financiers can get back to the roots of their trade in the old Villa Rothschild out at Königstein in the Taunus hills, now run by Kempinski, or celebrate the symbolic victory of capital over the aristocracy in the Schlosshotel in neighbouring Kronberg, formally the seat of the Princes of Hessia. The nightly rates in the priciest suites in such choice locations tip the scales at around €2,000 (an average monthly disposable salary for white-collar professionals), but are nothing compared to the latest breed of post-financial-crash investment madness: the central Palaisquartier, a development near Eschenheimer Tor featuring a fig-leaf reconstruction of the old Thurn und Taxis aristocratic residence and a cluster of mini-skyscrapers, can boast the tasteless Jumeirah Frankfurt Hotel, run by a hotel group belonging to the Dubai royal family and the first of their wildly decadent lodgings on the European mainland (London, of course, already having two at the time of opening in 2011). The presidential suite is advertised at €5,000 per night. The unique selling proposition is simple: it is the highest listed price for a hotel room in Germany (rumour has it that some suites elsewhere go for five-figure sums, but these figures are traditionally kept under wraps).

Inconspicuous Pursuits

Despite being subject to these incursions from the world of turbo-charged capitalism, Frankfurt remains nevertheless firmly anchored in one of Europe's most egalitarian and socially-minded societies, while its city government makes considerable efforts to preserve non-commercial space even as it gives permits to some of Germany's most expensive development projects. The effects of this political mood-music are that, while it is as easy to spend money in Frankfurt as in other banking metropolises, it is just as easy to fill one's leisure time with pursuits of a far less financially punishing nature.

German football, for example, has resisted the headlong charge towards profit margins which characterizes the English Premier League. Eintracht Frankfurt, which plays in the top Bundesliga, frequently sells match-day tickets for around €30, with season ticket holders getting an even better deal. Although this may be partly to do with the club's mediocre performance since its 1990s glory days, much is simply a result of the slower pace of commercialization in German football, even if the stadium is officially named after its sponsors: the Commerzbank-Arena. Idyllically situated in the green expanse of the city forests south of Sachsenhausen, the 1920s stadium was renovated in time for the World Cup of 2006 and is known by most Frankfurt football fans as the Waldstadion.

Completed in 1925 as part of the reformist, socially-minded planning policy of the Weimar Republic city government, the original stadium featured a swimming pool and cycling track around the central pitch, which was also used for athletics. The first summer games of the International Workers' Olympiads were held there, and when the pendulum swung the other way, the Nazis—who were quick to co-opt sports into their doctrine of white superiority—ensured not only its continuing use for track sports, but also for marches, parades and political rallies. Requisitioned by the American forces for their own sporting needs, it was returned to the city in the late 1940s and rebuilt to accommodate the growing crowds for football. With the increasing popularity of the newly-founded Bundesliga in the early 1960s, Eintracht Frankfurt moved there from their smaller premises at Riederwald.

The Riederwaldstadion between Bornheim and Seckbach is still in use by Eintracht Frankfurt, but not by its football arm. As with groups such as Bayer Leverkusen or Hamburger Sport Verein, Eintracht is not just a soccer club, but an overarching sports organization which fields teams in a variety of sports. Riederwald is home to Eintracht's tennis courts and ice-hockey hall, as well as a souvenir shop and café for the club's nostalgic "man-and-boy" football fans. It also houses Frankfurt's second soccer team, FSV Frankfurt 1899, in the old stadium, sponsored not by the mega-bucks Commerzbank, but by the building society Volksbank. While the area has an unpleasant past, having been used to sort rubble from the city centre—a process which lasted two decades—it is nowadays associated entirely with pleasurable pursuits: as well as the sporting facilities, it is home to the twice-yearly Dippemess fair. Held once in spring and once in autumn, the Dippemess also stems from the annual markets which became the trade fairs: while these became known simply as the Messe, the Dippemess, more of a market for local peasants and townsfolk than for Hanseatic brokers and Venetian merchants, was named after the pottery stalls which where once its defining feature (*Dippe* is Hessian dialect for earthenware). Until the 1960s, the Dippemess was held on the Römer market-place, but its continuing transformation from an old-fashioned fair to a modern fairground meant that it quickly outgrew the narrow confines of the city centre as wooden carousels were replaced with large metal Ferris wheels. With the rubble clearing programme nearing its end, the unused space to the east of the city was the ideal location for what is now the largest fairground in Frankfurt and its surroundings.

One recurrent fair which has not moved away from the Römer, however, is the Frankfurt Christmas Market. Yuletide fairs are a tra-dition in Frankfurt which reaches back almost as far as the city itself: the first mystery plays were probably held in the city during the reign of Otto the Great, and the Christmas market is documented from 1393 on. While the largest, most famous German *Christkind-markt* has always been held in Nuremburg—the city from where the archetypal *Lebkuchen* gingerbread comes—Frankfurt's festivities have developed and retained a beguiling local character: alongside the unimpressive, pricey standard-issue mulled wine and the gen-eral tit-tat one has come to expect from commercialized Christmas markets, Frankfurters can by their *Bethmännchen*, also known as *Quetchemännchen*, bite-sized almond pastries baked with three nuts around the outside that were once sent by suitors to the objects of their desire: if they were returned, then a proposition of marriage would not be accepted. Goethe was so fond of this almond delights that he had his mother send him a packet of them to Weimar every Christmas. The Christmas market today runs for the four weeks of Advent through to 22 December and is popular as a place to meet friends or go out for office drinks after work—it is also used by businessmen looking to impress visiting contacts from warmer climes with its picturesque, fairy-tale look (and to render them incapable of negotiating after the second mulled wine with a shot of rum kicks in). The market means big business for the city, too, as footfall increases for city-centre shops and the city council reaps in money for stall licences. The company which runs the Frankfurt market was also the pioneer of Christmas markets in English-speaking countries, single-handedly starting the current British craze for them after it set up in Frankfurt's twinned city Birmingham with 24 stalls in 2001 (it now counts hundreds of stalls and runs for six weeks, attracting almost five million visitors).

Äppelwoi: More than Just a Drink

Although Frankfurt's thirsty can only enjoy piping hot *Glühwein* for three weeks each year, there is another drink that gets them through the other eleven months: *Apfelwein*, or literally "apple wine", lovingly referred to in local dialect as *Äppelwoi*, *Ebbelwoi*, *Evvelwei*, or—especially in reference to a glass of the substance—*Schobbe*. Made from fermented apple juice, in drink classification terms Äppelwoi is a cider, but is usually far more tart than many English speakers would be led to expect from the word; indeed, most Frankfurters drink it as a spritzer with either lemonade or mineral water, although some craft Äppelwoi brews are made using sweeter apples for a more balanced flavour.

To say that Frankfurt is fond of Äppelwoi would be a gross understatement: it is part of the city's identity in the same way that brown ale is part of what makes people from Newcastle-on-Tyne Geordies or whisky contributes to defining the Scottish national feeling. As such, drinking Äppelwoi is a pastime as much as it is a simple matter of quenching thirst, and comes with its own range of accessories, the most important of which is the *Bembel*, a stoneware jar—generally liveried in grey with blue floral decoration—which can hold several glasses of the brew and is therefore generally named according to servings: *Achterbembel* jugs hold above two litres, enough for eight servings, while a *Viererbembel*, at around a litre, is enough for four. From this pitcher, Äppelwoi drinkers in the group can serve themselves and dilute their glass to their own taste. The glass, referred to as a *Schobbe* (high German *Schoppen*, from the word for barrel in turn related to the English word "shop"), is thick and patterned with a cross-hatch on the outside referred to as "ribbed" in German. Traditionally, it held a 300ml measure, but many locations have turned to serving in 250ml glasses—a move viewed with disdain by fans of the drink who refer to 250ml beakers as *Beschissergläser*, perhaps best translated from an etymological standpoint as "shyster glasses".

Especially served in pitchers, Äppelwoi is a shared drinking experience that Frankfurters associate with warm summer evenings in pub gardens or blustery autumn nights in a cosy inn. The most traditional places for it to be drunk are in a part of Sachsenhausen known as the *Ebbelweiviertel* based around Große Ritterstraße, a surviving patch of old-style two-to-three story houses, some with wattle-and-daub and timber-beamed façades. The interiors of real "apple wineries" should be panelled in dark wood and be hung floor-to-ceiling with yellowed prints and cracked old paintings; dingy net curtains from the days before smoking bans help, too; outside, shady courtyards with ivy-covered walls and large chestnut trees are *de rigueur*.

With its sour kick, Äppelwoi is perfect for washing down the heavier elements of traditional Frankfurt cuisine: shoulder of pork (a whole shoulder counts as an individual serving) and dumplings, pork chops on sauerkraut and mashed potato, and—what else?—the traditional sausages to which the city gave its name. At the same time, its refreshing fizziness also makes it the perfect accompaniment for spring and summer dishes served cold such as *Frankfurter Grüne Soße*, literally "green sauce", made of salad oil, minced boiled eggs and anywhere between seven and nine herbs (chives, parsley, cress, dill, chervil, borage, lovage, sorrel and pimpinella are all listed as possible ingredients). What is more, its tart sweetness also lends itself to being drunk with desserts, meaning that a *Bembel* can be put on the table at any time of year and refreshed at any point during a meal. Last but not least, heated up with spices and sugar, it can even serve as a winter dessert in its own right, or indeed as a general all-purpose "grandma cure" hot-toddy. In this latter variant, it is of course available at the Frankfurt Christmas Market.

For those who really take their local beverage seriously, there is the *Ebbelwei-Expreß*, a set of old two-axle tram units which were taken out of regular service in 1977. Intended as a last goodbye to the old cars, a circular route with all-you-can-drink *Apfelwein* was offered one Sunday that year—and extended due to popular demand. Soon the weekend expeditions had become something of an institution and, instead of being retired, the cars were given a new, colourful livery and refitted as leisure units. Although they generally operate in pairs, one motorized and one dummy car, their thirtieth anniversary in 2007 saw the longest ever, ten-car *Ebbelwei-Expreß* formation trundle along every Frankfurt drinker's favourite route, and all of these vintage units are still going strong as they head for their fortieth: in the particularly cold winters of the early 2010s their robustly over-engineered pantographs were used to clear the ice from the overhead electricity supply wires after several of the more modern units had come unstuck. They can be found on Sundays and bank holidays, starting at the turning loop outside the zoo before heading through the city centre on a sight-seeing tour, up to the Messe and then over the Main into Sachsenhausen past the *Apfelwein* area, and then back up across the river to the zoo. Since they run at least every half hour and ticketing is on a hop-on-hop-off basis, the trams are both an excellent way for tourists to see the city and for locals to tour their favourite cider spots.

Parks and Gardens

Fans of vintage rail vehicles are certainly never short of things to do in Frankfurt: although still used by some freight traffic today, the single-track line along the northern bank of the Main linking the main station and western harbour with the eastern docks and station is now more often than not used for excursions with old diesel rail-buses and even the odd steam engine. Passing the Nizza gardens in the west and then going under the Eisener Steg bridge and all the way along to the new ECBs headquarters, this is an unusual stretch and trains have to keep to a very low speed limit due to the fact that the line passes through what is essentially a public embankment park used by joggers, walkers and businessmen needing a quiet place to eat a sandwich.

Indeed, for all its urban intensity and homages to concrete and steel, Frankfurt has no shortage of greenery. Besides the green strip along the river, the gardens along the old route of the city walls (see Chapters 2 and 3) provide a green belt around the city centre which for almost the entire working population of the city is within a ten-minute walk. As soon as the fortifications were removed in the early 1800s, a stroll through the *Wallanlagen* immediately became a popular way to spend an idle hour, and the same is true to this day. Starting at the eastern end of the Nizza gardens (named, perhaps somewhat optimistically, for Nice), the Taunusanlage section of the green belt heads due north to Willy-Brandt-Platz, passing the Jewish museum and then the Städtische Bühnen to its right before entering into a canyon of skyscrapers as it heads north-west. This section of the gardens contains monumental busts commemorating Schiller, Heine and Beethoven, as well as a daringly abstract "house for Goethe" which bears no resemblance either to a house or the man of letters himself.

At the end of the Taunusanlage section, the Alte Oper hoves into view opposite the Marshall fountains, an oddly fitting reminder of the man who made the money flow into post-war Europe and Frankfurt in particular (see Chapters 4 and 10), framed by the towers of banks such as UBS which, if the water in the fountain represents flowing money, may be deemed to be sculptures hewn of ice. After the Oper, the green ring turns east into the Bockenheimer Anlage. This part of the gardens, broad and still clearly showing the triangular shape of the old bastions, is an oasis of peace and quiet in this active part of the city—the Stock Exchange is just one street in—and features charming landscaped sweeps of green interspersed with fountains and the Nebbiensche Gartenhaus exhibition space, a small garden pavilion put up by the Danish publisher Nebbien in the 1800s.

At Eschenheimer Tor, the old medieval gatehouse tower feels lost in the lanes of traffic surrounding it and with the vulgar bulk of the Jumeirah rising behind it, but the ensuing Eschenheimer Anlage portion of the green belt soon swallows walkers back up again, taking them on a slightly northeasterly course past a memorial to Philipp Reis (1834-1874), one of several individuals to be credited with having invented the telephone (and one of several men who is probably thus regularly cursed by harried lunch-breakers). The park becomes more residential, with kindergarten vegetable patches and a small *Trinkhalle* kiosk guaranteeing a supply of cool beer for impromptu summer get-togethers on the grass. Passed unwittingly by most stands a somewhat isolated memorial bust to Anton Kirchner (1779-1834), one of the first historians of Frankfurt itself.

The next juncture is Friedberger Tor, where the residential stretch once again gives way to city-centre bustle as trams emerge by the minute from an underpass and traffic roars past. Calm can be found a few feet away in the Bethmannpark, however, salvaged from what was once a huge English country garden belonging to the Bethmann banker dynasty and through which Prussian King Frederick William III, Napoleon and Goethe have wandered. A part of this patch of green was transformed into a Chinese garden in 1989, named the Gardens of Heavenly Peace out of solidarity with the protestors of Tiananmen Square who died in the same year, and provides a sense of utter tranquillity. Over the walls of the garden, however, war is never far away: the Hessendenkmal commemorates the successful defence by Hessian troops of the Frankfurt city walls on which these gardens were laid out at the beginning of the French Revolutionary Wars in 1792 (see page 87).

The Bethmannpark is complemented by the Bethmannweiher, a large pond popular with street drinkers of the uniquely harmless German kind; and indeed, with their 1980s haircuts, punk clothing and straggly mutts, the groups seem to fit in with the next section of the green belt, the Friedberger Anlage, which is lined by housing tower-blocks and decidedly grubbier than other stretches of the ring; refreshingly, however, the park becomes busier: this is, after all, a densely populated residential area and which children play football and families take walks. Crossing Allerheiligentor in the hastily reconstructed 1950s Ostenend, the green belt heads due south to the Main past the Rechneigraben, a tranche of the ditch in front of the city walls left and filled in to make a pond by the park's mastermind Sebastian Rinz (1782-1861), who is himself remembered by a statue in the preceding Friedberger section. In this last part of the ring, the Obermainanlage, are statues of Gotthold Ephraim Lessing (1729-81), the father of the German Enlightenment, and Arthur Schopenhauer (1788-1860), credited by many with ending it. Only Schopenhauer actually lived in Frankfurt, and did so nearby in not-so-genteel poverty on Schöne Aussicht on the Main, alongside many of the city's fishermen, to whom the park also features a memorial statue. After 5km, the park finishes next to the Literaturhaus, a cultural association in the neoclassical Villa Hoffmann.

Besides this central space, Frankfurters looking to enjoy tranquil greenery have several options. The Rothschildpark just across from the Alte Oper is a small but tranquil spot on the cusp of the Westend banking district, bordered on the north by the green expanse composed of Grüneburgpark, Botanischer Garten, and Palmengarten. The Grüneburgpark around the Poelzig building on the university campus is a gently sloping, open parkland space, while the Gardens and the Palmengarten offer a more specifically botanical experience, featuring exotic plants and greenhouses open all year round. Other popular spots for open air relaxation are the Günthersburgpark in between Nordend and Bornheim, which features theatre, poetry, music and author appearances free of charge every summer, as well as the expansive Ostpark, built in the early twentieth century very much in the spirit of the times to provide the working classes of Ostend and the Riederwald estates with fresh air and a healthy, non-alcohol-related recreational space. Ostend also houses the Frankfurt Zoo, Germany's oldest after Berlin, known for its success in breeding gorillas: Matze (1958-2008) became the eldest male stud in the world after 51 years of mating, 39 of them in Frankfurt, in which time he had 18 young with four females. Its impressive central offices, completed in 1876, today house the zoo restaurant and the Fritz-Rémond-Theater (see above).

Some of Frankfurt's most striking open spaces, however, are its lidos. As in the rest of Germany, open air swimming pools have been accorded far higher priority than in many other countries, meaning that the city of Frankfurt runs seven *Freibäder* in the summer, i.e. one lido per 100,000 inhabitants. The outdoor pools form a ring around the city, most frequently set in parkland and woods, and are often full to bursting point on hot summer days. While Frankfurt certainly has no shortage of private swimming pools, none of them can offer 50m of open air swimming and a lawn on which to enjoy a picnic—and perhaps a glass of Äppelwoi.

Nightlife: Bankers versus Students

Due to constant contact with other banking centres such as London, terms such as "work hard, play hard" have made their way into Frankfurt argot. While nightlife in Berlin is characterized by the general feeling that being seen anywhere before midnight is the equivalent of social death, Frankfurt is a city in which people are always thinking about tomorrow—and getting up early to make the most of it. In what is otherwise a rare sight in Germany, the bars to the north and west of the city centre, as well as those on the way home for many city workers in Sachsenhausen, fill up in the early evening with the suited and booted, ties loosened and shirt-sleeves rolled up in summer. Even midweek, there will be plenty of people eating out or enjoying an after-work tipple, but bars of this type tend to empty as midnight approaches.

At the same time, Frankfurt has a university of considerable size, an established and growing community of artists and trendy media types and—perhaps most crucially—lax German licensing laws. For those intent on so doing, there is no barrier to drinking 24 hours a day, and especially in the student quarter of Bockenheim and in the newly-trendy Bahnhofsviertel there is a profusion of bars and clubs for a young, style-conscious target group that either does not have to be at work early the next day—or does not have to be at work at all. While the small size of the city often leads people to expect that the straight-laced bankers and the alternative types might mix more often, it still seems to be the case that those who work in the finance industry within sight of the Bahnhofsviertel prefer to stick to their after-work locations—and that those who frequent the trendy scene there and elsewhere like it that way. Certainly, one won't find a large number of the exceptionally wealthy nodding their heads to the techno beats of Frankfurt DJs such as Sven Väth, Marc Spoon, and DJ Dag (some Frankfurters claim the city actually invented the genre before Berlin)—just as it is unusual to find many an all-night-party-goer warming up at the Opera. Unusual, but not impossible.

Plünderung der Iudengassen zu Franckfurt am Main den 22 Augustj 1614. Nach Mittag umb 8 uhr von den Handtwerck gesellen angefangen, und die gantze Nacht durch Continuirt, da dan ein Bürger und 2 Iuden gar todt blieben, viel aber beiderseits beschedigt worden, biß ihn entlich / als sie biß in die helfft der gassen komen / von der Bürgerschafft gentzlich abge= wehrt worden.

A contemporary engraving of the chaos of the Fettmilch Uprising and Pogrom in 1614 (Institut für Stadtgeschichte Frankfurt)

8 | Changing Faces
Faith, Persecution, Immigration

A History of Tolerance and Hatred

For a city today reputed to worship only Mammon, religion has played so great a role in the history and development of Frankfurt that it sometimes seems as if at certain times little else of interest was happening. Founded by a monarch who drew his legitimacy directly from Rome and then the seat of the Holy Roman Emperors, Frankfurt was one of the key strongholds of the Church in the Middle Ages. Yet its worldly preoccupations also made it fertile ground for the Reformation and the ensuing separation of Church and state—and indeed allowed it quickly to find a form of coexistence between the two branches of Christianity as practicalities took pride of place before ideologies. This pragmatism also explains how the city, despite regularly recurrent anti-Semitism, managed to attract and keep Germany's most prominent Jewish community and how, despite restrictions on smaller Christian denominations, it became a popular refuge for persecuted Reformists and Calvinists from across the continent.

Yet all of Frankfurt's history of putting pecuniary and practical concerns ahead of religious feeling was not enough to immunize it against the cancerous intolerance of Nazi ideology: Frankfurt dispossessed, dehumanized and deported its Jews just like every other German city and destroyed in the process a community which had made the city what it had become. The Holocaust left Frankfurt with a hole in its identity more gaping than almost any other part of Germany—one that is still noticeable at every turn. Perhaps it was in part the experience of this deep wound that led the post-war city to become the welcoming and proudly international place it is today: from the arrival of the first "guest workers" onwards, post-war Frankfurt has seen more—and more variations of—immigration than almost any other part of Germany. Today, over forty per cent of Frankfurt's inhabitants are either immigrants or the children of immigrants, with people of 173 various nationalities calling the city home. In a way, this is a return to what Frankfurt has always been: the city, after all, owes its very existence to a migrant.

The First Millennium: From the Capital of Christendom to Religious Plurality

If not a migrant in the traditional sense, Charlemagne was certainly peripatetic. Little is known about his early years, although he is assumed to have been born somewhere between Liège in modern-day Belgium and his later Imperial capital Aachen. He spent much of his life, however, "migrating" through Europe and adding territories to his empire, a rapaciousness he legitimized by becoming the protector of the papacy. Indeed, by modern standards, the history of Frankfurt—first mentioned in the chronicles due to Charlemagne spending Christmas 793 AD and holding the Church synod the following year there—begins under a religious fanatic. For it is difficult to apply any other term to a man who put those who refused to convert to Christian teachings to the sword: his subjugation of Saxony was brutal, culminating in the massacre of 4,500 captive pagans at Verden on the Aller river in 782; in 797 his Frankish forces occupied Barcelona and fought their way down through Catalonia against the Moors, beginning the centuries of the *Reconquista* supported by religious authority.

Given this background, it goes without saying that early Frankfurt was a very Christian place indeed. The original Carolingian palace, presumed to have been built on the orders of Charlemagne's son, Louis the Pious, was complemented by a large chapel just to the west of where today's cathedral stands on Domhügel; the rest of the settlement would have been entirely dwarfed by this house of God, and certainly several of the early events recorded in Frankfurt's history are of a religious nature. At Christmas 941, for example, Otto the Great is said to have forgiven his wayward brother Henry I, Duke of Bavaria, for planning to assassinate him, celebrating their reconciliation with a fair which would go on to become today's Christmas Market (see page 163); in 1007 Henry's son, Henry II, founded the Bishopric of Bamberg in the city in order to continue campaigns against the unconverted Slavs to the east. In 1146 the first Hohenstaufen king, Conrad III, heard the fanatic Bernhard of Clairvaux preach the Second Crusade at Speyer and immediately whisked the clerical firebrand off with him to Frankfurt, where he whipped up the assembled crowd into a frenzy while Conrad had his son Henry Berengar elected as his successor in the event of his death in the Holy Land. Conrad's religious fervour is thus to thank for the precedent of electing rulers in Frankfurt—and for the city's oldest surviving building, the Saalhofkapelle, which he had built along with a new palace directly on the Main.

While the old palace on Domhügel had fallen into disrepair, the church on the site of today's cathedral had remained in continuous use. Louis the German, son of Louis the Pious, had made Frankfurt his residence in the 850s and endowed the city with the land on which to build a place of worship for the townspeople. This Salvatorkirche was financed by Frankfurters (to what extent they donated willingly is, of course, unrecorded) and is said to have been a magnificent building; a testament to its importance is that its provost was nominated either by the powerful Archbishop of Mainz or, on occasion, directly from Rome.

The abeyance of the city as a place of residence until Conrad III led to a form of stasis, however, and it was not until the early 1200s that a population sufficient to require a second church had accumulated. In 1219 Frederick II, son of the formidable Barbarossa, gifted the city the land on which today's Leonhardskirche stands for a small chapel as part of the first town charter. Meanwhile, the powerful bishop of nearby Münzenberg, Kuno I, had founded a hospice and chapel in Sachsenhausen in the late 1190s in which he blessed the Teutonic Knights on their way to subdue the pagan East with the sword; the religious order inherited the land on his death in 1207. With the city's rapidly growing importance in the Holy Roman Empire, Church interest in Frankfurt increased and the rate at which new ecclesiastical institutions were set up accelerated: in 1223 city land was donated to the Cistercian monastery of Arnsberg to the north of Frankfurt, also founded by Kunos I, and records show that in 1228 monks of the order who had immigrated to the city were considered Frankfurt citizens. In this same year, the Emperor's son Henry settled an order of nuns in the city, too, and historians assume that the medieval city's two most important charitable institutions date from the 1220s: Heiliggeistspital (the Hospice of the Holy Ghost), a poorhouse and hospital for Frankfurt's populace, and the Gutleuthof, a leper sanctuary (and set up in the eponymous Gutleutviertel, then outside the city). Throughout this period, the Salvatorkirche was being rebuilt to a larger plan and was re-consecrated in 1239 as the Bartholomäuskirche (Church of St. Bartholomew).

There is considerable evidence that the city was unhappy at the speed with which religious orders were securing themselves chunks of land and erecting pompous new buildings: newly empowered by their town charter, officials made countless attempts to negotiate about precisely which parcels of land the Church would be given, and generally had to be overruled by Imperial decree. For while the Church's presence relieved the city of many social responsibilities such as poor relief, it also took land and resources out of the tax base. Indeed, growing dissatisfaction in the city may well have been the motive behind Henry VII granting Frankfurt increasing rights—and revenues from the royal mint—in the 1230s.

Yet it was not just the presence of a powerful Christian Church backed up by the Holy Roman Emperor that was unpopular: Frankfurt had had a Jewish population from its earliest years, and this population had long benefited from special Imperial protection. This community is first recorded, along with those of other cities in the region such as Worms, in 1074 in a dispensation from paying tolls authorized by Emperor Henry IV. At this time Jewish people actually within the city numbered handfuls; the Rabbi of Mainz wrote in the early 1100s that Frankfurt had no notable Jewish community. Jews probably lived spread across the surrounding area: they are referred to collectively as the "Jews of Wetterau" in the 1241 tax register of Conrad IV, a sort of Domesday Book for the Holy Roman Empire at that moment.

Yet by this very year, at least 150 Jews must have been living in Frankfurt itself, because between 159 and 173 Frankfurt Jews were killed in the city's first pogrom in the night of 29 to 30 May (not counting Jewish house servants, who are not recorded in any sources); around 25 of them are reported to have been spared death by converting to Christianity. Although the precise cause of the slaughter cannot be known, it is likely to have been the usual heady mixture of financial strain, external threats and religious fundamentalism that generally leads to the scapegoating and persecution of the Jews. What can be said for certain is that the Jewish population enjoyed enviable Imperial privileges of a substantial financial value and were, of course, due to Christian doctrine, the city's only legal moneylenders; furthermore, the approaching Mongol hordes of Genghis Kahn may well have served to make simple souls more suspicious of Semitic features than usual.

The Emperor—whose grandfather Frederick II had given all the Jews of the Holy Roman Empire Imperial protection in 1236, but secured their taxes for his own coffers—was furious and demanded damages from the city for his tax losses. Yet he was not so furious as to refuse to confirm the town charter in 1242; in fact, in 1246 he dropped his case altogether, persuaded that the pogrom had been a regrettable exception and that the city elders had not actively encouraged it, but rather been lax in their duty of care. This is an early show of the ambivalence of the Holy Roman Emperors towards "their Jews": Imperial protection for them was coupled to their utility as cash cows and was in practice often neglected or negotiated away. Nevertheless, from the 1250s onwards the Jewish community slowly returned to the city, and the presence of a new rabbi is recorded in 1288. The streets between what was now the Bartholomäuskirche and the river, Saalgasse and Fahrgasse, had a particular concentration of Jewish merchants, and a short golden age for the Jewish community began: for the last time until the 1800s, they had precisely the same rights and legal situation as other Frankfurters.

It was not to last: in 1349 King Charles of Bohemia, struggling for the title of Holy Roman Emperor, was looking to secure support from the Imperial cities, and Frankfurt drove a hard bargain: he pawned his rights to the substantial Jewish tax revenue in the city and charged the city fathers with protecting the Jews, but without holding them responsible for any harm that might come to them; worse still, the property of any Jews killed would automatically accrue to the city. The result was predictable: less than two weeks after he had left Frankfurt with its support that summer, the Jews were mercilessly slaughtered. The "rationale" that they had brought in the Black Death was retrospectively applied to the pogrom, but since the plague did not reach the city until that autumn, it can safely be assumed that purely financial motives were behind the barbarity. The fact that the Bartholomäuskirche swiftly expanded onto what had been Jewish property suggests that the Church was complicit in the violence.

Yet at the same moment, Frankfurt's city fathers found themselves increasingly in conflict with the Church. The 1300s saw another expansion of new ecclesiastical building: the Liebfrauenkirche and cloister (1318, 1325), the St. Catherine's hospice and cloister (1313, 1354), the Dreikönigskirche (Church of the Magi) to replace the old chapel of the Teutonic Knights in Sachsenhausen (1338), and the St. Peterskirche (1393). At the same time, the Golden Bull of 1356, which was a papal decree but more or less dictated by (the now newly crowned Emperor) Charles IV and the Imperial Diet, had weakened the Church's power; moreover, the nearby Archbishop of Mainz was in dire financial straits. In 1395, the time was ripe for the city to demand more tax contributions from the Church, to which the archbishop responded by placing an interdiction on the city; but this was swiftly lifted in 1398 following negotiations, and the system for taxing the Church was completely reordered in 1407. City procurators were sent into the check on Church accounts, and throughout the fifteenth century the city would take increasing control of clerical finances; by the time the Reformation came in the 1520s, secularizing Church property was simply a case of acknowledging the status quo.

Despite the butchery of 1349, by the 1360s Jews were once again returning to Frankfurt, yet under threat from growing anti-Semitism: new arrivals owed income tax to Emperor Charles IV and had to buy protection from the city through supplementary taxes; moreover, the Emperor ordered his personal representatives in the city to make sure that the Jews did not apply their own law and did not enter into competition with the tradesmen of the city. Soon a panoply of further Imperial and municipal rules were applied to Jewish settlement: Jews were forbidden by the city from employing Christian servants, for instance, while the successor to Charles IV, Wenceslaus IV, declared an amnesty on debts to Jews in 1390. A precise list of these regulations was eventually collated in 1424 under the *Judenstättigkeit*, a kind of constitution for the Jews which codified discrimination against them.

Yet anti-Jewish sentiment in the city continued to grow. Jews were considered fair game for insults or violence on the street: when one was murdered in 1446, the city scribe annotated his entry with three crosses and the words *Te deum laudamus*. King Frederick III, meanwhile, took umbrage at the proximity of the synagogue to the Bartholomäuskirche, now one of the Empire's key churches, and demanded that the Jewish place of worship be resettled elsewhere. In a chilling prelude to the Nazis' "Final Solution", in 1458, the city council met several times with the express aim of discussing how they could "be rid of the Jews", who had already been told by the Archbishop of Mainz to wear yellow bands on their arms. Despite the swagger of its pronouncements, however, the city did not actually want to be entirely devoid of Jews, who were by now paying most of their deductions directly to the city after it had bought the rights to Imperial tax collection in 1372: the proposition was to build a ghetto to the north east of the walls, which the city even did at its own expense (although the Jews had to stump up for their synagogue and baths). The gated street, Judengasse, would become the turbulent centre of Jewish life in Frankfurt for centuries to come.

Originally built to house one hundred people, the ghetto was soon overcrowded. As intolerant as Frankfurt's policy seems today, it was lax for its time, as the overall climate of anti-Semitism in Europe saw a wave of expulsions from other cities across the Empire: beginning in Trier in 1418, Jews were banned from Vienna, Cologne, Augsburg, Breslau and Magdeburg, with Nuremburg closing the century with an expulsion in 1499; Regensburg was the last major Imperial town to throw out its Jews in 1519. In this climate, a walled community (however unsanitary) with a constitution (however discriminatory) must have seemed promising. The effect of the Jewish immigration throughout the century was to concentrate their financial understanding in the city and establish it as a banking centre, with the correspondingly positive effects on the city treasury. As such, it is unsurprising that the city fathers allowed the ghetto to expand twice, once in 1552 and again in 1579. In 1585, the first Frankfurt Stock Exchange was founded.

In the 1500s attention had in any case turned away from the Jews as the Holy Roman Empire was split by the Reformation. The atmosphere in the city was tense: religion had become increasingly important in both private and public affairs throughout the 1400s, as both the surge in anti-Semitism and the volume of religious works commissioned from the likes of Dürer, Holbein and Grünewald testify. With its wealthy merchant class, Frankfurt was a particularly lucrative market for these artists, and a particularly fertile ground for Protestant anger at Church extravagance on taxpayers' expense. Despite the inroads Frankfurt's city council had made into clerical finances, the population as a whole welcomed the Reformation and it was all the government could do stop serious civil unrest in Frankfurt in the mid-1520s (see page 76). With its proximity to the events—the Diet of Worms, the Peasants' Revolt in southern Germany—the city was in a powder-keg, and left the authorities little choice but to make concessions to Reformationist demands: in 1526 Protestant preaching was officially permitted. Yet at the same time, it remained the city in which Catholic Holy Roman Emperors were made, and was dependent for its livelihood on their good-will: in 1529 it refused to sign the Speyer Protestation which defined the new eponymous Church. The result of this double game was that in the early 1530s the majority of the city's churches had turned *de facto* Lutheran, but the prestigious Bartholomäuskirche remained Catholic, a situation which was, simply put, fooling no-one. The city's populace, imbued with Lutheran righteousness, rioted three Christmases in a row, from 1530 to 1532, breaking into the Bartholomäuskirche and destroying Catholic icons and imagery, and the city government was forced in 1533 to face facts and declare the city Protestant. All Church property that had not already been donated to the city (such as the Monastery of the Discalced Friars, see page 37), was confiscated. Yet even in this act, however, the city fathers left themselves a path of retreat, forbidding Catholicism on a temporary basis for 15 years only. The city, now officially against the Restorationist Emperor, hesitantly joined the Protestant Schmalkadic League, whose armies it financed, but was quick to switch allegiance back to the Catholic empire when occupied by the almighty Emperor Charles V in 1547.

Yet despite the swings to and fro, the Reformation allowed the city to take permanent control of the vestiges of Church authority. The council now ran the charitable institutions and poor relief provided by the Heiliggeistspital and the various parish councils, and began to use the clerical infrastructure and funds to build up something approaching a welfare state. This development also meant that the city could take control of the religious transformation, imposing a particularly Lutheran form of Protestantism as a quasi-state religion. When the Peace of Augsburg of 1555 came—which provided for the existence of both Catholicism and Protestantism in the Holy Roman Empire, but required that the rulers of each constituent state opt for one or the other (*cuius region, eius religio*)—the transition in Frankfurt was so complete that it was out of the question for the city to return to Catholicism. Yet, given that the city had not permanently forbidden Catholic preaching, and in view of the importance of the Bartholomäuskirche, the Imperial city was subject to an exception in the peace treaty: in territories in which two religions had been exercised to date, the two would coexist. No further new confessions would be allowed, however.

The result of this balance of regulations, intended to cement the status quo and prevent future quarrels, was that for the coming centuries Frankfurt was an officially Protestant city of Lutheran confession, but one in which Catholic services were permitted. Catholics, however, were not allowed to become citizens, or to open up new congregations, and no new forms of Protestantism could be tolerated either. The effect was that the stream of Calvinist refugees coming in from the Low Countries and France, although arriving in a reformed city, could not exercise their religion freely.

Such was the bizarre mixture of tolerance and intolerance which marked Frankfurt's religious situation through until the end of the Holy Roman Empire: although by modern standards repressive, the city was in fact a safe haven for Calvinists who, facing the Inquisition in the Spanish Netherlands or burning at the stake by England's Bloody Mary, were little concerned about whether they would be able to apply for citizenship or build a new church on city property. By the time the flow of refugees had stopped in the late 1500s, the city's population had increased by between ten and twenty per cent, leading to a strain on resources, while banking and trade were booming with the influx of wealthy Flemish families fleeing persecution. This rapid growth produced an increasingly unequal distribution of income, and once again, the mixture of financial strain and religious fanaticism had its predictable effect: rather than turning on the newly-arrived Calvinist immigrants, in 1614, the populace burned down the Jewish ghetto and threw the Jews out of the city in the Fettmilch Uprising (see Chapters 4 and 11).

By this stage, the Frankfurt ghetto had become one of the centres of Jewish life in the empire. The Judengasse now counted 2,700 inhabitants, housed a Talmudic academy and hosted an empire-wide conference of head rabbis in 1603. This gathering, however, was deemed to be a conspiracy and broken up on the order of Emperor Rudolph II, who then sued the Jews of the empire as a whole in a case lasting 25 years. During this period, the customary Imperial protection for the Jews seemed weaker than ever, and this was no doubt a contributing factor in the Fettmilch pogrom: Frankfurters were demanding a debt haircut and quite possibly expected the Emperor to declare an amnesty on Jewish debts as he had in 1390. They were, however, sorely mistaken: in contrast to his predecessors, the new Emperor Matthias took his duty of protection towards the Jewish community quite seriously, brutally putting down the civil unrest in Frankfurt and having the expelled Jews marched back into the city under Imperial guard in 1616. Times had changed:

Christian clergy in the city spoke in favour of the Jews and condemned the brutality of the mob.

Thus the characteristic mixture of tolerance and intolerance
remained. A new *Judenstättigkeit* was written, which although more
liberal in some respects—it now allowed the returning Jews to work
as wholesalers in competition to Christians, for example—limited
the number of households in the ghetto and the number of mar-
riages permitted among Jews. It goes almost without saying that
they paid higher taxes and could not become citizens. It would be
wrong, however, to assume that this sort of treatment was meted out
to only the Jews: peasants from the surrounding villages living in
the city, as well as apprentices and several other groups not eligible
for citizenry, were also subject to rules regarding personal conduct
and dress, marriage and family life, as well as specific tolls and taxes.
The mixture of acceptance and singling-out also affected the new
Christian arrivals: Calvinists such as Theodor de Bry (1528-1598)
for example, an engraver from Liège who fled to Frankfurt in the
1570s, often set up outside the city where they were allowed to
practise their religion by princely dispensation. His grandson-in-
law, Matthäus Merian (1593-1650), from a Swiss Calvinist family,
would convert to Lutheranism so he could move the workshop into
Frankfurt—and became the city's most famous artist of the period
(see Chapter 6).

As the seventeenth century wore on, tolerance gained the
upper hand. The butchery of the Thirty Years' War, combined with
the memory of the Wars of Religion, served to show all but the
most fanatical that religious conflict was simply too dangerous a
genie to let out of the bottle. The city remained decidedly neutral
during the long war, and—remarkably in view of the general climate across Europe—there was not a single witch trial in Frankfurt.
In this increasingly relaxed religious and intellectual atmosphere,
Philipp Jakob Spener (1635-1705), a Strasbourg theologian who
preached in the city from 1666 to 1686, felt able to write two books
criticizing the state of the Lutheran Church, essentially founding
Pietism. While he himself did not advocate anything as radical
as forming a new confession, his followers, calling themselves the

Saalhof-Pietisten, increasingly distanced themselves from Lutheranism, founding a company to purchase land in America, to where they planned to emigrate and set up a new denomination. As they did not openly call the established Church in Frankfurt into question, the city allowed them to collect donations, and it was perhaps this undogmatic attitude that led the congregation to finally cancel their travel plans. Instead, they passed their money on to thirteen Quaker families from Krefeld on the Rhine, who left for the New World and founded Germantown, today a suburb of Philadelphia.

The Huguenots fleeing France following the revocation of the Edict of Nantes in 1685 therefore arrived in a far more liberal religious atmosphere than their Flemish and Dutch predecessors a century beforehand. Around 70,000 of them passed through the city on their flight from religious persecution between 1685 and 1695 alone, yet most moved on—both Calvinist and French church services remained forbidden, while other parts of Germany, as well as the Netherlands and Britain, were more welcoming in their approach: many went on into Prussia, where they became a key part of the growing capital, Berlin. Yet it was not only Frankfurt's government, but its people whose tolerance was stretched: once again an influx of refugees, coupled with high rates of economic growth and price rises, were leading to discontent among tradesmen and workers; and once again, the Jews were a promising scapegoat. Due to the cramped nature of the ghetto, some Jewish traders had been given leave by the city to acquire business premises outside the Judengasse: a group of angry Christian competitors petitioned Emperor Joseph I to make the city rescind these permits. When the city did not, and when the Emperor took the side of the city authorities and the Jewish merchants, the citizens sued for their charter and the repressive arrangements for Jews (the *Judenstättigkeit* of 1616) to be upheld. The argument dragged on for another thirty years (see page 84), during which time the ghetto burned down twice, in 1711 and again in 1721. While neither case seems to have been arson—the close quarters, overpopulation and entirely wooden construction of its houses made the ghetto into a veritable tinderbox—looters and plunderers were quick to take advantage of the situation, especially following the second fire: the Emperor, Charles VI, had to remind the city authorities to protect the Jewish community, most of whose members were now dispersed across the city and living for extortionate rents in Christian houses. Although rebuilding for the second time in ten years was a financial strain almost beyond the resources of the now decreasing Jewish population, the city authorities once again forced Jewish families back into the ghetto by decree in 1729.

The pattern of previous centuries repeated itself in another way, however: the city authorities, aware of the importance of Jewish financial expertise, once again adopted laxer regulations and applied restrictions selectively. It was at this time that the first of the modern banking dynasties began to develop: Mayer Amschel Rothschild (1744-1812), named after the Judengasse house of his ancestors (*Zum roten Schild*—"at the red sign"), was born in the ghetto and was, by the end of the century, the official Court Factor—essentially the financial advisor—to the Prince of Hesse. Jewish families in finance from elsewhere in Germany, such as the Oppenheimers of Hanover, bought homes in the Judengasse too. Indeed, the rapid climb of the likes of Rothschild led to tensions within the ghetto, which had become divided between the haves and the have-nots, forced to live so close to one another.

For even as other German cities were loosening legislation relating to Jews, Frankfurt's government remained—perhaps out of fear of renewed social tension—intransigent: Jews were not allowed to leave the ghetto on Sundays, and Enlightenment works promoting religious tolerance such as Lessing's *Nathan the Wise* were banned. Indeed, it would take the third destruction of the ghetto within a century for the city to finally lift restrictions on Jewish settlement. When the French Revolutionary forces fired on Frankfurt in the summer of 1796, the northern half of the street burned to the ground. For several years, the city was more concerned with defending itself and trying to preserve its position within the crumbling European order than with regulating the particulars of Jewish life. When in 1806 the city was integrated into the Confederation of the Rhine and the enlightened dictatorship of Karl von Dalberg began, one of his first actions was to lift restrictions on citizenship: members of all religions could now become citizens of Frankfurt, and in 1811 he abolished the obligation for Jews to live in the ghetto. Although it was rebuilt and remained a centre of Jewish life in the city, the Judengasse was no longer a prison.

The Tolerant Nineteenth Century, and Hateful Twentieth Century

Although short, Dalberg's reign as an enlightened despot, terminated early by the defeat of Napoleon and the restoration of Frankfurt as a Free City in 1815, had a lasting effect on the various religious and immigrant communities present in Frankfurt. During the death throes of the Holy Roman Empire in 1803, the city had gained all of the property which had been returned to the Catholic Church following the Peace of Augsburg. Dalberg institutionalized this in a French secularism in which the state guaranteed the religious freedom of all denominations from 1811 onwards. By early 1812 almost 650 Jews had secured rights as citizens (but only following a one-off collective payment of 440,000 Guilders); they were soon followed by Catholics, Calvinists and members of other minority denominations.

While the restoration of the old order brought a temporary regress in these citizen's rights—Jews and Catholics were once again disenfranchised in 1815—the winds of change had already blown away the dust in the city. Restrictions on settlement were not reintroduced, for example, and the new government moved of its own accord back towards a secular model, reinstating Jewish rights in two waves in 1824 and 1853. Meanwhile, the *Dotationsvertrag* of 1830 was signed between the eight churches on city territory and the council, finally formalizing the role of the city as the owner of ecclesiastical property but also obliging it to pay for the upkeep of the churches and to take on their personnel as civil servants: this contract, unique in Germany, has remained in force to this day.

In the first decades of the nineteenth century, with the end of the ghetto restrictions, the Jewish community began to develop from a single entity into a range of groups divided according to income and beliefs. The emancipation of the Jews was a development following on from the Enlightenment, and Enlightenment philosophy had not passed Jewish intellectuals by: Berlin's Moses Mendelssohn (1729-86) has come to represent a new willingness among Germany's Jews to consider less orthodox ways of life, and the tensions created in the Jewish community by secular ideas led to a split in Frankfurt in 1851. Thenceforth, the synagogue housed both an orthodox and a reformed congregation: the former was generally poorer and less educated, and remained in the Judengasse, which quickly became one of the most run-down and unsanitary areas of the city as the financial families moved away: the Rothschilds, for example, moved to a new address on Neue Mainzer Straße in 1818 (the street remains at the centre of the banking industry to this day), leaving only Gutele Rotschild (1753-1849), widow of the dynasty's founder Mayer Amschel, in the old house, which she refused to leave until her death. It was one of the few remaining old houses which was not torn down when the street, which had become both a form of olde-worlde tourist attraction of its day (see George Eliot on page 125) and a headache for the city's planning department, was rebuilt in the 1870s and 1880s.

The old synagogue had already been knocked down and rebuilt in the late 1850s, becoming the Hauptsynagoge, or Main Synagogue. With the reconstruction of the 1880s, the orthodox community acquired a new plot on the market square at the southern end of the street and opened their own synagogue, which became known as Börneplatzsynagoge when Judengasse and Judenmarkt were renamed Börnestraße and Börneplatz after Ludwig Börne (1786-1837), one of Germany's leading literary intellectuals in the first half of the nineteenth century, and himself issued from the ghetto (see Chapter 5).

Like his contemporary Heinrich Heine (1797-1856), Börne was a reformed Jew with radical democratic politics who fled Germany for France during the political repressions following the end of the Napoleonic interlude. That his name was applied to the street in 1885 shows both to what extent the city and the new Prussian overlords had become accepting of political dissent and how the

Jewish community had become a part of the city like any other: the idea that a street should be reserved and named for Jews seemed then—more than sixty years following the end of the ghetto—somehow wrong. Yet just over sixty years later, the city would be deporting its Jewish community to their deaths.

For all its political authoritarianism, the spirit of Wilhelmine Germany was relaxed in religious matters. The general feeling in Germany's Jewish population was of finally being accepted: on the completion of the new synagogue in Frankfurt's neighbouring city Offenbach in 1916, the rabbi urged his congregation to integrate as much as possible into German society, famously saying that the Jews in Germany had finally found their "place in the sun". As odd as it seems in hindsight, at that very moment, Jewish soldiers were fighting on the Western and Eastern Fronts in the First World War alongside their gentile comrades in arms: how could anyone foresee what was to come?

It is from this "time in the sun" that the Westend-Synagoge dates, the only Jewish place of worship in Frankfurt to survive both the Nazi persecution and the Allied bombs. The imposing structure, built in the popular *Jugendstil* of the time with Oriental details reminiscent of Egyptian or Assyrian architecture, housed a liberal, reformed congregation with considerable social and financial capital, as its location just to the north of the city's banking quarter demonstrates.

The story of one man born in Westend not far from the new synagogue shows how unexpected the persecution of the Jews was in Germany and how stubbornly the survivors fought to anchor the memory of what happened in the minds of post-war society: Otto Frank (1889-1980). For the first forty years of his life, Otto Frank was a German and a Frankfurter like many others: after graduating from grammar school in 1908, he worked in business and served in the military during the First World War, demobilized at the rank of officer and decorated with an Iron Cross. After the war he continued his career through the volatile 1920s, starting a family with his wife Edith, like him from a reformed Jewish family: their two children were named Margot and Anne.

Frank left Frankfurt soon after the Nazi seizure of power in 1933, the year of the high-water mark of the Jewish community in the city, which numbered roughly 28,000 people and was Germany's second largest. Like many others, he feared that Hitler was not simply a big-mouth who would be tempered by power and responsibility, but a diabolical dictator who would persecute the Jews in precisely that way he had described in his writings and speeches. Yet Frank and those who left were by no means in the great majority: many in the city felt that Jewish integration into German society could surely not be undone by one man, that surely Nazism was so outlandish and so out of touch with reality that it would prove to be a short-lived phenomenon. While emigration rates went up and remained high throughout the 1930s, the Jewish community in Frankfurt still counted around 12,000 at the beginning of the "Final Solution": the half of Frankfurt's Jewish population who remained in the city in 1940 had resisted the violent removal of Jews from public service and prominent positions in 1933 and 1934, the enactment of the Nuremberg laws from 1935 onwards, as well as the *Kristallnacht* pogrom ("The Night of Shattered Glass") and the first deportations of Jews with Polish passports in autumn 1938. Those who did not leave were a mixture of those who believed that things would take a turn for the better, those who did not have the means to leave and start afresh and those who were simply stubborn and refused to be thrown out of their city.

Over 10,000 Jewish inhabitants were deported over the course of eleven months between October 1941 and September 1942 to concentration camps in the east, and several hundred of the roughly 1,000 Jews remaining in the city were forcibly removed in smaller sweeps up until last weeks of Nazi rule in March 1945. (The precise details of how Frankfurt's Jewish community was destroyed are a matter for Chapter 11 of this book): by 1945, 11,000 of the them had been murdered in extermination camps; 400 Frankfurt Jews were liberated from their hellish prisons alive, and in the city itself 160 members of the Jewish community had somehow survived both National Socialist genocide and the war in the air.

Among the 11,000 Frankfurt Jews who died in the camps were Otto Frank's wife and two daughters, who had been captured in their Amsterdam attic hide-out. Otto Frank himself returned to the Netherlands after liberation, where he published his daughter's diaries, moving to Basel in 1953, where he would dedicate the rest of his life to the charitable organization he set up for her. Many of the Frankfurt Jews who had left the city before the Nazi extermination campaigns were able to escape the long arm of the Gestapo, moving from country to country until they had found asylum either in neutral countries such as Switzerland or had managed to establish themselves further afield: Siegfried Kracauer (see Chapters 5 and 6), for example, lived out his days in New York. Yet there is a horrible irony in the fact that Frankfurters fled up the Rhine to Basel or down it into the Netherlands: in previous centuries, persecuted minorities such as the Calvinists and the Huguenots had been travelling in the opposite direction.

During the Nazi years even the city's established Lutheran churches came to feel the weight of persecution. Despite the shameful (if cautious) welcome accorded to the National Socialist seizure of power by the city's Protestant diocese—the conservative congregation at Paulskirche was especially sympathetic to nationalist and reactionary sentiments—the new regime was suspicious of Christianity, and its distrust was only strengthened by a breakaway group of priests, many of who went on to join the *Bekennende Kirche* ("Confessing Church") movement of anti-Nazi clergy and congregations: in the autumn of 1934 some 12,000 Frankfurt Christians came to services denouncing racism and despotism. Yet this stance led to tensions within the denomination, and in 1939, afraid of the consequences of a new split, the protest group was officially disbanded and its clergy returned to the conservative fold.

The Catholic Church, too, was split by the Nazi ascent. Since the advent of Protestant Prussia in the 1860s, Catholicism had, in contrast to its role in countries such as Spain or Italy, not been close to the old establishment. As such, the tradition of left-leaning, socialist, anti-authoritarian Catholic teaching which had developed in the Rhine and Main regions made this denomination particularly suspect to Nazi officials, who—despite their contempt for any religion except their own fanaticism—saw the ascetic forbearance and glory in nationalism preached by the Protestant Church as more useful to their cause. Action against Catholics following the seizure of power was thus immediate: newspapers with Catholic leanings were shut down and Catholic clergy harassed in their community work. Aloys Eckert, head of the St. Bernard Church in Nordend, was a particularly fervent critic of Nazi oppression, demanding several times from his bishop at Limburg a clear positioning of the Catholic Church in Germany against the persecution of the Jews (eventually, Pope Pius XI published a veiled and weak encyclical against Nazi ideology), an outspokenness which earned him arrest and imprisonment.

Yet these acts of individual resistance were in vain: there was a renewed Nazi crackdown in 1938 and 1939 which outlawed Catholic workers' and youth groups and pushed community organization into illicit secrecy. And above all, the vast majority of Frankfurters who were, on paper at least, Christian, stood by as those of other religions and belonging to minorities were deported and murdered; many who were in the churches at Easter and Christmas must have themselves been party members. At the end of the Nazi period, churches not just in Frankfurt but all over Germany were faced with an uncomfortable dilemma: they could either continue to claim to speak for society as a whole and accept complicity in the industrialized genocide of the Nazi years, or they could claim to have been one of the persecuted minorities, thus accepting their marginalized status. It is a quandary that remains unresolved to this day.

The Present Day: a Global City and a City of the Globe

Seen from the darkness of the Nazi years, Frankfurt's development into Germany's most multicultural, most international city seems highly improbable: yet the successes cannot be denied. With over 200,000 inhabitants who were born in 173 various countries outside Germany, the city's population is one third foreign-born; a further 100,000 are first-generation Frankfurters whose parents have come from abroad. While Germany as a whole has attracted several waves of immigration since the end of the Second World War, no city in the country can compete with the sheer variety of migrants which Frankfurt enjoys: Berlin and the cities of the Rhine and Ruhr have their large Turkish communities, while Munich has historically attracted Italian immigration and the northern port city of Hamburg is home to some of the country's small but vibrant African communities. But Frankfurt has welcomed all of these cultures—and more.

The melting-pot atmosphere of the city comes from the fact that its migrants have arrived in the city from various places for various reasons. The industrial Ruhr cities primarily attracted labourers from southern Europe and Turkey, and while many such *Gastarbeiter* also came to work in the chemicals and metals industry in the Main region in the post-war period, the airport, the financial sector and the American military presence provided three further reliable motors of immigration into the area. Japanese bankers, Saudi Arabian stewardesses, Afro-American GIs: many have ended up settling in Frankfurt despite initially being posted to the city for only days, weeks or months at a time. Frankfurt today houses communities that are simply not found elsewhere in Germany: the city and the surrounding region have one of the only notable concentrations of Indians and Pakistanis in the country (and what is for Germany a very strong cricketing tradition). Today, Frankfurt counts around 30,000 Turks, 13,000 Italians and over 10,000 Croatians and Poles. The fifth largest foreign-born group is made up of the city's 9,000 Serbians, followed by Greeks, Moroccans and Bosnians, all of whom number around 5,000. Then there are the Spanish and Romanian communities, who round off the top ten. Bulgarians and French number around 4,000 each, followed by Portuguese, Indian, American, and Japanese inhabitants (each in the 2,000s). There are 2,600 British people in Frankfurt (seventeenth place), along with sizeable Austrian, Russian and Chinese populations.

This multiculturalism makes itself felt in the broad range of religions which have premises in or near the city: the only Bahá'í house of worship in Europe is located in Langenhain just outside

Frankfurt, while the city itself is home to one of only two Hindu temples in Germany and has a Sikh cultural centre (most of the city's Sikhs are Afghan refugees from the 1980s and newer arrivals following the turmoil of the last decade). Meanwhile, the city was the third in Germany in which a mosque was built: the Nuur Mosque in Sachsenhausen, opened in 1959; today, all the major Islamic confessions have places of worship in the city. In 1955 the German Buddhist Union was founded in Frankfurt, and today there are various Buddhist places of worship for Korean, Thai, Chinese and several other groups such as the Vietnamese and Tibetan Buddhists.

The range of Christian denominations is bewildering: beyond the Lutheran Protestant and Catholic churches which held a monopoly on Christian preaching until secularization, the city has gathered an array of other churches over the last two centuries. Anglicans were present from early on due to Frankfurt's trading relationship with Britain, and today's community is primarily composed of Anglican American military families who were in the city after 1945. The post-war American presence also brought congregations of Adventists and Baptists, who found small but lively communities of Mennonites and Methodists already present. The years following the war also saw immigration from Christians at odds with the communist regimes in Eastern Europe, with Russian and Serbian orthodox churches springing up along with several Greek and Syrian orthodox congregations. Various denominations of Coptic Christians are also present, primarily from Egypt and Ethiopia, as was the Armenian Church. The Christian offering in the city is rounded off by evangelical groups such as the Mormons, who built their first temple in Germany here in 1981, and the Jehovah's Witnesses, who value the city's central location in Europe as a base for their bell-ringing operations.

Perhaps the most surprising religious grouping of all present in Frankfurt is the Jewish community, which now numbers roughly 7,000. In May 1945 the city authorities sent buses to Theresienstadt to bring home the 300 or so Jewish survivors there who wanted to return, and their rabbi Leopold Neuhaus (1879-1954) immediately went about setting up a provisional synagogue in a Jewish kinder-garten confiscated with all other Jewish property in the late 1930s. In September 1950 the surviving yet desecrated Westend-Synagoge was returned to its original purpose, its restoration financed by the new Hesse state government, but Rabbi Neuhaus had already emi-grated to the United States by this stage, and the general feeling was the Jewish life in Germany was all but over. The synagogue, and the *Zentralrat der Juden in Deutschland*—the Central Council of Jews in Germany, founded in 1950—saw their *raison d'être* as being to help Jews in Germany emigrate, expecting to close their organiza-tion once the last member of a Jewish congregation had left for Israel or America.

As history's ironies would have it, however, the years imme-diately following the Second World War actually saw Jewish immigration into Germany increase as communist governments in Eastern Europe proved to share the Nazi's taste for totalitarianism and anti-Semitism: the community grew rapidly to several thou-sand, numbering 4,500 by 1989. One of those fleeing was Ignatz Bubis (1927-99), who, after going to West Berlin in 1949, settled in Frankfurt in 1956, becoming head of the city's Jewish community in 1966 and head of the *Zentralrat* in 1992 until his death. Bubis, whose high-value property investment deals were deeply unpopular in the city during the left-wing 1970s and led to several contro-versial public discussions (see page 208), became something of a German national treasure during his final years, stridently speaking out for tolerance of all faiths and races at every opportunity: what used to be the Obermainbrücke bridge now carries his name.

Bubis was an important figure because he broke with the pre-vailing assumption—both among many in the Jewish community and among many Germans either of an unthinking or latently anti-Semitic bent—that Jews in Germany could only have one goal: to move to Israel. Bubis repeatedly stressed that he was German and would remain in Germany at a time when the Jewish commu-nity was growing exponentially: the fall of communism had led to waves of Jewish immigrants after the Federal German Republic had announced it would give them citizenship on a no-questions-asked basis. Between 1989 and 2009 the number of Jews in Frankfurt almost doubled to over 7,000, making it Germany's third largest community after Berlin and Munich, and the city's vibrant economy now even attracts emigration from Israel. In complete contrast to previous eras, the city today pays to keep the Jewish community's infrastructure running, subsidizing synagogues, educational institutions and measures to integrate the new arrivals from the former communist East.

Today Frankfurt is without a doubt Germany's most tolerant city. Much of this is probably down to a mix of the same blasé attitude which can be observed in other heavily international cities and the generally worldly orientation of German and European society in general: church attendance is at an all-time low, replaced by atheism, agnosticism and a range of vaguely Buddhist convictions about karma and pacifism; Frankfurt's population is too busy earning money to need to scapegoat immigrants who contribute so much to the city. The worrying outbursts of violence against asylum seekers and migrants in the 1990s were limited to the country's rustbelt regions, and although the right-wing politician Roland Koch was able to win the 1999 election for Hesse's State Parliament on the back of a thinly-veiled campaign of xenophobia purportedly against allowing dual nationality, his support was weaker in Frankfurt than in the surrounding countryside.

If it were needed, however, the ultimate proof of Frankfurt's tolerance at the time of writing is the utter failure of the xenophobic PEGIDA movement (*Patriotische Europäer gegen die Islamisierung des Abendlandes*—"Patriotic Europeans against the Islamization of the Occident") to gain traction in the city at all: this loose alliance of neo-Nazis, Europhobes and assorted misfits started in Dresden in late 2014 and then spread to other cities, leading a sizeable proportion of the German political class to discredit itself in attempts to show understanding for its mixture of resentment and slander. Yet attempts to set up a large-scale PEGIDA demonstration in Frankfurt failed miserably as hundreds of protesters for tolerance and respect hammered on the panes of the hotel restaurant in which the fourteen would-be populists were trying to hold their inaugural meeting.

The departures hall at Terminal 1 of Frankfurt Airport, Germany's largest (Rainer Ebert/Wikimedia Commons)

9 | Internationalism
A Modern-day Babel

rankfurt has always been a place of international importance. The clue is in the name as much as anything else: the city was founded by the Franks, a Germanic tribe who went on to create France and turn the Latin dialects spoken there into French. Frankfurt, in turn, went on to become the cultural centre of the German lands, then bound together as the Holy Roman Empire, a would-be successor to the world's most cosmopolitan state to date. Frankfurt has always resounded to the sounds of Latin liturgies, German dialects and languages spoken all over Europe. As such, its post-Cold-War reinvention as Europe's financial capital is only the latest chapter in its history at the centre of the continent.

Frankfurt today is also one of the most central places in the world. Its airport is the eleventh busiest on the planet and, after London Heathrow and Paris Charles de Gaulle, Europe's third. Annually, over three million passengers depart from Frankfurt Airport for the United States; 1.6 million leave for Spain, 1.5 for Italy and 1.3 for the United Kingdom. Just under one million fly annually to Turkey, France and Austria, while 800,000 depart for China. With almost 270 destinations in 113 countries at the last count, Frankfurt can boast the largest number of international routes of any airport in the world.

The importance of the airport to the city is almost impossible to underestimate: oversized in comparison to the population of the city and the surrounding urban region, it is Frankfurt's largest employer, is home to Germany's flagship airline Lufthansa and—as the busiest cargo airport in Europe—plays a crucial role in the country's booming export economy. The airport even plays a cultural role: while New York JFK and London Heathrow are unloved and preferably avoided, Frankfurt airport is more closely integrated into the city, and even featured a legendary (and legendarily louche) night-club named the Dorian Grey, located under Terminal 1, from

1978 to 2000. On Sundays, the airport's supermarkets and shops are full—not just with employees and passengers, but with Frankfurters who did not get round to doing the weekly shop before close of business on Saturday. Germany still has strict Sunday closing, with exceptions for transport hubs and petrol stations, and the airport marts are especially valued by the city's English-speaking population, many of whom struggle for years to get used to the antiquated German opening hours—or simply to get out of the office in time. Despite its somewhat unprepossessing physical characteristics typical of a major international transit centres, Frankfurt Airport has even made it onto German stamps, cementing its importance to the country as a whole. Although officially referred to as Flughafen Frankfurt am Main or Rhein-Main-Flughafen, it brands itself as "Frankfurt Airport" and is referred to by almost everyone in in the city, regardless of their native tongue, simply as "airport".

Frankfurters do not have to travel far to hear a foreign language. In the ten years since 2005 the number of hotel stays in Frankfurt has doubled; already Germany's only Alpha-category global city, it was also the only one in Germany to make it onto the *New York Times* list of "52 Places You Have to See in 2014". The city has the largest number of foreign students in Germany, too, and a full third of its total population was born outside Germany (see page 192). At peak times such as the Book Fair and the Frankfurt Motor Show (the world's largest automotive trade fair), the city's native language seems to become English, as every shop assistant, restaurant waiter and taxi-driver in town switches into the worldwide lingua-franca.

The railway station, too, is an international hub. With around 350 trains daily arriving around the clock, it is perhaps the one part of the city that genuinely never sleeps: the first of five direct trains for Paris leaves just before 6am; half an hour later the first service of the day to Brussels departs. Other international destinations reachable by rail without a change of trains include Basel and Zürich, Vienna, Amsterdam and—perhaps most exotically—Marseille. With one or two changes of trains, passengers can leave Frankfurt Hauptbahnhof for places as far flung as Madrid, Budapest and Stockholm. On the roads the city is also an international centre: with over 320,000 vehicles passing daily, the Frankfurter Kreuz motorway interchange between the autobahns 3 and 5 near the airport is the busiest in Europe, and one of the continent's only stretches of ten-lane highway.

In world affairs, Frankfurt's importance is such that the German Reuters news agency offices are located there, as are those of Bloomberg, the financial network. International companies, too, are clustered in and around Frankfurt—especially in the suburb of Eschborn, not officially a part of the city and attractive due to its lower rate of corporation tax, Ernst & Young being the most prominent of the legitimate tax avoiders. Vodafone and Randstad both run their German operations from Eschborn, while the city proper hosts the country headquarters for a range of internationals: big-name advertising firms such as McCann-Erickson, Saatchi & Saatchi and Publicis jostle for space with the top three worldwide credit rating agencies (Standard & Poor's, Moody's, Fitch) and accounting firms such as PricewaterhouseCoopers (who created this compound-noun name even *before* moving into Germany) and KPMG, who run their European operations out of the trendily-monikered "The Squaire" office precinct near the airport. Frankfurt also has Germany's highest concentration of lawyers (one per one hundred inhabitants), thanks to a range of country or city offices for magic-circle and lesser legal firms, as well as the German headquarters of the world's largest food company, Nestlé, and indeed Ferrero, who cater to the German love of chocolate-hazelnut paste from Frankfurt.

While Berlin's former mayor, Klaus Wowereit, made waves worldwide with his comment that Berlin was "*arm, aber sexy*"—"poor, but sexy"—Frankfurters have long been chuckling to themselves that their city is "*reich* und *sexy*"—"rich *and* sexy". Although there may be room for disagreement on how precisely to define the word "sexy", there is no denying the city's supreme attractiveness for both investors and ambitious workers across the planet.

Frankfurt Stock Exchange in the *Alte Börse* building of the 1840s
(Wikimedia Commons)

10 | Consuming Interests
Banks, Finance and Counter-culture

Frankfurt has always been a city in which consumption has trumped production. Except for the brief industrial period during the late nineteenth and first half of the twentieth centuries, the businesses that have held sway have always been those related to the selling of goods and the financing of production, not to production itself. Yet for all the city's dependence on finance today, it retains a strong left-wing, proletarian, anti-capitalist counter-culture: much like London or New York, Frankfurt is in a love-hate relationship with its role in the world of money.

A Brief History of Banking and the Stock Exchange

With its central location on trade routes and early royal dispensations, Frankfurt grew as a market town to which goods were brought and exchanged. This role as a trading centre in turn required an elementary banking structure: especially during the autumn and spring trade fairs, up to 200 different types of coinage from as far afield as England, Russia and Italy could be in circulation at any one time; indeed, the Holy Roman Empire alone was composed of more than a hundred states, each entitled to mint its own coins. To avoid a confusing profusion of currencies and denominations, in the twelfth century the city fixed three sorts of coin that could be used as legal tender during the Messe weeks: the earliest bankers in Frankfurt were in fact currency exchangers.

It was the importance to the Messe of having transparent rates of exchange between currencies that led to the early founding of the Frankfurt Exchange, which was set up in 1585 in order to fix rates for the autumn trade fair. In the same year Johann von Bodeck (1555-1631), an Antwerp trader, arrived in the city fleeing the Spanish occupation of the Low Countries (see page 78); Antwerp at the time had the most advanced stock market in Europe, and Bodeck was instrumental in extending the Frankfurt Exchange from a twice-yearly to a permanent institution. He also introduced the concept of a deposit bank, taking on money and lending it many times over, and used his international connections to dominate currency exchange between the major European trading centres of Amsterdam, Antwerp, Hamburg, Frankfurt and Venice. By the time of his death the exchange had blossomed and he personally had amassed an enormous fortune totalling over one million Guilders, making him Frankfurt's first genuine millionaire.

In this unleashing of creativity in the early 1600s, the first of the city's banks were founded: Johann Goll & Söhne, opened in 1602, is the oldest known, followed by D. & J. de Neufville (1634, bought up by Goll in 1721), whose Francophone name indicates the continued importance of immigration to the city's banking sector. As the seventeenth century turned into the eighteenth and European states started to professionalize tax collection and government finances, a new market for state loans developed aside from money required by traders, and a new wave of banks was set up: Schmid & Co. (1723), Willemer & Co. (1748) and Metzler seel. Sohn & Co. (1760, and the only one still in business today). The most important newcomer was, however, the Bethmann Bank, opened by the brothers Simon Moritz (1721-82) and Johann Philipp Bethmann (1715-93) to earn from the trade in textiles and paints in 1748, but which grew large on loans to the Imperial government at Vienna; in 1792 it became the first Frankfurt banking house to lend to Prussia, too. The real innovation for Frankfurt as a financial centre came when Bethmann brokered a 200,000 Guilder Austrian Imperial bond in 1779, putting it onto the market in 200 single fractions: dividing the debt into a series of small, equal shares allowed a broader set of potential investors to buy, thus expanding the range of capital the bank could tap, and meant that the shares could be priced and traded, i.e. as stock. As such, the Frankfurt Exchange progressed from being a simple currency exchange to being a stock exchange.

After a brief dip in their fortunes as the French Revolutionary Wars broke out in the 1790s, the Frankfurt banks and exchange were soon back in business and doing better than ever before. With the emancipation of the Jews in the early 1800s, the Rothschild family was able to seize its opportunity and move from lending to small German states such as Hessia into the international big leagues. The patriarch Mayer Amschel Rothschild (1744-1812) had, in a manner similar to royal alliances, married off his five sons to important European centres of trade and banking: while his firstborn Amschel stayed in Frankfurt, the second eldest Salomon went to Vienna, Nathan to London, Calmann to Naples and the youngest Jakob to Paris. This unique international network allowed Rothschild to quickly move capital through Europe—even past the Continental Blockade during the Napoleonic Wars—and to loan gigantic sums to states where no other bank was in a position to broker the deal. The five brothers communicated with the Frankfurt headquarters by carrier pigeon, and their international network was the source both of their financial strength and of their invincibility: while Jewish money-lenders had previously been subject to periodic pogroms or prejudicial measures, the Rothschild family had, with its spread across Europe, made itself quite visibly immune to national crises.

With the Rothschild's immense balance sheet of state borrowing and the Bethmanns, Metzlers and several other dynasties now concentrating on commercial bonds to companies at the dawn of the industrial revolution, the Frankfurt Stock Exchange grew rapidly: by the time Frankfurt was annexed to Prussia, it was the premier exchange in the German-speaking world and, alongside London, Paris and New York one of the world's first rank. Yet it did not have its own building until 1845, having taken place until that stage on a twice-weekly basis in the Römer town hall (see Coryate's description on page 119); indeed, the city fathers were sceptical of financial innovation, refusing the licence to trade stock on a daily basis in 1825 on the basis that speculative business would catapult "the families of foolish men into ruin". It would take until 1845 for the Stock Exchange to get its own premises—usefully enough, in the same building at the telegraph office—opposite the Römer and the Paulskirche, by which point daily trading had finally been allowed.

Yet the purpose-built trading floor soon proved to be too small: following the proclamation of the Second German Empire in 1871, an unprecedented economic boom led to a rapid multiplication in public offerings as companies rushed to capitalize at high value, and in 1879 the new exchange was opened—called *Neue Börse* to this day despite the fact that the *Alte Börse* was destroyed during the bombing raids of 1944. Yet only a few decades later the new exchange would prove to be outsized as the city's stock market was battered first by the First World War—during which trading links to foreign exchanges were cut—and then by hyperinflation, which rendered vast numbers of securities representing fixed sums of money worthless; the Nazis then redirected capital into armaments production, viewing all forms of investment on the stock market as a Jewish and therefore thoroughly immoral waste of resources and limiting trading to the point of irrelevance. Indeed, the seizure of power by the NSDAP in 1933 had already led to such uncertainty among Frankfurt's economic elite that the entire board of the Chamber of Commerce, Germany's second oldest, resigned in late March. In the absence of the adventurous enterprising spirit that had become a key part of the city's identity, the National Socialist governor of Frankfurt Jakob Sprenger, went to absurd lengths to try and define its role: while Munich titled itself "Capital of the Movement" and Nuremburg was the "City of the Reich Party Rallies", Frankfurt (known in Hitler's inner circle as the "nest of Jews and democrats") was bizarrely and parochially rebranded as the "City of German Craftsmanship" (*Stadt des deutschen Handwerks*).

It was only following the Second World War and the 1948 currency reform prepared in Frankfurt that the city's capital markets returned to their former importance, especially once foreign trading was allowed again in 1956. Furthermore, the uncertainty with regard to Berlin—which had formerly rivalled Frankfurt as Germany's banking centre and housed a formidable stock exchange—and eastern Germany as a whole led to an influx of banks to the city: Deutsche Bank, Commerzbank and the (now-defunct) Dresdner Bank all moved from the Soviet sectors in the 1950s. With the *Wirtschaftswunder* in full swing, German manufacturers were both reliable debtors for banks and safe bets for traders, while German workers were heaping money into savings and pensions which institutional fund managers were looking to place as investments: almost all of this money started to flow through Frankfurt, its banks and its stock exchange—and still does to this day.

In 2015 the Frankfurt Stock Exchange is the tenth largest in the world by market capitalization and the largest in continental Europe, handling ninety per cent of stock trades in Germany. Companies from across the world are listed on the exchange, whose best known index is the DAX (*Deutsche Aktien Index*) of the German top 30. The banking sector, too, is concentrated in Frankfurt, which has Germany's top four banks by total assets: with €1.6 billion, Deutsche Bank, the world's largest foreign exchange dealer, is three times the size of its nearest rival, Commerzbank; in third place follows the German government-owned development bank KfW, *Kreditanstalt für Wiederaufbau* (quite literally the "credit institute for reconstruction") originally set up to distribute Marshall Plan funds and now an investor in small and medium-sized business and a provider of export finance; the fourth largest is the German cooperative bank DZ, or *Deutsche Zentral-Genossenschaftsbank*; over forty international banks also have offices in the city. Germany, which is perhaps the world's most stable and powerful economy, carries out its foreign exchange, its business investment and its all-important export development through Frankfurt's banks, while Germany's savers, some of the world's most diligent, deposit much of their capital here. With all this money lying around, it should not come as much of a surprise that Frankfurt is, by most measures, the country's most expensive city in terms of cost of living and Germany's only "alpha" city in globalization rankings (Munich makes "alpha minus", while Berlin lags behind Hamburg and Düsseldorf—both "beta plus"—in the "beta minus" category). This kind of ranking hypothesizes that if a nuclear bomb were to suddenly explode over Berlin, the effect on the global economy would be lower than if one were to knock out Frankfurt.

Unions and Students

As New Yorkers and Londoners will testify, life in an "Alpha plus" city is not all beer and skittles. For those not earning a good banking salary or outside the workforce entirely (students, the long-term unemployed, pensioners) it can be downright difficult. Yet Frankfurt has a strong commitment to these groups, both institutional and societal, and has often resolutely fought for their place in the city.

With banks and companies relocating to Frankfurt *en masse* in the early 1950s and making it the young Federal Republic's *de facto* economic capital, their adversaries soon followed. Unions, for example, frequently set up in the city, and some of the country's most powerful remain here to this day: the construction, farming and ecology union IG BAU, for instance, as well as the mighty IG Metall, Germany's largest union with almost two millions members in the metalworking industry. While their heartlands lie elsewhere, generally in the rust-belt Ruhr to the north or in industrious Swabia, Frankfurt guarantees union bosses easy access both to decision-makers and to rumours and political-economic mood-music. The smaller but no less influential education and knowledge workers' union GEW also resides in Frankfurt, whose university is the third largest in Germany and employs over 3,000 people with around 46,000 students.

In the post-war years the university has been at the centre of much of the counter-cultural reaction to the city's new-found role as a global financial metropolis. Not only did the famous 1968 demonstrations and occupation of the campus stand for the alternative stance of its student body, but this early fight was also directed against a phenomenon today circumscribed as gentrification.

By the mid-1960s the centre of Frankfurt was quite literally full, while office space was in high demand. Although companies started to build upwards, there was still a huge amount of pressure on property prices around the core of banks to the immediate west of the city centre on the Taunusanlage. At the inauguration of the 210ft Zürich insurance tower (now replaced by the shiny new 500ft Opernturm) just across from the *Alte Oper*—then still a crumbling ruin—Social Democrat Mayor Werner Bockelmann declared that nearby Westend, filled with roomy bankers' villas and open green space, would be more densely developed following a "five finger plan" by which skyscrapers would radiate out from the new tower, which would be "the palm".

It was the kind of initiative that only the 1960s could have produced: what were considered in the city planning department to be little more than dingy, outdated nineteenth-century piles were to be sacrificed for a gleaming future of broad, car-filled streets and towers made of metal and concrete. Unashamedly referring back to the 1920s utopia of Ernst May (see Chapters 3 and 12), planners aimed to separate work and living, relocating the inner-city population to green suburbs and opening up office space in a rationalized city centre. The huge high-rise development at Nordweststadt, just completed, was the new ideal: municipal planners saw no need for dilapidated old buildings in the centre to be renovated when cheap and plentiful accommodation could be erected on greenfield land at the city limits.

Although misguided, it was an entirely noble idea in the spirit of its time; yet as with all such noble ideas, there was no shortage of sly, cash-rich folk happy to capitalize on it. With the new building regulations for Westend now specifying skyscrapers, wealthy residents and speculative investors entered into a bidding war, trying desperately to buy up enough contiguous land for high-rise development. In view of the inevitable growth of the city and the planning regulations, the nearby banks were more than happy to provide generous lines of credit for such a safe investment, and by the late 1960s all of the land up for redevelopment had been bought by seven consortiums numbering fewer than thirty well-connected people.

Tenants in the buildings on the parcels of land bought up—frequently villas and townhouses divided into smaller apartments—were forced out as quickly as possible and the buildings turned into offices awaiting permission to demolish and rebuild them. Buildings not yet given planning clearance for commercial use were let to gangmasters who packed the *Gastarbeiter* arriving from southern Europe into the buildings four or five to a room: the aim was both to prevent stable tenancies from being established and allow the buildings to become so dilapidated that they could be torn down and rebuilt with new planning permission. Year after year, stately piles fell into deliberate disrepair.

Students at the university, whose campus was on the other side of Westend in Bockenheim, were some of the first to be affected by this strategy. Many rented rooms in the old Westend villas and were swept from building to building as, throughout the late 1960s the tide of speculation and new-build rolled out along Bockenheimer Landstraße. By 1969 the population of Westend had declined from 40,000 in the mid-1960s to 20,000, yet many of the buildings were empty as investors continued their game of monopoly. That summer, 700 of those remaining, many of whom were students active in the occupation of the university buildings and the student protests, united to form a residents' initiative: empty buildings were turned into squats for students and immigrant families, while trees slated for felling along the Westend's broad avenues were watered.

Many in the Social Democratic Party who felt uncomfortable with the effects of its policy of inner-city redevelopment and suburban rebuilding were delighted with the initiative, and it took until 1971 for the investors to build up enough pressure on the city authorities to have the squats cleared: the results were high-profile protests and heavily publicized civil disobedience. It was the beginning of what became known as the *Frankfurter Häuserkampf* (the Frankfurt Fight for Houses), a landmark political conflict and one of the first in Europe in which the prevailing 1960s/1970s orthodoxy of demolish-and-rebuild was successfully challenged.

Many who went on to play important roles in German society were part of the *Häuserkampf*: Daniel Cohn-Bendit and Joschka Fischer (born 1945 and 1948 respectively), later politicians in the Green Party, lined up among the squatters in an underground organization named "Revolutionary Struggle", while Ignatz Bubis (1927-1999), who went on to become head of Germany's Jewish Council, was one of the most high-profile and most maligned of the investors. In 1972, Fischer, who would later make history by entering the Bundestag as the first Green elected member (wearing trainers), was one of the squatters in three-storey set of mid-1800s buildings on the corner of Bockenheimer Landstraße and Schumannstraße belonging to Bubis. The investor had them torn down to make way for office space only to—much to the delight of many in Westend—fail to find anyone interested in building on the site.

Although by the mid-1970s a series of protection orders and new state laws had stemmed the tide of speculation and calmed the situation, Bubis had become a hate-figure and was involved in further controversy in 1975 when stage and film director Rainer Werner Fassbinder (1945-1982) tried to premiere a play he had written entitled *Der Müll, die Stadt und der Tod* ("Rubbish, City and Death") in the city. One of its key characters is a greedy and amoral Jewish property investor, who was most likely based on Bubis, and although the work as a whole is perhaps more complex than is usually assumed (the former Nazi murderer is not shown in any better a light), Fassbinder was unable—and indeed unwilling—fully to dispel accusations of anti-Semitism. Bubis, already a leader in the Frankfurt Jewish community at the time (see page 194), arranged a demonstration to sabotage the premiere, and the play was not performed for the first time until 1987 in New York; it was not staged anywhere in Germany until 2009 (a performance planned for 1985 in Frankfurt was also cancelled following protests).

The effects of the *Häuserkampf* were lasting: the squats in West Berlin's Kreuzberg and on Hamburg's harbour front were directly inspired and informed by the pioneering Frankfurt experience, which managed to save around twenty buildings from being turned into offices. Meanwhile, planning policy as a whole in Frankfurt changed: the conservative Christian Democrats gained a majority in the town hall for the first time in 1977 (see page 110) and began to reconstruct historic areas of the city like the Römerberg. The assumption that "new is always better" had been convincingly challenged. As with so many counter-culture initiatives, however, the final fate of both the *Häuserkampf* and many of its members was to be co-opted into the system they fought: many of the most beautiful old buildings in Westend are now used by high-powered legal practices or as bank reception spaces. Their genteel nineteenth-century charm has now been recognized by those who once considered it out of date as a statement of style and a clear competitive advantage.

Joschka Fischer now frequents such buildings, in black leather shoes as a lobbyist for German industrial concerns such as Siemens and BMW. As divisive as Bubis was, however, he went on to become a figure of reconciliation and today has a bridge named after him close to Frankfurt's up-and-coming Ostend. There is much anger in Frankfurt about the new headquarters for the European Central Bank and the luxury flats in what was previously a sanctuary for low-earning Frankfurters, but the times, they are a-changing, and today's students are too busy doing internships—and too pressured by a spoon-fed, tightly-timed syllabus—to start occupying anything. Anti-capitalist protests on the opening of the ECB's new headquarters in early 2015 were large and surprisingly violent, but mainly due to an international hard core of radical left-wing activists and a worrying neo-Nazi insurgency. Yet whatever the political make-up of today's demonstrators, the brief and fragile flame of the worldwide Occupy movement in the wake of the 2008 financial crisis, which was at its strongest in Germany on the Taunusanlage park in front of the former ECB headquarters, shows that Frankfurt is still the centre of indignation at speculative capitalist structures in the country.

11 | The Dark Side
From Barbarity to White-collar Crime

O ne of the driving forces behind both the 1968 student movement in Frankfurt and the 1980s opposition to the expansion of the city's airport was the uncomfortable feeling that below the surface of a well-ordered society, frightening undercurrents of thoughtlessness, criminality and barbarity were lurking. The 1968 revolutionaries occupying the halls of Frankfurt University told everyone to ask their parents and their grandparents what they had done in the war: soon the whole of Germany was wondering if the amicable old gentleman with a felt hat who always had a sweet in his pocket for passing youngsters had, 25 years beforehand, been responsible for gassing Jewish children. In the 1980s this epistemological discord went further: the previous generation had carried on about its daily business with genocide happening in its midst; was this generation now similarly sleepwalking into the abyss as the Western capitalist system of transforming natural resources into money led to the destruction of the entire planet? The Green movement in Germany was seized by the idea that, just as during the Nazi years, everyday life was a veneer behind which a chasm lurked. This radical fear has marked German public life ever since: the country was the first to elect a Green party into its parliament, the first to put them into government and one of the first to plan a nuclear power phase-out.

That the 1968 and 1980s disruptions were initiated in Frankfurt was in some ways a product of chance: the speed with which the movements spread across Germany showed that the entire country was grappling with the same issues of trust in previous generations and doubt about the prevailing economic model. In another way, however, Frankfurt's history as the pre-eminent centre of Jewish life in western Germany and new role as the captain's bridge of capitalism in the post-war Federal Republic meant that the conflicts had

The wheel is prepared on which this condemned man is to be broken at the Frankfurt gallows, 1741 (Wikimedia Commons)

necessarily to emanate from the city. Yet although it plays the role of Sodom and Gomorrah for leftist activists today, for much of its history Frankfurt has been no more criminal or immoral than other European cities. That, however, is not saying much.

Medieval Frankfurt: Witch-hunts and Hangings

Like any other city in the Middle Ages, Frankfurt's criminal justice development in its early centuries was comparable with that of today's Islamist militias: all sorts of barbaric punishments were meted out as deterrents with all manner of abstruse religious justifications. The most common method of executing the death penalty, hanging, was comparatively humane, and remains anchored in the geography of the city today: the area named "Gallus" draws its name from a dialect shortening of the German word *Galgen*, or gallows. At this time, Gallus was way out to the west of the city walls—as was its neighbouring area Gutleut, once a leper colony—and was passed by travellers coming in from cities downriver such as Mainz.

One such traveller, Thomas Coryat (see Chapter 5) describes the impression Gallus made in the early seventeenth century:

> A little on this side the townes end of Franckford I observed a most rufull spectacle that stroke a certaine horror into me, and so I thinke did into the hearts of most other relenting travellers that passed that way: the bodies of sixteene men hanging upon a great stonie gallows hard by the high way side, supported with many great stony pillars.

Thankfully, Coryat does not go into his usual detail on the precise state of decay of the corpses: the custom was to leave them as carrion and not take them down until the city was next visited by a dignitary or royal. In 1561, however, those on Frankfurt's "death row" had had an unlikely reprieve in the form of a hurricane, which damaged the gallows beyond repair; the city's guilds were contractually obliged to rebuild them, and to avoid individual craftsmen being plagued by their consciences, each and every woodworker, rope-maker and joiner in the city was made to contribute to the reconstruction (even those with no suitable trade were required to hammer in at least one symbolic nail).

Another form of communally sanctioned punishment were the various stocks and pillories installed on Hauptwache, including a moveable cage in which those sentenced were locked and which could be spun by all who passed—a tradition which lasted well into the 1700s. Other less amusing sentences were also carried out on public squares: Roßmarkt, for example, was the site of choice for beheadings, while Rabenstein on today's Mainzer Landstraße was used for the most cruel and unusual punishments medieval Europe had to offer: the unfortunate men who found themselves here were blinded with red-hot pokers or had their hands, ears and noses cut off; convicted swindlers were branded with the city's eagle on their forehead: the name *Rabenstein* (raven stone) comes from the black birds which circled in search of discarded flesh. Women, meanwhile, were most often drowned in the Main, tied to boards or shut into barrels on the Old Bridge and thrown over into a particularly deep channel. The last sight they were meant to see was the golden *Brickegickel*, the statue of a strutting cock—a reminder of the existence of the devil, who was said to have slammed into the stonework a chicken sent over the bridge by a mason with whom he had struck a bizarre Faustian pact (see page 49). Truly the Middle Ages were dark times.

One of the most gruesome executions in Frankfurt was that of Vizenz Fettmilch (1565-1616), the principal figure behind the pogrom of 1614 and the man after whom the civil disorder of those years was named. Fettmilch had begun as the leader of a populist citizens' movement with a series of demands, some more, some less legitimate (see page 80), yet the situation escalated and soon this grocer and gingerbread baker found himself leading a vigilante band who terrorized the authorities, cornering them in the Römer town hall until they agreed under duress to the citizens' demands and, later, deposing them. When the Emperor Matthias I attempted to restore order by issuing an Imperial ban on the continuing protests in 1614, all hell broke loose: a march for "Bread and Work" on 22 August ended in a drunken mêlée in which a mob stormed the Jewish ghetto, forced its population onto the nearby cemetery and then ransacked their homes, forcing them to leave the city the next day.

When an Imperial herald arrived in late October declaring Fettmilch a wanted man, along with his two accomplices Konrad Schopp and Korand Gerngroß (this wonderful second name translates literally as "wannabe big"), the rioting population started to have second thoughts, yet the charismatic Fettmilch remained so popular that it took a month for an Imperial magistrate to pluck up the courage to arrest him; and indeed he was promptly freed by supporters from his dungeon in the Bornheim tower. Yet order was soon restored by Imperial troops and Fettmilch was handed over to a magistrate in nearby Mainz, whence he was sent to Aschaffenburg for trial while the last of the uprising in Frankfurt was put down. After a lengthy hearing in which was eventually condemned for *lèse majesté*, he was sentenced to death and executed on Roßmarkt on 28 February 1616: his two oath fingers were sliced off before he was beheaded and then quartered in front of the voyeuristic mob (his accomplices' corpses were, aside from their heads, left intact). Goethe records seeing his bleached skull on spikes on the Old Bridge 150 years later:

Among the many old-fashioned relics on the bridge, from my earliest days, I was struck by the skull of a capital felon stuck onto the bridge tower which, to judge by the three or four empty spikes beside it, was the one which had managed to brave time and all of the elements since 1616. Whenever one returned to Frankfurt from Sachsenhausen, the tower would rise up before one and one would notice the skull.

By Goethe's time, capital punishment was in decline, however. He himself was fascinated by the dark fate of Susanna Margaretha Brandt (his "Gretchen", see page 122), who was beheaded at the age of 26 in 1772 for infanticide, yet throughout the 1700s the death penalty was used ever more sparingly. The last execution in the city before the Nazi years took place in 1799, when a potter convicted of murdering his wife was beheaded on Roßmarkt. In 1806 the French Army tore down the gallows, celebrating Napoleon's birthday with a firework display on the field, and a century later the memory of the area's grim purpose had been erased by the iron and steel of the railways: it was re-etymologized in Bowdlerian fashion as having been named after St. Gall.

The 1800s: Rare Uprisings

With the *de facto* abolition of the death penalty in the Napoleonic years, the city of Frankfurt was a good deal more civilized than many others in the nineteenth century. Even more astoundingly, up to the First World War its population quadrupled without much by way of civil strife. Yet brief flare-ups of mob mentality at key moments of political rupture reminded the city of the potential for unrest among its downtrodden working folk. The 1840s had seen a smouldering resentment across Germany in which, unusually in historical terms, left-wing and democratic politics melded with nationalism: young intellectuals and the new working classes across German-speaking Europe saw their only way to freedom from state oppression and economic penury in a united, democratic German state. In Frankfurt there were regular "Monday coffee mornings" led by citizens' initiatives agitating for more democracy, and several events of importance for all of Germany such as the inauguration of the Goethe memorial in 1844 were accompanied by protests against authoritarian structures.

By 1848, the Year of Revolutions, the powder keg was ready to explode: despite liberalized regulations on freedom of the press and religious minorities on 3 March, the presence of the German National Assembly in the city from the end of that month gave a focus to protests for suffrage, democracy and a new constitution. Throughout the summer activists from across the German-speaking lands flooded into Frankfurt, creating an increasingly febrile atmosphere as the deliberations of the assembly dragged on. When war between the German Confederation and Demark came in August and the new parliament agreed to what was seen as too lenient a compromise, nationalist sentiment erupted and the city went into revolt: on 18

September a mob tore up paving stones at more than forty locations to create barricades. Confederation troops from surrounding Hessia were called in, and when two conservative Prussian members of the parliament rode out to meet and take command of them at Friedberger Warte, the mob turned on them, shooting Waterloohero General von Auerswald (1792-1848) and beating Felix von Lichnowsky (1814-48) so badly that he died the following day. By this stage the uprising had been quelled by the approaching troops: the barricades, although numerous, had been erected hastily and not on any major arteries, and after short but intense fighting the discredited mob disappeared into the night. Indeed, the death of the two members of the Frankfurt parliament—and the twelve soldiers who died in putting down the revolt—shook citizens who had seen so little violence in recent decades and lastingly damaged the cause of democracy in Germany. Reactionary Arthur Schopenhauer (1788-1860), for example, who spent the last decades of his life in Frankfurt, left a legacy to the families of the dead soldiers in his will.

The Weimar Years and Nazi Frankfurt: Regression into Barbarity

The next time Frankfurt—and Germany as a whole—saw serious violence on the streets was at the end of the First World War. With central government weakened in late 1918 after surrender and the country full of armed and angry demobilized men, it was almost inevitable that there would be a revolution. Throughout the winter and into 1919, law and order in the city broke down entirely as the municipal police force, military policemen and various vigilante groups clashed. The economy was in tatters and bartering was rife: when Naval police tried to break up a the thriving black market on Börneplatz on 31 March 1919, tensions erupted and the entire city centre sank into violence as Naval and regular police units fought one another, all the while struggling to restrain rioting crowds. The mob broke into the Hammelstraße cells, where prisoners were held on remand, releasing 200 detainees awaiting trial onto the streets, where they promptly disarmed the municipal police approaching the scene. In the ensuing mayhem shops were plundered and buildings occupied by armed groups; only after they started using grenades and machine guns could the municipal police regain control of the city, although they had to tolerate the continued presence of the Naval police, who were armed, dangerous and savage: it transpired that, during the chaos, they had turned on one of their own, beating the man senseless and throwing him into the Main in a sack weighed down with paving stones (making the luckless sailor the first recorded non-suicidal drowning in the river since the late 1600s—and the last to date). Unrest continued throughout the year and into 1920, and by the time something approaching normality was restored in spring of that year, the chaotic early-Weimar period had seen around fifty violent deaths in the city.

Throughout the 1920s, civil disorder continued on a low level, part of the corrosive uncertainty which ate away at the fabric of the young Weimar Republic. Especially following the inflationary crisis of 1923, the young National Socialist German Workers' Party, led by Hitler from 1921 onwards, and the German Communist Party frequently engaged in planned confrontations, especially in outlying areas of the city (although these were by no means as violent as the pitched battles held in Berlin's working-class districts). As the Nazis grew and became more organized, however, their terrorizing presence on the streets increased: for much of the late 1920s barely a month went by in Frankfurt without at least one act of criminal damage carried out by party activists; each Nazi demonstration was accompanied by brawls, often with stabbings and beatings. Later, when the Frankfurt NSDAP wrote its own official chronicle, it said of those years: "Our ranks were strengthened by those in whose nature it was to fight; they sensed that the banners of our movement was where the fight was."

The Nazi party in Frankfurt was led by Jakob Sprenger (see Chapter 4), a post office clerk who headed the Hessen-Nassau district from the suburb of Bockenheim—ironically, a primarily social-democratic area. Elected to the Reichstag for the NSDAP, this rabid anti-Semite was made ruler of Hessia after the Nazi seizure of power and proceeded to rule his fiefdom with an iron first. As soon as Hitler had been made chancellor on 31st January

1933, Sprenger, like other Nazi district leaders, began to move to consolidate the Führer's position. That night, a torchlight procession of SA men marched along the Kaiserstraße, up the Zeil and into Bornheim: in a mere foretaste of what was to come, one of the marching thugs thrust his burning torch into the face of woman watching the demonstration on a street corner.

In their grasp for power in the city, which was still officially governed by the Social Democrat Ludwig Landmann (1868-1945) until the local elections of early March 1933, Sprenger's men were inspired by a tradition of populist movements: on the day in which they won the election, the Nazis sent the SA into the Römer town hall to occupy it in the same way as Fettmilch had in 1614; the new NSDAP mayor, a man named Krebs (fittingly enough, "Cancer") immediately removed all Jews from municipal positions. Thus, 81 people lost their jobs overnight, including the preceding Mayor Landmann, who was in the country with friends and had been warned not to return to the city, now swarming with Nazi thugs. Hoping to sink into anonymity in Berlin, Landmann arrived there only to suffer a heart attack; while in hospital recuperating that summer, news reached him that the Nazi city council had cancelled his pension, and although a scrutiny commission for municipal finances forced the city to reinstate it in November, the former mayor was in penury by 1935 after the Nuremberg laws imposed swingeing tax-grabs on Jews. A few months before the outbreak of the Second World War, Landmann, like so many other Frankfurt Jews, headed for Amsterdam (after paying a hefty emigration tax); his wife had been born there and the couple managed to avoid deportation, although Landmann died of malnutrition and a heart condition in hiding in March 1945, never living to see the demise of the regime.

Meanwhile, in the summer of 1933 the city fell entirely into the grip of the Nazis in what German historians refer to as the *Gleichschaltung*—literally, the synchronization. Jews everywhere were criminally removed from office (until the Nuremberg race laws there was not even a "legal" basis for this): in April Jewish lawyers lost their right to enter court buildings, for example. Soon after, the city's union offices were occupied by SA units in preparation for

1 May, which was to become a National Socialist holiday rather than a celebration of workers' solidarity. The university was forced to remove all suspect art teachers from its staff, and on 3 May, the NSDAP students stood guard at the entrance to the lecture halls, confiscating Jewish student passes; a week later, the students helped the SA organize the great book burning on the Römer. Two oxen pulled a dung cart filled with books by authors such as Bertolt Brecht, Thomas Mann and Siegfried Kracauer from the university to the central square, where they were consumed on a funeral pyre to liberal Germany.

In its combination of age-old prejudice and violence with bureaucracy and technological sophistication, the barbarity of Nazi rule revealed itself to be a horrific mixture of the medieval and modern. In Frankfurt, the inspiration from previous, less enlightened ages was made very clear by Sprenger's writings, in which he praised peasant pogroms against Jews (he published an "analysis" of anti-Semitic tendencies in German country-folk in 1933), while the modern aspect of Nazi terror was illustrated by his embrace of Hitler's grand plans: an early publicity photo of Sprenger in office shows him next to Hitler at the ground-breaking ceremony for Germany's first *Autobahn* just outside the city in September 1933.

Despite the injustices, the atmosphere in Frankfurt in the years leading up to the Second World War was one of pragmatism. Following the turmoil and uncertainty of the Weimar years, not only the party faithful but Frankfurters generally were by and large willing to obey orders from on high. Once the *Gleichschaltung* was complete, there was very little by way of active resistance. Both the municipal police and the newly set-up Gestapo were frequently provided with information from a willingly cooperative population, driven as often by petty personal conflicts to become informers as by genuine Nazi conviction. The secret services certainly never had difficulty acquiring incriminating material: when, for instance, the Hessen-Nassau leader of the Social Democrats, now operating illicitly, lost a list of party members and their addresses from the back of his motorbike in 1934, it was handed in to the Gestapo almost immediately and he was punished with lengthy prison sentences—along with most of the other leading party members.

Meanwhile, the regime's stranglehold on Germany's Jewish population grew tighter and tighter. By 1935 over a fifth of Frankfurt's roughly 25,000 remaining Jews were reliant on state aid after having been terrorized out of their jobs. The Nuremburg laws and the "Ayranization of the German economy" meant nothing less than a step-by-step criminal confiscation of money and property—and with the size and wealth of its Jewish community, nowhere was this more evident than in Frankfurt. The fate of Maximilian von Goldschmidt-Rothschild (1843-1940) shows not only how much the Nazi regime coerced out of Jews who remained in the country, but also how compliant so many of them were—especially older residents who did not have the heart to escape and start anew elsewhere. Born Goldschmidt in Frankfurt, in 1878 Maximilian had married Minna Karoline Frelin von Rothschild, who stood to inherit much of the family fortune; this made him the richest man in the German Empire (his wealth exceeded that of Emperor William II). Although his banking operation suffered in the world economic crisis and had to be nationalized in 1932, he remained enormously wealthy, and was a lucrative target for the Nazi kleptomaniacs: in June 1937 he was forced to sell his Westend villa, acquired in 1917 for 670,000 Gold Marks, to the city at a knockdown rate of 190,000 Reichsmarks; in September 1938 he was then pressured into selling the dynastic Rothschild-Palais and the parkland around it for a pitiful 620,000 Reichsmarks. Given leave to remain as a tenant in a small suite of rooms in the stately home, Goldschmidt-Rothschild narrowly avoided deportation—by dying at the age of 96 in 1940.

It was a fate that 11,000 Frankfurt Jews would not escape between 1941 and 1945. Following the *Kristallnacht* pogrom in the night of 9/10 November 1938, the Gestapo had secured from the ruins of the Jewish centre in Fahrgasse a list of the 23,000 practising Jews still living in the city, a list which would later serve in their rounding-up and forcible removal. The November "Night of Shattered Glass" saw the Börneplatz and Friedberger Anlage synagogues in the east of the city totally destroyed: both were demolished as beyond repair (at the expense of the Jewish community), while the other two synagogues in the city in Westend and Nordend were severely damaged; hundreds of Jewish shops, too, were in ruins.

Following this pogrom, the slow trickle of Jewish emigrants from Frankfurt turned into a flood, while at the same time, the regime tightened controls on those leaving: a punitive tax was levied on emigrants, who were only allowed to take with them what they could prove to have acquired before 1933. Thus, most of those who left Germany did so with little more than the clothes they were wearing: yet leave they did. The census of 1939, the first to define Jewishness by race rather than religion, showed that there were only 14,461 Jews by Nazi definition left in the city, with 1879 "half-Jews" and 857 "quarter-Jews" also still present.

For those Jews who were still in Frankfurt by the outbreak of war, persecution began in earnest in 1940: they were forced to hand in all valuable made of gold or silver, all their driving licences and vehicle papers and their radios. They were allowed to shop only in specific places at specific times and as of 19 September 1941 were required to wear the yellow *Judenstern* Star of David: the first deportations followed exactly four weeks later on 19 October 1941, as 1,200 Frankfurt Jews were sent to the Łódź ghetto. They were taken from their flats and houses at 7am with no warning, marched through Ostend to the wholesale market and loaded into cattle trucks. In November two further transports left for Minsk and Riga, and in the summer of 1942 a further seven large-scale deportations took place. Most of these went straight to concentration camps such as Theresienstadt. Including smaller transports until early 1944, mostly to Auschwitz, 9,415 Jews were deported from Frankfurt; 700 killed themselves before they could be taken. Altogether, over 11,000 Jews from Frankfurt met their death in the east in the Nazi machinery of exploitation and extermination.

Among those who died was Arthur von Weinberg (1860-1943), a celebrated chemical industrialist and horse-racing fanatic who in 1933 had been forced to resign from his position on the board of IG Farben, the company which went on to help develop the gas chambers. Arrested at the age of 82 in Bavaria after having been forced to sell his Frankfurt home, he was transported to the Theresienstadt concentration camp, where he died a broken man.

In the city itself the populace took little notice of the deportations: by 1942 repressive regime measures and summary justice were widespread. The reintroduction of the death penalty by Nazi courts led to spates of executions which became so frequent that the Frankfurt prosecutor was soon complaining that they had lost all deterrent effect. Everyday life became increasingly horrific: everywhere groups of emaciated foreign forced labourers were kept in prison-like conditions under armed guard. The situation grew worse as the war went on, and by 1944 large metal works were staffed almost entirely by underfed Russian prisoners of war, while the Adlerwerk car factory even set up its own branch of the Natzweiler concentration camp in Alsace to receive prisoners: of the 1,600 who were sent to forced labour there, 528 died. Captive workers also suffered disproportionately in the Allied air-strikes, as they were not allowed to use air-raid shelters and frequently made to carry out dangerous tasks such as clearing bombed-out sites.

Despite the madness—or perhaps due to its dulling effect—acts of resistance were few and far between. Indeed, the city's "poster girl" freedom fighter Johanna Kirchner (1889-1944), whose bravery is commemorated by a plaque in the Paulskirche, fled Frankfurt in 1933, leaving her children behind to continue her work as the SPD (Social Democrat) party secretary in the Saarland (which was still under French control) and later in France itself, where she helped to organize the SPD in exile and produce illicit political material for distribution in Germany. Hiding out in a nunnery in unoccupied France, she narrowly escaped the Vichy secret police in 1941, only to fall into their hands in 1942 and be extradited to Germany, where she was executed in a Berlin prison in June 1944 following a half-hour show-trial.

Post-war Frankfurt: *Aufarbeitung*

With its shameful record of collaboration and consent in the Nazi dictatorship, much like the rest of Germany, in the late 1940s and 1950s Frankfurt was in a mood to forget. What is more, following an initial period of denazification, the Allied occupiers soon started to integrate their three zones of occupation into the Western economic, political and military alliance. The motives behind this switch to business-as-usual were both laudable (the Allies had learned the lessons of history and realized that Germany would need a stable political system and material wealth in order to prevent renewed unrest) and cynical—a remilitarized and economically powerful Germany would act as a buffer against Soviet aggression and be less of a drain on Allied resources. It was therefore the wish both of the vast majority of people in Frankfurt and of their political overlords to move on swiftly from the crimes of the Nazi years. Gestures of reconciliation such as the refurbishment of the Westend-Synagoge (see page 194) or the resettling of the Institute for Social Research (see page 137) were made quietly.

Yet not everyone was happy with this silent collusion. Fritz von Unruh (1885-1970), for example, a Frankfurt writer who went into exile in America in 1933 after his books were burned on the Römer square, was asked to return by Mayor Kolb in 1948 to give a speech in the newly restored Paulskirche. Von Unruh, who had, oddly enough, lived in the Rententurm until leaving and whose name, suitably, translates word for word as "of disquiet", fulminated against what he saw as a resurgence of Nazis who had either survived the immediate postwar purges or were on their way back to the top. His angry, apposite accusations left the crowd stunned; his opinions were uncomfortable and he quickly became unpopular. Although he resettled in Germany in 1952, he left once again in 1955 after its rearmament had been announced. Unable to settle anywhere, he returned again in 1962, promptly losing his home in a hurricane and dying a lonely and forgotten man in a village on the Lahn river.

Another victim of Nazi persecution invited to Frankfurt was Fritz Bauer (1903-68), a Jewish state prosecutor who had fled to Denmark and then Sweden after eight months in a concentration camp in 1933. Returning to Germany after the war with a determination to bring the perpetrators of Nazi terror to justice, he had made a name for himself in Braunschweig (Brunswick) in 1952 by establishing the precedent that legal provisions from the days of

Hitler's regime could not be used as justifications under the laws in the new Federal Republic, coining the word *Unrechtsstaat* ("illegitimate state") for Nazi Germany.

Impressed by Bauer, in 1956 the Social Democrat President of Hesse, Georg August Zinn, made him chief Hessian state prosecutor in Frankfurt, from where he decided to try and use the laws of the fledgling Federal Republic to bring some of the most brutal Auschwitz criminals to justice. In order to avoid a proliferation of smaller cases held in local courts against each of the perpetrators individually, Bauer managed to get agreement from the Federal High Court to concentrate all Auschwitz trials in Frankfurt. His aim was not only to see justice done, but to publicize what the Nazi extermination camps had been and how they had worked in a country full of those who genuinely did not know about them—and those who pretended not to know.

In years of painstaking and painful research, Bauer and three prosecutors Joachim Kügler, Georg Friedrich Vogel and Gerhard Wiese, gathered cases of murder and cruelty, located and prepared witnesses and showed remarkable fortitude in the face of threats: "When I leave this office, I'm in enemy territory", Bauer—a regular recipient of vile hate-mail—is famous for saying. Sometimes serendipity helped: a survivor gave journalist Thomas Gnielka (1928-65, see page 133) protocols taken from the camp of prisoners shot at will by SS guards and passed these on to Bauer; the lists proved key in securing convictions.

By the time the first trial was opened in the plenary room in the Römer on 20 December 1963, 23 former Auschwitz officials stood accused of murder and mass murder in what was the biggest court case in the history of the young Federal Republic: 176 days in court later, the judges retired to deliberate, delivering their verdicts over two days on 19 and 20 August 1965, sending six of the accused down for life sentences and dealing out a further eleven prison sentences; only three of those in the dock could not be proven guilty to the satisfaction of the judges.

Two further Auschwitz trials were held in Frankfurt from 1965 to 1968, and although the publicity they attracted was enormous,

Bauer himself was disappointed in the reception they received, complaining that the media had overstressed the inhumane characteristics of the criminals, thus allowing German society to reassure itself that they were monstrous exceptions, not the products of a system they themselves had supported and tolerated. He was also unconvinced by the judges' statements which, he thought, also overly exonerated ordinary Germans by making the Third Reich sound like it was an occupied country, rather than a dictatorship which had been democratically legitimated in 1933 and in which the populace had remained complicit. Yet Bauer's arguments, although perhaps not accepted in the courtroom, had been aired by it, and became part of the core credo of the 1968 generation: "don't trust anyone over thirty!" they proclaimed as they revolutionized Germany, establishing a cultural swing away from deference to authority whose momentum has continued through to this day. The Frankfurt Auschwitz trials are in the DNA of today's deeply liberal, deeply anti-authoritarian German society.

Frankfurt under Fire: the Red Army Faction

Indeed, the swing of the *Achtundsechziger*, "the 68ers", can be said to have gone too far towards anarchism. Impatient with change in society and unwilling to compromise on their far-left views, the more radical among the student movement developed a philosophy of "armed resistance" to the capitalist system. Weeks before the city's students occupied the university on 2 April, what would become the *Rote Armee Fraktion* (Red Army Faction, RAF) around Andreas Baader (1943-77), Gudrun Ensslin (1940-77) and Ulrike Meinhof (1934-76) carried out its first terrorist attack, firebombing two Frankfurt department stores. As the centre of post-war capitalism—which the group considered little more than a continuation of Nazism—Frankfurt was a symbolic choice, and would frequently be their location of choice for their decade-long terrorist campaign.

The American headquarters in the city were a particularly high-value target. Not only had the occupiers, in their view, colluded with the German elites to re-impose a democratically legitimated form of fascism on the country, but as leader of the Western capitalist system, the US was the epitome of everything the RAF despised; moreover, the US military's location in the former IG Farben building stood as a symbol of the continuum from Nazi Germany to the modern Federal Republic. During their "May offensive" of 1972, the RAF bombed the (then publically accessible) foyer of the US headquarters, killing one soldier and injuring thirteen.

The next wave of terror came in 1976: with the original RAF behind bars, a "second generation" of competing cells started a new campaign. A second bomb went off at the IG Farben building, injuring 16 American personnel, while in the summer of 1977 another group tried to kidnap Jürgen Ponto, chairman of the board of directors of Deutsche Bank. The unwitting Ponto opened the door to the daughter of a family friend, Susanne Albrecht, who—unbeknownst to him—was a member of an RAF cell; two of her accomplices then entered his sumptuous Oberursel villa and tried to kidnap him. Ponto, however, did not agree to go quietly and, trying to defend himself, was fatally shot before the terrorists fled.

This was the beginning of what became known as the *Deutscher Herbst* (German autumn), during which the very fabric of the young West German democracy seemed in danger. The president of the leading German employers' association, Hanns Martin Schleyer, was kidnapped in Cologne, held for six weeks and killed; a plane was hijacked and diverted to Mogadishu, where it was stormed by German special forces. Meanwhile, Baader and Meinhof had killed themselves in their prison cells (Ensslin had already committed suicide the previous year), and the situation deescalated.

Yet Frankfurt military personnel and high-profile bankers could not sleep easily in their beds: sporadic attacks continued (against NATO chief Haig in Belgium in 1979, for example, or against the heads of arms manufacturers). In 1985 the "third generation" RAF carried out the group's most audacious attack for some time, murdered an American soldier late on 8 August and used his forces identification card to gain access to the Rhein-Main Air Base south of Frankfurt Airport, where they planted a bomb which killed one US soldier and a civilian employee the following day, injuring a further eleven people. Even from within the RAF milieu the fact that the victims were all simple soldiers or employees drew criticism, and so turning their attention to prominent managers, civil servants and bankers, the terrorists carried out a series of high-profile attacks throughout the late 1980s.

Early on 30 November 1989, for example, Alfred Herrhausen, head of Deutsche Bank, was being chauffeured into Frankfurt from his home in Bad Homburg. As the company Mercedes passed a bicycle on the roadside, a bomb on the back-wheel rack exploded, killing the banker who had made a name for himself by demanding the cancellation of Third World debt. It was the last such attack the group laid claim to; to sighs of relief in the Frankfurt banking industry, it officially announced that it had disbanded in the 1990s.

Frankfurt Today: Capital of White-collar Crime

Frankfurt's banking sector has nevertheless not reduced the security precautions its takes, especially after 9/11 2001, one of the few occasions on which the mighty towers of the financial metropolis have seemed vulnerable. Visitors wishing access to the Main Tower viewing platform, for example, go through airport-style security; most other towers do not permit entry to anyone except members of staff.

In recent years, however, Deutsche Bank has been forced to admit a series of rather unwelcome visitors: crime investigation squads. The years from 2012 to 2015 have seen a spate of high-profile raids on the bank's mirror-glass headquarters on Taunusanlage as part of ongoing investigations into perjury: the head of legal at Deutsche Bank stands under suspicion of having misled courts to protect bank managers during preceding cases regarding the Kirch insolvency. Investigations have even been launched into the role of previous heads of the bank, Jürgen Fitschen and Josef Ackermann.

Certainly, difficulties for Ackermann are accompanied by no small measure of *Schadenfreude*, both within the banking sector and in Germany as a whole. The Swiss banker became notorious for his ambition, declaring the old rear to be the new front as he set profit targets of 25 per cent and transformed Deutsche Bank from the lender of choice for German business into an investment bank on the Anglo-American model: the extent to which the New York and London arms of the bank gained the upper hand over the classic lending business under his reign is demonstrated by the fact that he was succeeded by a duo, the aforementioned Jürgen Fitschen and British-Indian Anshu Jain, the latter of whom has a background in the New York hedge fund scene and had never lived in Germany during his nineteen years of working for the bank before becoming its (short-lived) co-CEO.

Thus Ackermann became something of a hate-figure among critics of Germany's mid-2000s economic reorientation towards market forces, being seen as the incarnation of the new and less friendly form of capitalism unleashed on the country by the Schröder reforms. When the financial crash of 2008 came, he won himself few friends by boasting about the bank's continuing profits as other institutes went bust; Ackermann became controversial even among the turbo-capitalist bankers of Frankfurt he claimed to champion by frequently referring to the fact that Deutsche had not required state aid, all the while refusing to admit that taxpayers' support for other ailing organizations in the banking sector as a whole was indirectly contributing to the bank's positive balance sheet.

Regardless of whether actual criminal activity can be proven, much of Germany is convinced that Frankfurt's wheeler-dealers are among the country's most amoral inhabitants; the continuous trickle of news about embezzlement, miss-selling and tax-dodging do little to dispel what finance industry public-relations officers like to refer to as "myths and conspiracy theories". Indeed, even the most extravagant of accusations seem to find echoes in reality: the city's tax offices—Germany's largest, housed in the extensively renovated Gutleutkaserne barracks—are never short of cases of evasion, and have themselves been accused of criminal goings-on after four of their top tax inspectors were abruptly declared unfit for work between 2007 and 2009 after questionable psychological profiling. Coincidentally enough, all four were working on high-profile cases involving big-leagues banks and see their dismissals as politically motivated: it is literally a question of "how far up does this thing go?"

Those looking to score easy points can always refer to the city's crime statistics; at 16 crimes registered per 100,000 inhabitants annually, Frankfurt is Germany's crime capital, yet only 3.4 per cent of the incidents recorded are violent crimes (which puts the city below even the exceptionally low German average figures for murder, bodily harm and rape). As such, the general suspicion is that these figures show Frankfurt's propensity for white-collar crime such as banking fraud. As tempting as this analysis may be, however, the vast majority of this statistical blip seems to come from the airport (smuggling, customs offences or in-air incidents are booked on city territory) and from the fact that most credit card payments, and therefore most credit-card fraud, goes through Frankfurt. Most genuinely creative white-collar crime in Germany probably does involve Frankfurt, but is even more probably never brought to light.

One thing, however, is for sure: criminality in Frankfurt today is less barbarous and more illicit than ever before.

12 | Escape
Estates, Forests and Ancient Towns

For all the self-consciously urban feel to its centre, Frankfurt remains a relatively small city in which one is never more than half an hour away from picturesque villages and deep green woods. Besides the city's parks, its extensive forests to the south provide plenty of pleasant recreational space, while a range of small towns—some within the Frankfurt urban authority and some slightly further afield—afford genteel living conditions to the professional classes as well as discretion and seclusion for the city's super-rich. Slightly further afield, the unspoiled surroundings of the hilly Hessian countryside beckon: the Taunuswald to the north and the outlying foothills of the Sauerland and central Germany's uplands offer typically Central European panoramas of wooded valleys, craggy cliffs and mighty castles. Yet some of Frankfurt's best escapes are actually average suburban streets.

The Ernst May Estates

Nowhere does Frankfurt seem calmer and greener than in the eight housing estates built by city planner Ernst May (1886-1970) in the *neues Frankfurt* ("New Frankfurt") years of 1926-30. During this period, with a worker-friendly Social Democratic local government in power and a measure of economic stability until the Wall Street Crash of 1929 (see Chapter 4), the municipal authorities embarked on an enormous home-building programme intended to lessen pressure on the crowded city centre and—very much in the spirit of its time—to provide a greener, healthier lived environment which would, it was thought, help to create nothing less than a new and better kind of citizen.

May was in almost every respect the right man for the job: born in Frankfurt and emotionally invested in the city, he had gone to Britain to work for Raymond Unwin and Barry Parker on the garden city projects to the north of London in the early 1910s; fascinated

The Gutenbergdenkmal and Cathedral in Mainz
(Ingo Staudacher/Wikimedia Commons)

by the Parker-Unwin planning philosophy, he translated one of the partners' books on town planning into German and then started to apply their ideas in Germany, creating garden suburbs in Breslau and developing his ideas under the new coinage *Trabantenstadt*, "satellite settlement". This was the German version of the planning concept prevailing across Europe and America in the decades between 1920 and 1980, in which a functional city centre is filled with offices and civil institutions, while rings of industrial estates and suburban settlements respectively keep polluters out of the centre and house the population in spacious, green surroundings. Now much-maligned, in view of the then crowded and unsanitary conditions of many large cities and the fact that the promise of individual motorized transport was still considered a blessing rather than a curse, it is easy to see how seductive this zoning concept was to early twentieth-century planners.

Invited to Frankfurt by progressive Mayor Ludwig Landmann (1868-1945, see pages 101 and 219) in 1925 and given the financial resources and the political power to build fast, May had the opportunity of his life: and the ring of 12,000 simple, cheap and yet high-quality new homes spread across eight sites in less than five years can be considered his masterpiece—and a *tour de force* of modern urban planning. Built before the excesses of the post-war period, in which the megalomaniac high-rise ideas of Charles-Edouard "le Corbusier" Jeanneret Gris (1887-1965) gained the upper hand and entered into an unholy alliance with a cost-cutting, poured concrete approach to public housing, the brick-built *May-Siedlungen* or "May Estates" of low-rise apartments in communal green spaces and terraced houses with gardens are human in scale and have remained eminently liveable to this day. The eight estates erected between 1926 and 1930 cluster in nodes around the city centre and are now quiet quarters populated by elderly couples and young families (with whom the houses are very popular), standing as excellent examples of a bygone age of publically-minded planning and a clear commitment to quality social housing. To the northwest of the city, Römerstadt, Praunheim, and Westhausen form an almost contiguous ensemble, while the Bornheimer Hang and Riederwald estates to the east are particularly well-preserved. To the south, the Niederrad estate is the most visually striking, with its apartments blocks stacked up against each other on diagonals around a central garden in a zigzag fashion (they are referred to colloquially as the *Zickzackhäuser*); slightly closer towards the centre are the horse-shoe curved blocks of the Heimatsiedlung (literally "home settlement") in Sachsenhausen; to the west in Gallus, the linear Hellerhof flats round off the May Estates.

For those looking to really breathe in the spirit of the May system, however, the idyllically situated Römerstadt (so named because traces of Roman settlement were found during construction work) is the most interesting excursion. The Ernst-May-Haus on the estate is one of his archetypal two-up, two-down terraced houses; kept in an almost entirely original condition by its tenant until her death aged ninety, it has now been opened as a museum. Besides marvelling at how oddly un-German—and typically British—the suburban street seems with its row of terraced houses featuring front and back gardens, visitors can admire one of May's most important innovations, the *Frankfurter Küche*—the Frankfurt Kitchen.

The Frankfurt Kitchen is considered one of the forerunners of the modern fitted kitchen. Until the 1920s, most working-class kitchens were simply corners of one of the living rooms, thrown together out of whichever pieces of equipment and furniture the household could afford; cooking, washing, and cleaning were generally carried out in the same space, which was generally poorly ventilated and badly-lit and, more often than not, also used by at least one member of the household as a bedroom. In the philosophy of *neues Bauen*—the new way of building—which went with the *neues Frankfurt* concept, however, the occupants were to benefit not just from warm, dry, bright spaces, but to live better lives within them.

May thus charged a young interior designer from Vienna, Margarete Schütte-Lihotzky (1897-2000, the first Austrian woman to complete a degree in architecture) with creating a mass-producible kitchen set that could be fitted into all of the new homes, which would all have a separate space designed for housework and cooking. Nevertheless, the financial resources and spaces accorded to May were not inexhaustible, and both the houses in general and the kitchen especially had to be small so that as many homes as possible could be built: Lihotzky would have to fit as much as feasible into a room measuring two by three metres (six by ten feet). Working on the scientific management principles of Taylorism, Lihotzky observed housewives in the kitchen so that she could document their workflow and then understand how it could be optimized and compacted; in view of the limited space available, she investigated galley kitchens in other situations, eventually adopting the facilities in railway restaurant cars as her model for the cooking area. The design she came up with was ergonomic, versatile and affordable: it was the birth of the modern kitchen.

The Frankfurt Kitchen was installed in around 10,000 homes, and small, rationalized versions inspired by or referring to it found their way into many hundreds of thousands of spaces in social housing developments across Europe in the decades that followed. Much as in the case of May's Estates as a whole, later incarnations of the concept often discredited the original: both in Germany and beyond, the high-quality wood and metal materials Lihotzky had used were often replaced with cheaper, newer substitutes, while space was squeezed even more as new domestic appliances entered the home (while the original version did take account of gas piping and electricity, refrigerators, for instance, would only become standard in the 1950s). What is more, Lihotzky had to offer introductory courses to women moving into the new homes since her design, while versatile, was inflexible and could only be used in the exact way she intended—for left-handed housewives especially, the ironing-board fixed to the wall must have been utter torture. Later, feminists would criticize the concept of concentrating all housework activities in the kitchen as having shut women off from the rest of the household, yet Lihotzky—herself an emancipated woman of communist convictions—remained convinced that her kitchen had created a comfortable domain, not a prison, for housewives.

With the rise of right-wing sentiment in the early 1930s, May and Lihotzky formed a group of progressively-minded architects and designers who left Germany for the Soviet Union, creating Stalin's gigantic industrial new-town of Magnitogorsk. Stateless after the Nazi seizure of power, May set himself up in Africa and Lihotzky in Turkey, and they did not return to Germany and Austria respectively until the 1950s. May resettled in Hamburg, where he continued his planning career. His work in Frankfurt had—thanks to its "satellite" location outside the city centre—survived the war intact, and his Bornheimer Hang and Riederwald settlements were even extended by post-war planners.

Offenbach

Those interested in following the spread, exaggeration and decline of May's town-planning ideas will find Offenbach of great interest. Although a city of 120,000 people in its own right, Offenbach flows directly into south-eastern Frankfurt and is, to all intents and purposes, a part of the city. Indeed, the earliest record of the town of Offenbach dates to 977 when Emperor Otto II gifted it to the Salvatorkirche of Frankfurt, the forerunner of the cathedral in which the Holy Roman Emperors would be crowned. Offenbach was shunted back and forth between various rulers from then on, being pawned back to Frankfurt from the Counts of Hanau for the princely sum of 1,000 Guilders in 1372. Less than a century later, however, it was returned to the Falkenstein counts, who erected a castle there and started to mint coins: Frankfurt felt provoked by this step and the city's official relationship with Offenbach has been generally strained—sometimes more, sometimes less—since then.

In the 1700s especially, Offenbach started to overtake its prestigious neighbour in a variety of areas: while Frankfurt remained resolute on religious questions (see Chapters 4 and 8), from 1698 onwards Offenbach allowed Huguenot refugees to settle and open churches in their denomination. The effect was to rapidly increase the size of the town and to anchor skilled traders and craftsmen from the world's most advanced economy in the city (*ancien régime* France was, at that point, Europe's powerhouse). The new arrivals were experienced in the importing and processing of tobacco, for example, the growth segment in the eighteenth century *par excellence*, and the fledgling industrial city soon started to attract emigrants from Frankfurt, too, which still limited access to the trades. By 1803, when Offenbach abolished special taxes on Jews several years ahead of its neighbour, the city had become an attractive alternative to Frankfurt with a flourishing leather industry, which in turn gave birth to the first chemicals companies. Throughout the 1800s Offenbach grew fast and, as Germany unified and the old borders were abolished, began to become ever more integrated into its larger neighbour.

In the Second World War the industrially important city was heavily bombed—one-third of it was damaged beyond repair in 1945. Throughout the 1950s and 1960s, however, even more of the Old Town was torn down as Offenbach implemented the post-war orthodoxy of building high and building boxy in a far more radical way than Frankfurt. Cars and pedestrians were separated using walkways and galleries as the city centre was filled with office blocks and the outlying districts with residential towers. Yet what looked shiny and new in the first few years soon started to appear rundown as the city fell victim early to deindustrialization: leather-processing was already disappearing from Europe in the 1970s, and Offenbach's strong electronics industry also fell victim to Asian competition early on. Even so, the city fought hard against its decline, attracting businesses from Frankfurt to fill its office towers and concentrating on the industries which remained (in a link to regional tradition, it is still a major producer of printing and typesetting machines). It has also made a virtue of its radically modern look, turning the Hochschule für Gestaltung, founded to train craftsmen in the 1830s, into a popular design university. Offenbach, whose leather industry especially attracted an above-average number of immigrant *Gastarbeiter* workers in the 1960s, has also made a point of celebrating its ethnic diversity.

Visitors who have seen the Frankfurt Ernst May Estates will be interested in the Lauterborn district, which features some of the post-war prefabricated housing designed by Egon Eiermann (1904-70), the architect behind the Berlin Memorial Church and the Olivetti office towers in Frankfurt, both masterpieces of architectural functionalism. Despite its importance for modern building, Offenbach also retains some more antiquated structures of interest, such as the French Protestant church and the 1916 synagogue, now a theatre—one of Germany's finest, and one of the last to be completed before the rise of anti-Semitism.

Höchst

Although actually further away from central Frankfurt than Offenbach and separated from the city by the River Nidda as it flows into the Main, Höchst was made part of Frankfurt by boundary reform in 1928 and is officially a district of the city. Nevertheless, it retains an entirely independent character: having escaped destruction in the Second World War, its timber-framed old-town dating from the sixteenth century is almost entirely preserved, as is the Justinuskirche, one of Germany's oldest in continuous use and in its original state. Most of the church building, which presides over the Main from a small but steep hillock, is original Carolingian, dating from 830-850; although somewhat unspectacular when compared to the gothic and baroque churches and cathedrals which have followed elsewhere, the Romanesque St. Justin's Church impresses by its sheer age and simple elegance.

The city walls, too, date from the town's earliest years, and give Höchst the impression of being one great fortress when seen from the Main. To the west of the church rises a tower which could be mistaken for a misplaced lighthouse, but is actually the early baroque tower of the 1500s Höchst castle—another stop on a sightseeing tour of this picturesque place which must also include the Bolongaro Palace. This high-baroque stately home was built by Giuseppe Bolongaro (1712-79), an Italian businessman who moved to Frankfurt in 1743 and built up a tobacco trading empire: his snuff factory was Europe's biggest for a period in the eighteenth century. The family settled in Höchst after several run-ins with the Frankfurt city authorities, who were unwilling to grant the merchant citizenship due to his loyalty to Catholicism.

Although tobacco production in Höchst was soon eclipsed by that of Offenbach upriver, the town became home to one of

Germany's most important industrial concerns—the Hoechst chemicals company, founded in 1863 and a worldwide exporter of paints and dyes by the outbreak of the First World War. It was also a pioneer in creating synthetic enzymes, and the world's first batch of man-made hormones was synthesized here in 1904 (the Hoechst works created artificial adrenaline). In 1925 Hoechst became part of the IG Farben conglomerate, returning to independence after the Allies confiscated and broke up the company in the aftermath of the Second World War; it remained in business as Hoechst AG until 2005, when it was restructured into a range of smaller companies. The gigantic Hoechst works were turned into an industrial park which today houses several businesses from a range of sectors: after Frankfurt Airport the park has the second largest concentration of jobs in Frankfurt, with 22,000 employees spread across the site. The Behrens building (named after its architect Peter Behrens, 1868-1940) is particularly striking: the Expressionist brick-built headquarters was opened in 1924 just before Hoechst merged into IG Farben and left for the Frankfurt Poelzig building (see page 61); its interior, featuring De Stijl artwork and a paternoster lift, has been returned almost entirely to its original state by the current corporate tenants.

The Stockbroker Belt and the Taunus Hills

To the north of Frankfurt, a series of picturesque towns in the Taunus foothills form the city's stockbroker belt: Königstein and its smaller neighbour Kronberg are divided by a strip of forest from Oberursel, further east, which in turn gives way to Bad Homburg, the best known of the chain.

The "Bad" in Bad Homburg marks it out as a spa town where the world's rich once went to take cures and do what bored aristocrats like to do more than anything else: drink and gamble. Its casino, opened along with the spa in 1841, was one of the first in Germany and turned this provincial small town into an international resort of the very first class. Run by two brothers from Luxemburg, who later went on to set up the Monte Carlo Casino in Monaco, their Spielbank today trades under the cheeky title of "the mother of Monte Carlo". The money lost by the type of languid aristocrats portrayed by Dostoyevsky in *The Gambler* (the novella is rumoured to have been based on his own time in Homburg) has now been largely replaced by bankers' bonuses, but the elaborately decorated façade of the spa buildings and the well-heeled gentility of the town make this bygone era seem close. Bad Homburg now markets itself with the unashamed motto *Champagnerluft und Tradition* ("a whiff of champagne and tradition").

Oberursel, by contrast, can seem almost down to earth, despite its equally high prices and the conspicuous density of sports cars. Lacking in aristocratic tradition, this outlying town relies more on its medieval charm to lure in bankers looking for a quiet retreat. It is also the only one of the "string of pearls" in Frankfurt's stockbroker belt to have a direct metro connection into the city, making it attractive to those who might not quite be able to afford that dream car just yet (or who do not have a parking space with their name on it).

Kronberg, the smallest of the Taunus suburbs, is also the second richest: with a purchasing power index of 189 per cent of the national average, Kronberg has been sought out by some of Frankfurt's most powerful bankers: Jean-Claude Trichet lived here during his years at the European Central Bank, coinciding with Josef Ackermann during his time as boss of Deutsche Bank. Neighbouring Königstein, meanwhile, can boast an unassailable purchasing power of 191 per cent above the average, a romantic ruined castle and one of Germany's most exclusive hotels, the Villa Rothschild, built in 1884 as the summer residence of Wilhelm Carl von Rothschild (1828-1901).

Just behind these four stockbroker towns, the Taunus hills rise, cut north to south by the Aar, Ems and Weil rivers, all left-hand tributaries of the picturesque River Lahn, which flows through the ancient town of Wetzlar and the bishopric of Limburg. Popular destinations include the Großer Feldberg peak, whose telecommunications tower affords a view down to Frankfurt (16km or 12 miles to the south); several other elevations also offer viewing platforms. Geological features such as the Eschbacher Klippen, an outcrop of 12m (40ft) craggy quartz cliffs, and the Kubacher Kristallhöhle caves—Germany's largest accessible underground cavities—are also attractions. Several of the Taunus peaks offer views of two of the region's most important cities besides Frankfurt, Wiesbaden and Mainz.

Wiesbaden and Mainz

The penultimate syllable of the name Wiesbaden hints at the city's beginnings as one of Europe's oldest spa towns, and even today the city retains the urbane charm of a place in which wealthy people came for relaxation. Most of Wiesbaden's characteristic buildings were put up in the *belle époque* Wilhelmine period: the Kurhaus (spa hall) of 1907, the Hesse State Theatre (1894) and the two principal churches, the Marktkirche and the Ringkirche (1862 and 1894) all speak of a bygone age of pan-European aristocratic *bons vivants*. Although Ernst May developed a blueprint for a "new Wiesbaden" along the lines of his commercial, industrial and residential zoning in Frankfurt, the plans were never implemented. Furthermore, the city was spared the level of destruction meted out to others in the Second World War: as such, with its impressive large-scale buildings and overall intactness, it was the ideal location for government in the immediate post-war period, and became the capital of the State of Hessen, a status it has retained to this day. The former residence of the Counts of Nassau, the Stadtschloss, has functioned as the Hesse State Assembly since 1946, and as such many policies which affect the much larger Frankfurt are developed and passed in this quiet spa town. Another centre of power is the American military administration: the US Air Force in Europe was headquartered here until 1973, and even after its relocation to Rammstein, Wiesbaden retained a US military presence; with the consolidation of American forces in Europe in the mid-2000s, Wiesbaden was selected as the location for their new headquarters and has seen a steady increase in military personnel since then. While the city coffers are all the better for it, disquiet has spread of late after the NSA scandal: the new Consolidated Intelligence Center being set up by American forces in the city will without a doubt be used by the controversial organization, as well as the CIA.

Just across the Rhine, which flows past but not through Wiesbaden, lies Mainz. In the early Middle Ages this old Roman market town was considerably more important than Frankfurt; as the seat of an archbishop, it retained jurisdiction over Frankfurt in religious matters until the Reformation. Yet the city steadily declined in importance against its erstwhile rival, and by the turn of the twentieth century its population of 100,000 meant that it was almost five times smaller than Frankfurt. Nevertheless, its comparative irrelevance did not save the city and its timber-framed centre from the inferno of the Second World War: the British Royal Air Force destroyed eighty per cent of the city after an air raid created a firestorm on 27 February 1945.

The post-war reconstruction of Mainz was one of West Germany's most loveless and insensitive efforts, although the cathedral and several other structures of historic importance were restored. Like Wiesbaden, the city is a state capital, heading Hesse's western neighbour Rhineland-Palatinate (Rheinland-Pfalz), and exercises a role of national importance as the headquarters of ZDF, Germany's second public service television broadcaster. Once a year, Mainz fills with Mardi Gras revellers from the surrounding region: along with Cologne, Düsseldorf and Bonn, the city is one of the centres of Rhenish Carnival, a week-long celebration dating back to the Middle Ages which is marked by processions through the city streets and livelier-than-usual nightlife. Frankfurt is entirely devoid of Carnival tradition, and those in the city wanting to enjoy its unique atmosphere are always happy to forget the age-old rivalry with this ancient city on the confluence of the Rhine and the Main.

Further Reading

For readers with good German and an interest in the history of the city, *Frankfurt am Main: Die Geschichte der Stadt*, a by-period collection of academic essays edited by Jan Thorbecke, should be both a first port of call and the key work of reference against which all others are compared; I worked from the lavishly illustrated 1994 edition. A highly readable *compte rendu* of the life of the city up to the early 1950s comes in the form of *Frankfurts Geschichte* by Hermann Meinert: written from a more emotionally involved point of view by a single author, the book makes up for in momentum what it lacks in distance and detail (I used the fifth edition of 1977). Several entertaining historical asides are contained in *Frankfurt am Main: Stadtführer-Geschichte-Kultur* by Alice Selinger (2011), perhaps the best off-the-shelf guidebook available on the city.

The following titles are worthy of note on specific aspects of Frankfurt history. *Kino und Film in Frankfurt am Main: Lebende Bilder einer Stadt* (1995, M. Schurig, R. & T. Worschech) is a lively account of Frankfurt and its cinematic history and was of particular use for Chapter 6 of this work; *Das "Neue" Frankfurt, Innovationen in der Frankfurter Kunst vom Mittelalter bis heute* (2010, C. Freigang, M. Dauss, E. Brockhof) is a comprehensive round-up of the art and design history of the city. Meanwhile, *Hochhausstadt Frankfurt: Bauten und Visionen seit 1945* (2014, P. Sturm, P. C. Schmal) offers information on the aims and actions of Frankfurt city planning in the modern era, as does essay no. 5 in *Towards Undivided Cities in Western Europe: New Challenges for Urban Policy* (M. de Winter, S. Musterd); a good starting point for those interested in the details of the Ernst May Estates is *May Siedlungen: Architekturführer durch acht Siedlungen des Neuen Frankfurt 1926-1930* (1994, D. W. Dreysse). A solid collection of work in the entertaining and homely Frankfurt dialect is available as *Ausgewählte Frankfurter Mundartdichtung* (1966, ed. Waldemar Kramer). For works of literature set in Frankfurt, see Chapter 5.

Index